Engaging 'Tweens and Teens

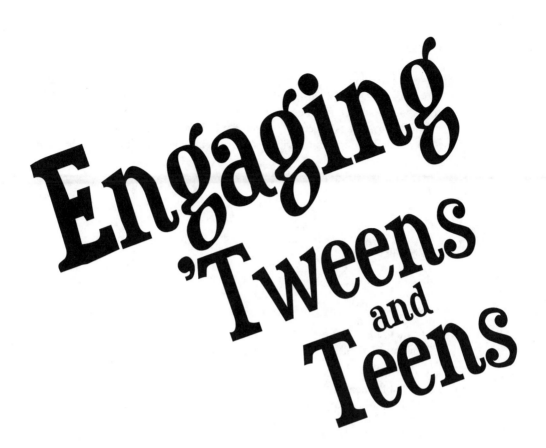

Engaging 'Tweens and Teens

A Brain-Compatible
Approach to Reaching
Middle and
High School Students

Raleigh Philp

CORWIN PRESS
A SAGE Publications Company
Thousand Oaks, CA 91320

For information:

Corwin Press
A Sage Publications Company
2455 Teller Road
Thousand Oaks, California 91320
www.corwinpress.com

Sage Publications Ltd.
1 Oliver's Yard
55 City Road
London EC1Y 1SP
United Kingdom

Sage Publications India Pvt. Ltd.
B-42, Panchsheel Enclave
Post Box 4109
New Delhi 110 017 India

Printed in the United States of America.

Library of Congress Cataloging-in-Publication Data

Philp, Raleigh.
Engaging 'tweens and teens : a brain-compatible approach to reaching middle and high school students / Raleigh Philp.
    p. cm.
Includes bibliographical references and index.
ISBN 1-4129-4483-X or 9-7814-1294-4830 (cloth : alk. paper) — ISBN 1-890460-49-4 or 9-7818-9046-0495 (pbk. : alk. paper)
    1. Cognitive neuroscience. 2. Learning, Psychology of. 3. Teenagers—Physiology.
4. Children—Physiology. I. Title.
QP360.5.P48 2007
612.8'2—dc22

                                        2006017034

This book is printed on acid-free paper.

06 07 08 09 10 10 9 8 7 6 5 4 3 2 1

Acquisitions Editor:	Stacy Wagner
Editorial Assistant:	Joanna Coelho
Production Editor:	Jenn Reese
Typesetter:	C&M Digitals (P) Ltd.
Proofreader:	Caryne Brown
Indexer:	Nara Wood
Cover Designer:	Michael Dubowe

Contents

Preface   vii

Acknowledgments   ix

About the Author   xi

1. What We Know About the Brain and Learning:
   Integrating Neuroscience, Psychology, and Education   1

2. Mapping the Brain: New Findings in Brain Research   19

3. Environmental and Genetic Effects on the Developing Brain   41

4. The Brain During Adolescence: Making Sense of Technology,
   Media, Social Status, and Education   63

5. Making Material Meaningful: Connecting Emotions and Learning   91

6. Stress and the Brain-Body Connection: Restoring Balance
   in the Classroom   109

7. Managing Students' Physiological States for Engaged Learning   125

8. Using Music Effectively to Enhance Learning   141

9. This Is Your Brain On . . . : Understanding and Curbing
   Adolescent Substance Abuse   157

10. Drugs That Enhance Student Achievement:
    Good Kids Making Bad Decisions   175

Conclusion   195

References   197

Index   207

Preface

This book is designed to help teachers of middle and secondary students understand the neurobiology behind the behaviors of those students. They often haven't a clue about why they act as they do—but you will, as you read this book. It offers a chance to update teachers and other youth providers with some of the most exciting research coming out of the laboratory and applies that knowledge to the classroom. If you couple this knowledge with the classroom applications I have added, you are bound to share my passion for connecting brain-compatible learning to others. This could be the linchpin that revitalizes your teaching career and helps you to do what good teachers do best: bring excitement into to the classroom!

Most teachers feel compelled in their own way to encourage each student's unique talents, to merge and connect with others. Believe it or not, the design of the human brain is organized precisely to help each of us reach our potential and, along the way, help others to reach theirs. If we can understand more about brain function and brain health, we can teach this in our classrooms.

About twelve years ago, I delivered my first workshop on how brain-compatible learning enhances teaching. The participants, a group of health educators, wanted immediate access to applications of the research, without having to slog through the research that justified those applications. While I designed the one-day workshop around their needs, I felt that if they could understand the research as I had, they would see why I had been so captivated studying the neuroscience findings that applied to education. During the past twelve years, I have learned that teachers need to be aware of the research that justifies this growing movement to appreciate where it's coming from and where it can take their instruction and, ultimately, student learning.

The beauty of this work is the translation from neuroscience to the classroom. Of course, while there are discoveries in the lab that cannot be used in the classroom, what can be applied in the classroom is very powerful. For the first time in history, the biological basis for learning and behavior is beginning to shape our teaching and training.

When I first started reading the research, I was entranced by the concept of neural plasticity, which essentially means that brain cells, or neurons, can change shape, size, chemistry, or even function as a result of *use*. Neurons, the tiny biological units of thought and learning, are at the core of this system. Tended by ten times the number of helpers, or glial cells, they function in ways we are only starting to figure out. Just think of the thirty or so youthful brains that are in your classroom. They love to grow in response to new learning, and they thrive on stimulation, challenge, change, appreciation, effective social interaction, and inquiry. The trouble is, they just don't know it!

From the initial stimuli received by the brain developing in utero until the last breath is taken, our behaviors shape our brains, and our brains influence our behaviors. Therefore we should view ourselves as teachers of healthy brain behaviors that promote learning, curiosity, creativity, passion, and information processing. As educators, this is what we are designed to do!

No matter how remarkable it is as an information processor, the brain is ultimately a meaning-making organ. If we can teach our students how to strengthen and nourish the integrity of the brain, then we can better equip them to fulfill their dreams and to reach their potentials. What scientists are saying is that each child has a unique brain profile and, when understood, it can explain brain behavior and subsequently act as a guide to modifying behavior for the good of the child. This understanding paints an encouraging picture for the future of today's generation of developing brains.

Now, please join me on this learning journey and share it with your students.

Acknowledgments

I would like to thank the generations of students I have been fortunate enough to have taught over the last forty years, for I have learned so much more from them than they of me. I would like to thank many dedicated professors and teachers, namely Eric Jensen, whose love of learning is probably even greater than mine. His guidance and creativity have made the knowledge and application about brain research a passion for me.

There are so many other dedicated teachers who have inspired me to write this book. It would have been impossible without Doug Dancer, my high-school biology teacher; Tim Hallinan, my inspiration for midlife learning; and Lew Miller and John Elfers, my dear friends who continue to influence me.

Sincere thanks are also due to Katie Franco, my wonderfully talented developmental editor for this project, and Rusty von Dyl, the man responsible for the superb layout of the book you now hold in your hands.

Finally, I would like to thank my lovely wife and life partner, Adrienne, and our children Sean and Heather for their love and support of everything I have tried.

About the Author

 Raleigh Philp has taught at every level of public and private school from grade school through graduate school. Currently, he is a consultant for the California State Department of Education's health-related programs and an adjunct professor at Pepperdine University, teaching science and health methods courses in the graduate school of education.

Over the last decade, Raleigh has devoted his academic efforts to studying the literature on brain research. He is primarily interested in the application of neuroscience to learning. He is committed to helping educators better understand adolescent brain development so they may focus their instruction on reaching students with varied learning methods. Raleigh has presented brain-compatible learning workshops and been a keynote speaker at universities, county offices of education, and school districts throughout California, Maryland, Nevada, New Mexico, Idaho, Washington, and Wyoming. He is a past recipient of the California Presidential Award for Excellence in Science Teaching, as well as a Fulbright grant.

He lives with his wife Adrienne in Arcadia, California.

What We Know About the Brain and Learning: Integrating Neuroscience, Psychology, and Education

Chapter 1
What We Know About the Brain and Learning:
Integrating Neuroscience, Psychology, and Education

In the past, educational methods . . . have never been based on neuroscience or any research based on an understanding of how the brain actually learns.
— Susan Y. Bookheimer, neuroscientist

Thousands of scientists from many disciplines have been on the great adventure of trying to figure out what's going on in the brain. One of the most exciting prospects of this new understanding has the power to help adolescents learn, live more productive lives, and achieve their maximum potential. Now that educators are caught up in the excitement, we are thinking about brain development with a different perspective.

For the first time we are beginning to look for neuroscience, psychology, and education to speak some common language, a language that communicates how we are bridging the gap between the three disciplines. Understanding the rudimentary anatomy and physiology of the brain will allow educators to talk to the neuroscientists and to transfer some discoveries into educational practice.

The Mechanic and the Neurosurgeon

Bob was a Volvo mechanic. To get where he was, Bob had years of experience and had training specifically for the computerized cars of today. Receiving his paycheck for the week, he realized again that his salary wasn't commensurate with what he valued his worth as a mechanic.

That afternoon as he was removing the computerized cylinder head from a newer model, he spotted a well-known neurosurgeon from UCLA in the customer waiting room. The surgeon was there waiting for the service manager to come take a look at his Volvo when the mechanic shouted across the hall, "Hey, Doc, can I ask you a question?" The neurosurgeon, a bit surprised, walked into the shop where the mechanic was working the cylinder head. The mechanic straightened up, wiped his hands on a rag, and asked, "So Doc, look at this engine. I open its heart, take the valves out, repair any damage, replace the computer, and then put it all back in, and when I finish, it works just like new. So how come I get such a meager salary and you get the really big bucks, when you and I are doing basically the same work?"

The neurosurgeon paused, smiled, and whispered to the mechanic, "Try doing it with the engine running!"

So it could be said of any understanding of the living, running human brain. When out of the skull, this nondescript-looking mass of reddish Jell-O has little to offer other than a mechanic's examination, but inside the skull, the living brain is probably the most complex structure on the earth. Let's take a brief look from the beginning.

It All Happened So Fast!

With the Internet at every student's fingertips, researching in the stacks has become outdated.

Education has remained the same for several decades, except for the impact of technology on the students and the classroom. In high school we still issue big colorful textbooks that overload backpacks, provide homework much as we always have, and give tests on Fridays and at the end of the chapter. Now you can read a book on the video monitor and find everything you ever needed by looking it up on the Internet. What ever happened to teaching kids to use the abstracting journals or to sit in the stacks for hours on end to research one topic? Much has happened since the days that students needed those skills.

A graduate student preparing for a teaching credential recently expressed some dismay to her professor when challenged to figure out a science problem in class. The class was shown the "dunking duck" and was requested to figure out the solution as a teacher-led inquiry problem progressed. After the activity, the frustrated student raised her hand and said, "I didn't care that we had to think. All I wanted to do was to 'Google it' to find the answer." This may typify our students' feelings toward taking advantage of the speedy technology so readily available. What happened to the value of having students think about a problem for a time?

We will need to adjust to the rapid flow of technological advances that will replace our traditional methodology in the classroom. With the aid of the world at their fingertips, adolescents will no longer tolerate a learning environment out of the last century. The research coming out of the neuroscience labs may be changing all of that.

In a short fifteen years, the study of neuroscience has morphed into an emerging source of information that would startle even the most forward thinking of yesteryear's scientists. Sigmund Freud would be baffled, B. F. Skinner would be perplexed, and Hans Selye would have been mystified. Even Einstein wouldn't have fathomed it! Jean Piaget, however, would have said, "Yes! Now they will believe me!"

The Caution Sign

Scientists have warned educators who have become fascinated with the latest findings in neuroscience that it is difficult to draw sweeping conclusions about learning in the classroom. Despite this, many educators sense a growing need to translate the findings from brain science to some sort of useful guidelines. Where's the guidance for educators? There is a need to look for a balance between the two concepts:

Generalization #1
"Brain-based learning is the answer."

Generalization #2
"Neuroscience research is speaking directly to educators."

One extreme from generalization #1 might be exemplified by the then-governor of Georgia Zell Miller's initiative to give every mother in the state a classical CD featuring Mozart music. This was to be played to her baby in an effort to enhance the child's intelligence. Extrapolated from the Mozart effect research at the University of California at Irvine (Rauscher, 1993), the actual findings just do not support the expense and effort. The term "Mozart effect" was coined by the media after a 1993 *Nature* publication showed that college students who listened to the Mozart Sonata for Two Pianos in D Major had short-term subsequent enhancement of their spatial-temporal reasoning. The popularization of neurological research findings in the educational community should be tempered by cautious application and recommendations.

In spite of the politics, many teachers are delighted to learn how some of the brain research applies to learning and the classroom. Just as elated are the neuroscientists who see how beneficial their work can be when used in a conservative and meaningful context. The caution sign still needs to be heeded, however, because all of this has happened so fast to an industry (Education) that moves so slowly.

How have we come so far in such a short time? The partial answer lies in the advancement of technology and the rapid development of high-speed computers. In Chapter 2 we will look at some of this technology in closer detail. These inventions have allowed advancement unparalleled in the history of man. One wonders if the next few decades will show a continued extrapolation of the rate of discovery. A rather scary thought educators should recognize is that the dynamics of discovery are often impeded by the sluggishness of changes in educational practices.

The Aims of This Book

It has been said that neuroscience literature older than eight or nine years has little application to education, and prior to that, very little overlap is seen in the literature from the two disciplines. Fortunately, translators like Eric Jensen, Robert Sylwester, Pat Wolfe, and David Sousa changed all of that. Understanding the significance of the 1990s "Decade of the Brain," these translators and many others focused on helping educators understand the momentous, albeit small, fraction of applications from neuroscience and psychology to education.

There has been an almost inevitable backlash from skeptics who claim the translators have oversimplified neuroscience research and overinterpreted the findings (Bruer, 1999). What John Bruer and others have failed to see is the overwhelming enthusiasm from educators for understanding how people learn. For those of us in the classroom, it's easy to support the arguments in favor of incorporating findings from neuroscience into the field of education.

To put this in perspective, there are three themes to be pursued in this book. First, the inner workings of the brain at a rudimentary level with examples applicable to teachers of secondary students. Aspects of biology, physiology, and chemistry can help teachers understand the primary underpinnings of the structure, organization, and development of the human brain at different stages of maturity.

Second, the brain has been considered a black box until recently and studied only from the outside. The input from psychology will help us understand the cognitive aspects of behavior in educational contexts. Again, the examples and stories focus on the target audience—middle- and high-school teachers.

Third, the practical application of knowledge about adolescent human behavior to promote more effective learning and teaching. Understanding the link between education as a social function and a scientific one helps a teacher adapt to today's adolescent population.

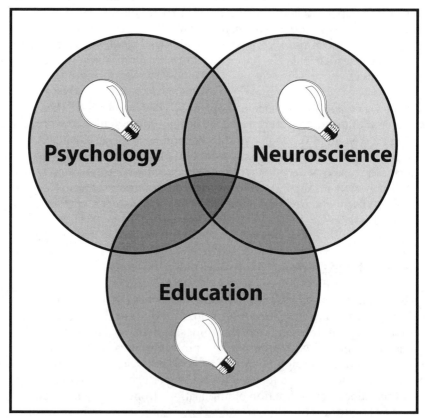

Thanks to the "Decade of the Brain," information from psychology and neuroscience is now having an impact on education.

It is important in this endeavor to be careful in distinguishing between what neuroscience, psychology, and education are saying. We also need to be cautious about how we translate findings from one area to another.

The Beginnings

In the early part of her pregnancy, almost every mother wonders what this growing creation inside her belly will become. The baby's brain metamorphosis begins early. A faint neural plate forms just days after conception from a small ball of beginning cells. If you could see it under a microscope, the tiny neural groove would become quite distinct in a few days to form a tubelike figure that begins to form the mysterious brain and spinal cord. The protoplasm of life now takes over. Getting surges of chemical instructions and blasts of protein that tell it to produce glial cells, the primordial brain-like tissue starts its life by changing into something else—a tradition that will follow it throughout its existence. The glial cells tend to the potent neurons all of their lives. Like ladies in waiting, the glial cells spend their early existence ensuring that the neurons are moved to just the right places to form the brain's organization. Racing around and helping neurons find partners, groups, layers, and organizational networks seems to be the primary job of the glial cell force that outnumbers neurons ten to one. They provide sufficient care to help the wondrous neuron population to multiply into more than one hundred billion copies by the time of birth (Scheibel, 1998).

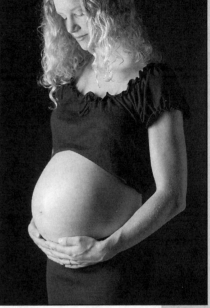

Foundational brain development takes place in the fetus during pregnancy.

The nine months that the individual's brain takes to develop in the womb are extremely critical. This is virtually the only time the person has to grow a full set of neurons. Called neurogenesis—*neuro* meaning "mind," *genesis* meaning "beginning"—the process was baffling to scientists when it was first discovered a few years ago. Here's why: At the rate of about 250,000 neurons a minute, the new brain starts building early. By about twenty-eight weeks, or seven months in utero, the fetal brain has proliferated about twice as many neurons as it will need when it is born. In the last two months of fetal development, genetically programmed cell death (apoptosis) takes place.

When scientists first discovered this seemingly wasteful procedure it was alarming. Yet we now know this happens during all normal brain development. In the last two months before birth, the brain prunes away about half of its cells. From that point on no appreciable number of neurons is lost in the healthy brain until adolescence, when another pruning takes place (Giedd, et al., 1999).

By the end of the human gestation period, an incredible mass of brain tissue in the soft, melonlike skull functions to provide the child with the potential for thinking, talking, feeling, and being a distinctively conscious human being.

The infant cortex, a mass of soft white matter, waits to be spun with insulating fatty material to cover the naked neurons that will allow a child to suckle, see, hear, touch, and curl tiny fingers. This process, called mylenation, is what allows nerve cells to conduct electrical messages. What joy there is to know that quadrillions of connections will be made to form a brain capable of becoming a fully formed child in just a few years!

While the anxious and dazed postpartum mother wants to view her infant immediately to check out whether her child has all the fingers and toes, it is the mysterious brain that every mother should wonder about after she has given birth. It's what's inside that downy covered sphere that counts most.

Each child is born with an extraordinary range of potential, especially when compared to any other living thing. With a bulging neocortex yet to be explored and a palate capable of making complex sounds in only a few years, the human child stands like a giant redwood when compared to the tiny seedlings of the animal world. Neural templates will, when formed, influence cognitive functioning throughout life. Social and emotional organization will follow with the enormous influence of experience. Perhaps to a greater extent, the experience of the first five years of life will dominate the direction of this primitive little mass of neurons.

The influence of experience in determining how the brain will develop is greatest in the first years of life. Consistent, predictable, nurturing, and enriching experiences help a child to develop personal potential. While this research says to middle- and high-school teachers that the die is already cast by the time students reach us, the influence of the adolescent years and the formation of neural networks from twelve to sixteen years of age hold great potential for changing the templates formed in the first few years. The research to substantiate this statement comes to us from brain scans recently derived and studied (Giedd, 1999).

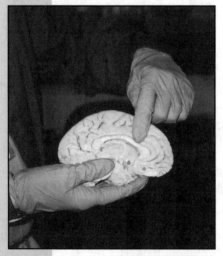

From the moment of birth, the brain has almost unlimited growth potential.

As the infant brain begins to grow, it starts to define who the person is. By the time a child begins to acquire rudimentary language, caretakers are making assumptions about what this person is going to be like. Like other illusionary correlations (people tend to remember times when two events co-occur and forget the times when they don't), mothers and fathers see their personalities and physical traits emerge in the infant. They see expressions, mannerisms similar to their own, and more important, a temperament beginning to form.

Multifunctioning Magic

The brain is the most complicated organ in the world. It consists of more than one hundred billion neurons and a trillion supporting cells. Every neuron is connected to hundreds, perhaps thousands of other neurons forming complex networks. These networks make more connections than stars in universe. The brain occupies only 2 percent of body's weight but uses 20 percent of the oxygen taken into the body. If you were to compare a piece of brain tissue to a sand grain at the beach, that tiny space would occupy about 100,000 neurons (Amen, 2001).

The brain is capable of doing many things at once. It can simultaneously drive a car, listen to music, see road signs, and complete unrelated tasks like developing a lesson plan while driving to school. Scientists are discovering how and where our brains analyze the environment by taking in data from all the senses—sight, hearing, touch, taste, and smell. The dilemma is how to find out what the brain does to bind all the elements of an event together and to interpret what is happening at a given time. For instance, we see a blue car pass us on the left. The shape, color, movement, and location are all processed in different parts of the brain, but we see the entire event as a whole without being conscious of the discrete input that is required to make the scene possible. How? How do you explain consciousness? Antonio Damasio in *The Feeling of What Happens: Body and Emotion in the Making of Consciousness* builds a model of how consciousness is constructed on emotional underpinnings. He is one of the first scientists to describe the neurobiology of consciousness. Scientists like Damasio are beginning to understand and describe what it means to "feel." This human endeavor points to an awareness of the past and an anticipated future along with a feeling of self, i.e., this is where I live, this is the kind of person I am (Damasio, 1999).

How amazing it is to sense the world around you! Every fragment of information is stored or discarded in this complex system. We remember almost nothing before the age of three years. The hippocampus, which embeds the starting place for long-term memory isn't mature enough yet to do its job (Carter, 1999). Emotional memories, however, are already being stored in the amygdala, which most likely begins working at birth.

Connecting to other human beings is possible only because of the associations the brain has made through the vehicles of language, religion, and technologies. As humans we have the distinct advantage of being able to record and reflect the synthesized experiences of hundreds of human generations that had brains before us.

The future is on the other side of the fulcrum point. It connects you to the next generation. If you have children, you pass on the gene pool and experiences of your own life to them through your persona and what you have taught them. Interestingly, teachers influence the experience part of the learning ledger as much as anyone, and possibly more than some parents.

It's a Jungle in There

In order to perform all of the things a brain must do, it has morphed from the early beginnings after birth into an astonishing and highly elegant structure. The brain is not just one single mass of tissue but a complex organization within its parameters and beyond. The great mediator qualities of the brain control systems far and wide. In general, the complexity of brain structure and the functions that these different structures mediate are organized in a bottom-to-top way.

All kinds of analogies have been proposed to describe the functioning brain, none better than well-known brain research translator Eric Jensen's "Human Brain, Human Jungle" from *Completing the Puzzle* (1996):

> The jungle is active at times, quiet at times, but always teeming with life. The brain is similar. It is very active at times, much less at others, but always alive and busy. The jungle has its own zones, regions, and sectors: the underground, the streams, the ground cover, the low plants and shrubs, the air, the taller plants, the trees, etc. The brain has its own sectors for thinking, sexuality, memory, survival, emotions, breathing, creativity, etc. While the jungle changes over time, one constant remains true—the law of the jungle is survival and no one's in charge. Just as no one runs the jungle, neuroscientist Michael Gazzaniga reminds us that no single region of the human brain is equipped to run our brain. It is well connected but there is no "command center" for best efficiency.

Jensen goes on to say, "Keep that concept in mind: that the brain is best at learning what it needs to survive—socially, economically, emotionally, and physically. From your typical student brain's point of view, remember that 'academic success' is often quite low on its list of to do's!"

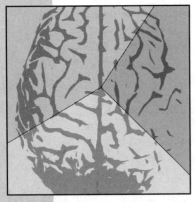

Paul MacLean's Triune Brain theory paved the way for recent neurological advances.

The Basic Parts

The brain has tons of parts! While this is not a book on brain anatomy and physiology, a brief treatment of some critical structures and functions of the brain may help the reader appreciate how marvelous this apparatus is. Before examining the major areas of the brain, let's spend a few moments exploring how we got there.

Paul MacLean, a pioneer of modern neuroscience, in 1970 defined three distinct systems within the brain that correspond to key evolutionary systems that have developed across various species. This model is known as the Triune Brain model.

The Triune Brain model defined the lower, less complex areas of the brain as being similar in structure and function to the "reptilian brain." For years this model seemed to predominate as the way to explain that emotion was confined to MacLean's second level of evolutionary organization, the limbic system. It also gave credence to the theory that the crude brains of reptilian forms may have given rise to high brain forms. In the last decade, Joseph LeDoux has urged that scientists drop that view and recognize that emotion engages many parts of the cortex. Credited with original research that traced the emotion of fear throughout the brain, LeDoux suggests that different emotions take different pathways and the use of MacLean's terms is outdated based on recent findings (LeDoux, 1996). Research continues to support the view that parts of the limbic system and emotion are related, if not exclusive (Zull, 2002).

Scientists would argue about any linear evolutionary trend from the primitive reptilian brain. The key observation in this organizational process is that, in all cases, the brain starts with the lowest complexity at the bottom and highest on top. The most complex part of the brain is the cortex. When compared to other animals, the frontal cortex (part of the neocortex) is the most uniquely human part of the brain. This big lump of brain tissue at the front of the head reminds us that we have no competitors here. Many animals have proportionally fairly large brains compared to their body weight, but they are all missing the large-sized neo- or "new" cortex in front of the head.

Each network processes a small segment of a brain function, but together in networks they process almost everything we think or feel.

For the purposes of this treatise we might divide the brain into three major areas: the finger-sized brain stem, the limbic system, and the largest part of the brain, the cerebrum. The little brain stem at the base of our brain regulates all of the input/output mechanics of the brain. We have little control or exhibit hardly any plasticity in this section of the brain. It's a good thing, too: Who would want to have a say about such basic self-regulated functions as blood circulation and respiration? Fortunately, we never have to worry about these processes because the brain stem takes care of them automatically.

Our limbic system is composed of several interconnected structures around the midbrain. Some of the important structures contained here are the amygdala, the hippocampus, and the cingulate gyrus. Below the occipital region (or sight area) and next to the brain stem, the cerebellum is responsible for balance, coordination, muscle movements—and a host of new findings suggests that some memory is located here.

Deep inside the brain, researchers have found a small structure called the nucleus accumbens. This region has been shown to be activated by drugs such as cocaine and amphetamines, suggesting that it is involved with the rewarding or pleasure cycle. Recently there have been findings that suggest it is also activated during laughter and joy (Winters, 2004).

The largest part of the brain is called the cerebrum, which comprises about 85 percent of the brain's mass. It is composed of the left and right hemispheres. Nestled beneath the cerebral cortex are the central lobes of the brain, identified as the frontal, parietal, temporal, and the occipital. They are responsible for critical daily activities such as hearing, vision, speech, and executive functions like decision making and cause-and-effect recognition.

The cerebral cortex is actually the gray, wrinkled surface encompassing the cerebrum. The cerebral cortex looks wrinkly because of its many folds.

There are ten to fourteen billion neurons contained within the cerebral cortex, and they are organized into several hundred million neural networks. Each network processes a small segment of a brain function, but together in networks they process almost everything we think or feel.

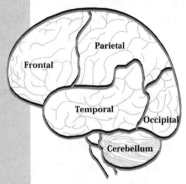

SOURCE: *Brain Mania! 50 Great Brains*

The Lobes

The frontal lobe has many functional areas, but it is probably best known for the containment of the prefrontal cortex, which is involved with just about everything human—the ability to form a personality, have insight and foresight, and make executive decisions are all here. The highest intellectual functions of thinking, planning, and problem solving dwell in this wonderful space. One of the key structures located primarily in the left cerebral hemisphere is Broca's area, which is important in the production of speech and written language.

The temporal lobe is associated with the primary auditory cortex and, as part of the limbic system, houses the hippocampus. Many complex aspects of learning and memory recall can be traced to this section of the brain.

Much of the interior of the parietal lobe of one hemisphere (usually the left), together with a portion of the temporal lobe, is Wernicke's area, which is involved with the comprehension of language.

The occipital lobe is concerned with visualization. Both the visual cortex and a visual association cortex are involved in higher-order processing of visual information.

Alphabetical Brain Connections (ABC)

The following definitions will be helpful to you as you look for ways to build confidence and knowledge about the brain.

ACTH Also called corticotropin, ACTH is a stress-related hormone produced by the pituitary gland. When released into the bloodstream, it reaches the adrenal gland (located just above the kidneys) and triggers the hormones that work when your body experiences stress.

Adrenaline This hormone is released from the adrenal gland into the bloodstream within seconds in response to stress of any sort. Also known as epinephrine, this hormone is backed up by a group of steroid hormones called glucocorticoids.

Axons These are the long fibers extending from the brain cells (neurons) that carry an electrical nerve impulse to other neurons. An axon can be up to three feet long in the human lower leg.

Cingulate gyrus This structure lies directly above the corpus callosum. It mediates communication between the cortex and midbrain structures.

Corpus callosum A massive band of white matter that connects the left and right hemispheres and allows them to communicate with each other.

Dendrites These are the strandlike fibers emanating from one end of the cell body. They are the receptor sites for axons; when they come close to each other they make a synapse. Each cell (neuron) can have upwards of one thousand connections.

Dopamine This neurotransmitter is found in the "pleasure pathway" of the brain. The work of dopamine is critically impacted by drug and alcohol interaction. This "feel-good" substance appears to be reduced in patients suffering from Parkinson's disease.

Endorphins A class of morphinelike substances or natural opiates, secreted by the pituitary gland and the brain. They can help reduce the sensation of pain.

Glial A "tending" cell, it is one of two types of brain cells. Glial cells outnumber neurons, the other brain cell, by ten to one, and are also known as interneurons. They carry nutrients, speed repair, and may form their own communication network.

Hypothalamus This structure controls appetite, body temperature, and other important functions. It's a complex collection of cell groups that also influences hormone secretion, digestion, sexuality, circulation, emotions, and sleep.

Lateralization Lateralization refers to the activity of using one side of the brain more than another. The term "relative lateralization" is more accurate since we are usually using at least some of the left and right sides of the brain at the same time.

Medulla Located in the brain stem, the medulla channels information between the cerebral hemispheres and the spinal cord. It controls respiration, circulation, wakefulness, breathing, and heart rate.

Myelin Myelin is a fatty white shield that coats and insulates axons. It can help make the cells (neurons) more efficient and without myelination—the process of depositing myelin around axons—the nerves aren't able to conduct their chemical messages.

Norepinephrine Formally known as noradrenaline, norepinephrine is a neurotransmitter primarily involved in our arousal states: fight or flight, metabolic rate, blood pressure, emotions, and mood.

Neurons One of two types of brain cells. We have about one hundred billion neurons. Neurons receive stimulation from their branches (known as dendrites) and communicate by firing a nerve impulse along an axon.

Neurotransmitters Our brain's biochemical messengers. There are more than two hundred known neurotransmitters in the brain and spinal cord. These are the stimuli that excite neighboring neurons or act as inhibitors to suppress activation.

Pons Located near the top of the brain stem, above the medulla, lays the pons. It's a critical relay station for our sensory information.

Reticular formation A small structure, located at the top of the brain stem and bottom of midbrain area. It's the regulator responsible for attention, arousal, sleep/awake states, and consciousness.

Serotonin A common neurotransmitter, most responsible for inducing relaxation, regulating mood, and sleep. Antidepressants like Prozac usually suppress the absorption of serotonin, making the user more active.

Synapse A synapse is the junction point or cleft where the axon of one neuron almost touches the dendrites of another. When an axon of one neuron releases neurotransmitters to stimulate the dendrites of another cell, the resulting junction point where the reaction occurs is a synapse. The adult human has approximately one hundred trillion synapses.

Thalamus Located deep within the midbrain, the thalamus is a key sensory relay station. Its functions are involved in hearing, muscle movement, and retrieving memories.

Vasopressin A stress-related hormone that is partly responsible for our aggression.

THE EDUCATIONAL CONNECTION

In today's middle and high schools there is a need to be realistic about our progress in the past few decades. Are we still teaching a 1970s curriculum with the tools of this century? If so, this would be comparable to equipping a new Toyota hybrid car with 1960s belted tires. Is there a need to change the use of instructional strategies popular in past generations? Do the findings and experience from neuroscience warrant changing the way we teach?

A common assumption in education is that if students are provided with enough information, they will make sense of most if it and put it to productive use. When weekly tests are given, however, it is evident that many of the students didn't understand the material. Looking for more effective ways to help us understand how the brain learns will improve our teaching.

Appreciating some of the basic structures and functions of the brain is important for teachers in today's secondary classrooms. It's equally as crucial to appreciate the complexity and the beauty found in the human brain. The brain doesn't like to take on dramatic changes or vast amounts of information straightaway; it prefers "nibbling" at small amounts of material (hence the very basic brain information in this chapter). By understanding the most rudimentary yet exciting structures and functions of the brain, teachers may begin to appreciate how valuable the care and feeding of the brain are to a successful life.

Summary of Chapter 1

- The "Decade of the Brain" led to increased interest in the implications of recent neuroscience research for education.

- It is important to recognize that neuroscience, psychology, and education are disciplines that need to work together.

- We must be careful in translating the findings from neuroscience to education.

- The brain is exceptionally complex and consists of structures and functions that are only now beginning to be understood.

ENGAGING THE BRAIN THROUGH ACTIVITIES

Applying the concepts of the content of each chapter is important. At the end of each succeeding chapter, the activities included are designed to engage students in the process of learning about the structure and function of the brain. Our challenge as teachers of adolescents is to encourage students to think about the relationships among knowledge of the brain, the choices they make, the behavior they display, and the enhancement of their personal health.

Activity #1

The Brain: A Road Map to the Mind
A wonderful illustrative resource for brain structures and functions can be found at MSNBC Interactive. Look for the box at the bottom of the article saying "Interactive." The menu includes internal, external, fear factors, memory manager, and sensory switchboard.
URL- http://www.msnbc.msn.com/id/6849058

Activity #2

A Guided Tour of the Human Brain
This is a great visual tutorial that offers a guided tour of the human brain. It's provided by the HOPES (Huntington's Outreach Project for Education, at Stanford). The tour starts with a brief description of brain cells (neurons and glia) and the ventricular system, and then explores the different lobes of the brain. The tutorial gets more detailed in its discussion of the limbic system, basal ganglia, and diencephalon. The ability to add or subtract structures will help you get an idea of the three-dimensional configuration of the brain.
URL- http://www.stanford.edu/group/hopes/basics/braintut/ab0.html

Activity #3

Musical Shares

This activity can be applied to teach any content. It allows each student to become an "expert" about a fact or concept. When students are given an opportunity to teach something, several things happen. First, the students take pride in the fact that they can teach something. Second, other students will listen and reciprocate because they also get to teach something. Third, by teaching this information to a number of students, an important brain-compatible learning principle is practiced. Repetition by teaching the concept to other students will create a better opportunity for long-term memory.

To Play Musical Shares:

1. Select some music with a beat to play on your stereo. Songs like "Tango," "In the Mood," "Hernando's Hideaway," or "Country Roads" will work well.

2. Give each student a 3" x 5" card with one brain factoid (use the definitions in this chapter). Independently, ask them to become an expert on their particular definition.

3. Allow a few minutes to absorb the material, and then ask them to teach a person sitting next to them the information on the card. Encourage them to paraphrase and use animated discussion in teaching the information. After a few minutes, say, "We are now going to play Musical Shares."

4. Use an overhead transparency or a PowerPoint slide to convey the following information:

Musical Shares

When the music begins, walk around the room silently.

When the music stops, find a partner and share the information that has been chosen to share.

When the music starts again, leave your partner and walk around the room.

When the music stops, find another partner and share the information that has been chosen to share.

Activity #4

Mind Mapping

Individual mind maps: Try using mind maps once with your middle- and high-school students, and you will find it becomes one of your staple strategies for assessment. Mind maps are creative ways to show a pattern of connected ideas.

A mind map uses both words and pictures to create a memorable pattern of how the brain interprets information. By adding colors, pictures, and symbols, the learner engages more of the brain than just the language centers. Most students say they understand the material much more when they have a chance to mind map as opposed to taking traditional notes.

To get started: Using a readily available supply of 8 ½" x 14" paper makes it easier for you to collect and return the mind maps to students. Provide students with colored pens and have them draw their own representation of the primary topic—in this case, the brain. Encourage them to make their own representation of what they think it should look like. While it's good for some students to branch curving lines off the center graphic, others may want to organize their mind maps differently. It's most important to allow students to express themselves. You will be surprised how different the finished products are from each other! It is only important that they create a picture, symbol, and some key words for every concept you want them to include. If they are mind mapping the structures and functions of the brain as discussed in this chapter, all the information is included here.

Selected Books for Enhancing This Chapter

Abraham, Carolyn	*Possessing Genius: The Bizarre Odyssey of Einstein's Brain.* St. Martin's Press: New York, 2002 This is a page-turner! Abraham provides the history and fascination that occupied Einstein's brain for forty years after his death. The saga is almost science fiction but true to account as her research supports. This is a must for brain junkies.
Damasio, Antonio R.	*The Feeling of What Happens: Body and Emotion in the Making of Consciousness.* Harcourt Brace: Orlando, FL, 1999 A landmark treatment of the underlying biology of how emotions and feelings are stored and translated in the brain. Damasio's treaty on consciousness is different from current views, and this results in a fascinating study of how the human brain relates to its environment. One of the most talked-about books of 1999 in brain science.
Jensen, Eric	*Teaching with the Brain in Mind,* Second Edition. ASCD: Alexandria, VA, 2005 The author provides an extensive catalog of practical applications so often missing in similar books. Designed for all teachers, Jensen's book provides the reader with practical and usable insights from the research. A valuable tool for enhancing teaching innovations.

2

Mapping the Brain:
New Findings in Brain Research

Chapter 2
Mapping the Brain: New Findings in Brain Research

In the last dozen years, there has been an exponential increase in the number of studies that have found differences in the brain. It's very exciting.

—Sandra Witelson, neuroscientist

After centuries of speculation and scientific exploration, many intriguing and exciting things have been discovered about the brain, and these ideas are fairly easy to understand. From the early workers of the sixteenth century to today's technologically driven labs, science has taken a remarkable journey, and the data are accumulating at an unprecedented rate. Much of the brain remains mysterious, but educators are seeing connections right now that can be used to help children learn.

It Made a Great Difference to the Students at Mel High

Mr. Daunas was considered by most of his students at Mel High School as the best teacher they had ever had. He had been ensconced in the same laboratory classroom since anyone could remember. Students always looked forward to entering his classroom to see what was novel that day. His collection of live animals and aquariums stocked with native fish and lizards commanded a look-see, but it was his little affirmation board that always caught the eye of students passing in and out between periods. Each day he changed the affirmation, and students loved reading them. The soft, yet stimulating, new age music emanating out of 1970s big box speakers between classes made them feel comfortable. He would even turn off the harsh fluorescent lights for afternoon classes and rely on just the overhead projector and flickering aquarium lights to illuminate the room.

Although the environment made a difference, it was Mr. Daunas's genuine enthusiasm for biology and his understanding attitude toward students who didn't get it the first time around that impressed generations of students who took his classes.

One morning in spring semester he was absent—not a total surprise for students but unusual because of the teacher's excellent attendance record. On this sad morning, his students would find out that Mr. Daunas had experienced a stroke.

Each year more than 500,000 Americans experience a stroke. A stroke happens when a blockage bursts or clogs the blood vessel bringing oxygen and nutrients to the head. Brain cells die. Mr. Daunas was a prime candidate for such a happening. A bit out of shape and a long history of high blood pressure placed him in a fairly high-risk group. Strokes are one of the leading causes of death in people fifty to seventy years of age (Society for Neuroscience, 2004).

Fortunately, Mr. Daunas survived the stroke and unlike stroke victims of the past was left without serious disabilities. He has since returned to school and teaches a full load of classes. Upon his return, the students were even more appreciative of his skill as a teacher.

The brain is amazingly plastic. In the past, it was commonly accepted that brain damage from a stroke was permanent. Once a brain region died, its function was gone forever. While the kind of stroke that Mr. Daunas experienced killed many neurons and cut many connections, some undamaged neurons took over, changing the number and strength of the messages they sent, rerouting traffic around the accident site. Rewiring is possible, even though age does make it harder to reroute and establish new circuits (Ratey, 2001).

Research and the new therapies that have been developed out of this research have allowed Mr. Daunas, and thousands of stroke victims like him, to make dramatic improvement after surviving a stroke. Brain scientists have found that fast reactions can make a great deal of difference. If given new therapies within hours of the onset of a stroke, the medical procedures can rapidly dissolve blockages, restore blood flow, and ward off additional brain damage. The new therapy can achieve a complete recovery when given within a short time of the attack. This translates into improved quality of life for patients and millions of dollars in savings for the health-care system.

What's most exciting here is how new brain discoveries are improving the chances of survival from all types of formerly fatal brain injuries. Young people suffering brain injuries from accidents are now being given a much better chance to live healthy and happy lives. This couldn't have happened without opening the black box of the brain.

Shocking Behavior

Today's urban athletes are pushing the envelop further than ever; in some very unusual places!

Every fifteen seconds, one person in America sustains a brain injury. Acquired brain injuries from car accidents, a fall, toxic inhalation, sport injuries, and abuse can produce a diminished or altered state of consciousness, which results in impairment of cognitive abilities or physical functioning. Other types of brain injuries or "brain insults" result from hereditary, congenital, or degenerative sources. Brain injuries of any sort can be serious. The brain was not meant to play contact sports without proper headgear, snowboard without a helmet, hit a soccer ball with the head, or ride a motorcycle bareheaded in the *Easy Rider* style. We have made some headway toward regulating dangerous activities for children, and it's cost us some freedoms. Most people would agree that it's worth the price.

There are other things that can hurt the brain besides physical trauma. Drugs and alcohol, malnutrition, chronic stress, infections such as those associated with the

THE EDUCATIONAL CONNECTION

Much of the science community and educators agree that we should be teaching brain science in school. It is important for teachers and students to know something about neuroscience and to understand that learning about the brain means knowing more about yourself. For students, this can be very helpful for the "predictive value" of why they might act the way they do. In Chapter 5 we will take a deeper look into why and how the teenage brain functions the way it does.

As researchers learned to map the anatomy of behavior, they realized that the brain is shaped by the interplay of genes and environment and is more malleable than anyone had guessed. Pathways forged, then continually revised by experience, link lattices of neurons. So intimate is this feedback that there is no way to separate the brain's neural structure from the influence of the world that surrounds it. Teachers have been aware of this for a long time even without understanding the science behind our conviction that environment shapes the brain.

HIV virus, and environmental toxins can cause damage; chronic depression also hurts the brain.

It's just as important to know that many things help the brain. We know that social connections, positive thinking, good diet, vitamins, exercise, proper sleep and relaxation, learning music, and staying in school are all helpful to keeping a brain happy.

The New Brain

As you read the pages of this book, new findings are making old ones obsolete, and more information is being added to the database at a pace never even dreamed of in the past. What has led us to understand so much about how the brain works? Why have we revised almost everything we know about the brain in the past ten to fifteen years?

The brain is the single most complicated structure known in the universe. It will to take time to figure out how it works. Understanding it is a slower process than the headlines might indicate since it's very difficult to learn about the living brain. The beauty of this work is in its "falsefiability." In other words, science is always subject to new discoveries that often render old discoveries incorrect or false. This factor is a good benchmark for separating science from nonscience. If it can't be falsified, it isn't science! The true strength of neuroscience is in the fact that new and improved explanations of structures and functions are continually replacing old explanations. When old ideas can no longer be substantiated by research, they fall like dead trees in the forest.

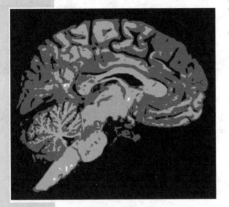

The brain wasn't always thought to be the source of cognition.

SOURCE: *Brain Mania! 50 Great Brains*

For example, Roger Sperry's discoveries and subsequent theories in the 1950s about right/left brain activity have been replaced by better fitting ideas through research. Paul MacLean's work on the Triune Brain theory of the '60s is now just a nice set of metaphors and has been updated to include newer findings. Albert Einstein in *The Practical Cogitator* said, "No amount of experimentation can ever prove me right; a single experiment may at any time, prove me wrong." Again, the strength of this science is centered on the fact that new discoveries help modify or repeal popularly held beliefs. It's self-correcting!

To understand the accelerated rate of development in brain science, let's return to our conception of the brain in the past. The ancient Egyptians described head injuries and their treatment but in their writings identified the heart as the seat of cognition. The operating principles by which the brain is organized and stores and retrieves information stayed well guarded for centuries.

In the sixteenth century, Andreas Vesalius's dissections of the human body and descriptions of his findings helped to correct misconceptions about the brain and other organs that had prevailed since ancient times. Vesalius wrote revolutionary texts on the subject of human anatomy. The seven volumes of his work were completely illustrated with fine engravings based on his own drawings and helped dispel the long-held idea of the heart being the seat of reasoning.

During the past century, the laboratories of the growing profession of neurology became the proving grounds for new information and knowledge about the brain. First, a readily available supply of wounded veterans from all the wars during the nineteenth and twentieth centuries provided more to researchers than ever before. Their severe and deadly head wounds spawned many research papers for the fledgling scientific journals of the time. Describing every brain insult and injury imaginable from looking at the injured and deceased, researchers wished that they could get feedback from patients remaining alive from brain injuries. (Most information was described postmortem since victims of open head injuries rarely lived, almost always dying from infection before sterile procedures were practiced.)

Case studies of brain injuries were frequently reported in the first part of the century. With the advent of better communication through scientific journals, the discovery of which structures might be responsible for certain functions increased greatly. The advent of using dangerous machinery long before regulations protected workers provided exciting, yet gory, times in the advancement of neurology. Newfangled machines and inventions like hay balers, harvesting combines, and blasting powers, all characteristic of the Industrial Revolution, put workers in harm's way for losing limbs and succumbing to head injuries.

Perhaps one of the most famous head injuries where the victim lived to tell about it was that of Phineas Gage. There is a wonderful account of it in Antonio Damasio's book *Descartes' Error*. In this depiction, Gage is said to be a well-respected twenty-five-year-old construction foreman in charge of a railroad project that required men to lay new tracks for railroad expansion. In 1848, because of almost fatal error while completing work on a blasting hole, dynamite exploded in his face. "Gage's iron tamping bar enters his left cheek, pierces the base of the skull, traverses in the front of his brain, and exits at high speed through the top of his head. The rod landed over 100 feet away, covered with blood and brains" (Damasio, 1994).

The fact that Gage lived and survived infection was very unusual for the time. Many accounts were prepared of the changes in his personality and his lack of reasoning power over the next thirteen final years of his sad life. His fame places Phineas Gage with few others that survived severe brain injury only to be changed markedly by the experience.

The neurologists of the day had to rely on data from brain insults and injuries to forge ahead with the research in this field. Case study by case study, the body of knowledge was progressing, albeit slowly and tediously, through the first part of the last century.

Based on observations of patients with brain damages, especially of loss of speech, Broca developed the concept of left-hemisphere dominance for speech, and accurately predicted the location of where speech is processed in the brain.

About the same time that Phineas Gage was traumatized by the loss of a good portion of his frontal lobe, Paul Broca, a Belgian anatomist, was successful in determining the loss of function as the result of brain injury. He is mainly remembered for his epoch-making works on the localization of brain functions. Based on observations of patients with brain damage, especially of loss of speech, Broca developed the concept of left-hemisphere dominance for speech, and accurately predicted the location of where speech is processed in the brain. Working independently from Broca was Carl Wernicke in Germany. Although it took the scientific community a while to understand the importance of their work, both Broca and Wernicke were credited with the discovery of where language is processed in the brain. Most of their research involved case studies in which brain injuries served as the lynchpins for discovery (Damasio, 1994).

Mapping the Brain

Beginning in the 1940s, Canadian brain surgeon Wilder Penfield mapped the brain's motor cortex—the area that controls the movement of the body's muscles. He did this by applying mild electric currents to the exposed brains of patients while they were in surgery. His work was pivotal for the entry of technology to study parts of the brain in living people. (See the activities at the end of the chapter to simulate Penfield's experiments.)

The use of x-rays in medicine was well known in the first half of the twentieth century and used widely to identify hard, dense material in the body. The problem with x-rays was that organs of the same density look the same. But British engineer Godfrey Hounsfield came up with an improvement on the old technology. It combined x-ray images with a computer. Referred to as Computerized Axil Tomography (CAT), this technology is especially useful for looking at head injuries and brain problems. The CAT scan uses x-rays, but instead of the image being recorded on photographic film, computers record the x-rays passing through the body. The scanner rotates around the entire body, taking a series of images that provide a three-dimensional image of the body. Since a CAT scan allows images to be taken on all sides of the body, it shows the exact location of a foreign object. With this equipment, scientists were able to clearly see a brain lesion as a dark, circular cyst the brain.

As helpful as CAT scans were, neuroscientists still needed to establish what was happening in the brain at the time it was happening. What was needed

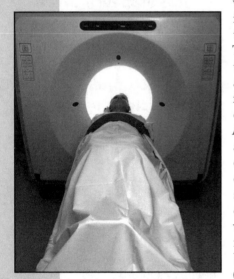

Brain-scanning technology has changed almost everything we thought we knew about the brain.

was more precise technology that would allow the imaging of blood flow and oxidation of glucose, the brain's main food item. Positron Emission Tomography (PET) was the first scanning method to provide information on brain function as well as anatomy. This information includes data on blood flow, oxygen consumption, glucose metabolism, and concentrations of various molecules in brain tissue. Although the process is not invasive, a very small amount of a radioactive compound is inhaled by or injected into the patient. The injected or inhaled compound accumulates in the brain tissue to be studied. As the radioactive atoms in the compound decay, they release smaller particles called positrons, which are positively charged. A scanner detects the radioactive material to produce an image of the brain. When a positron collides with an electron (negatively charged), they are both annihilated, and two photons (light particles) are emitted. The photons move in opposite directions and are picked up by the detector ring of the PET scanner. A high-speed computer uses this information to generate three-dimensional, cross-sectional images that represent the biological activity where the radioisotope compound has accumulated.

Like the PET scan, Single Photon Emission Computed Tomography (SPECT) scans are capable of evaluating brain blood flow and activity patterns. They are easier to perform, less expensive, and use less radiation then PET scans. New and improved machines now allow neurologists to see how the working brain really functions. Neurologists look for evidence of dementia, strokes, brain trauma, and drug abuse when compared to normal brains.

One of the most ardent supporters of SPECT scans and their diagnostic possibilities with types of ADD (attention deficit disorder) is Daniel Amen. His work in SPECT brain imaging and the children he treats for ADD has received a great deal of interest in the past ten years.

Developed in the 1980s, Magnetic Resonance Imaging (MRI) has added profoundly to helping understand what is happening in the brain. MRI is a technology that, using a gigantic magnet, can line up the protons—or nuclei of hydrogen atoms—in an object (or organism) to align with the north-south polarity of the magnet. A computer reads this to create an image known as MRI. MRI is excellent for observing soft tissues because they have a higher water (and therefore hydrogen) content than bone. MRI can give an image of any plane through the body, while the patient's experience consists of lying still in a body-sized tube and hearing the clicks of the machinery. MRI can focus within 1 mm in depth in all three planes. Like an optical camera using colored differential, scientists can interpret the values for different chemicals rapidly moving across the brain in three-dimensional photos (Hymen, 2000).

The problem with MRI in the late '80s was that it took so much computer function to read the output data. Computer size and capacity were limiting factors when the researcher needed to get real-time data. It might take hours or days to wait until the computers processed all the data.

Two factors dramatically increased the value of MRI for brain scientists. First, the breakthrough came with the development of supercomputers. Computers have become more powerful and less expensive. Be reminded that your PC laptop now possesses more power than computers taking up an entire room or house twenty years ago. Now, scientists can study data in real time. Second, a new type of MRI was discovered in 1992 (Bookheimer, 2004). Functional MRI (fMRI) shows what areas of the brain are working by showing indirectly which areas more blood is flowing to during a performance task. For instance, if you want to study a singular system like the system that distributes the neurotransmitter serotonin, you can eliminate all other systems and watch where and how this important substance is made, flows to, and works on (Slywester, 2001). If you wanted to know the effect of cocaine in the brain and in what regions, you could find out as the cocaine was coursing through the veins of the subject.

Neuroscientists now use both types of MRI. Structural MRI is used to obtain high-resolution images of brain structures while functional MRI provides images of what the brain is doing during mental activity.

For many situations, MRI is the preferred diagnostic tool—especially for brain imaging (although CAT scan is still chosen for strokes because it is better at detecting hemorrhaging). The drawback of MRI technology is that it is tremendously expensive and difficult for smaller hospitals to afford. This invention is probably the single most important advance in brain science. What inventions will be next in the rapidly developing science?

THE EDUCATIONAL CONNECTION

Now that scientific tools are emerging to unlock some of the mysteries of the brain, there is also great interest from educators in all educational settings. Educators are now rethinking the very foundation of how we teach and what we teach to children of all ages. There are an increasing number of significant principles about how people learn that are now being substantiated by brain research. Why some of the teaching strategies in the past have worked and why some strategies work better than others are now being understood. For instance, teachers now know why it's vital to frequently change the physiological state of their learners: Research about the habituation of neurons to the same stimuli has helped educators understand that (see Chapter 7). Effective teachers knew this intuitively but didn't understand why. What we have learned is that teachers can improve learning by becoming aware of how the brain works. When educators understand something about how the brain functions, they can translate this knowledge to skills useful for their students.

As brain-imaging technology has provided geometric increases in knowledge, and a lesser amount of application to the classroom, we are obligated as educators to seek a rudimentary understanding of how memory works from several levels.

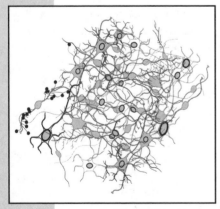

Neural network (used with permission of Eric Jensen).

The Mother of all Multitaskers!

Neurons are cells that specialize in receiving and transmitting signals. Glial cells support the neurons at a ratio of about ten glial cells to every neuron. Humans store DNA, our genetic material, in nerve cells. In each cell, at any given moment, only small portions of our DNA are being activated and producing proteins, while the rest remains unexpressed in that cell. Amazingly, each of the hundred billion neurons and the accompanying trillion glial cells of the brain contain the same DNA. Each cell will produce those genetic products that it needs to do its specific task. Scientists believe that billions of cells in the brain can coordinate, orchestrate, communicate, and cooperate to create the most complex of biological organs from these billions of parts.

Neurons are cells specialized to receive, store, and transmit information. The work of neurons is to communicate with each other. All neurons have some features that allow them to receive, process, store, and send messages that come from outside of the cells.

Besides the cell body, axons at one end and dendrites at the other make up the structure of the cell. The chemical part of any message allows neurons to receive a stream of chemical signals from other neurons, process these incoming signals, and change their chemical interior in response to these signals. This happens almost instantly as the messages are transmitted to other neurons. Networks of neurons are engaged in continuous dialogue with each other, and the resulting communication creates the way the brain mediates and directs its activities.

There are many kinds of neurons. They can be defined either by how they look or by what they do. In some areas of the brain, neurons are densely packed, while in others they are relatively distant. Most neurons form their connections with neurons that are close to each other; other neurons send axons to neurons in distant areas of the brain. A single neuron or group of neurons can send simultaneous signals to many areas, and since neurons can be "talking" to each other simultaneously while "talking" to thousands of other neurons, it can be said that they are masters at multitasking!

Fortunately, neurons are perfectly designed for making connections. Each neuron sends out signals to other neurons and receives input from other neurons. Some of the most exciting work on memory is now taking place at the neuron level of understanding, as neuroscientists consider how neurons talk to each other.

Concentrating on the neurons located in the hippocampus, scientists are beginning to hypothesize how memory is established in these cells. This is where short-term memory is stored and appears to be the linchpin organ for how some memories get forgotten, while others go to long-term memory in the cortex.

A special neurotransmitter, in this case a peptide compound called "glutamate," acts as excitatory neurotransmitter that appears to be one of the keys to cellular memory. It is the most excitatory of neurotransmitters, and the hippocampus seems to be the most "glutamatergic" of all the structures (Sapolsky, 1999).

When a neuron has received some information, gets excited, and wants to pass it on to another neuron, something amazing happens. A wave of electrical excitation sweeps over the neuron and triggers the release of neurotransmitters. Scientists now believe this is how neurons talk to each other!

According to Robert Sapolsky in his book *Why Zebras Don't Get Ulcers*, "the electrical excitation travels down the neuron through the axon and to the end of the dendrite. A little bit of glutamate is released and gets the other neuron a little excited. In other words, some glutamate is released and nothing happens. It isn't until a certain threshold of glutamate concentration is passed that suddenly all hell breaks loose in the second neuron and there is a massive wave of excitation. Calcium comes pouring in and all kinds of reactions occur. . . . And this is what learning is all about!"

Think of this analogy: A math teacher drones on, equations go in one ear and out the other. It's repeated again and again, and it fails to sink in. Finally for the hundredth time it is repeated, and a light bulb goes on. "Aha!" On the cellular level that threshold of glutamate excitation has been released.

According to Sapolsky, the second part of this idea has even more importance. Under the right conditions when there is enough glutamate-driven excitement,

the next time it takes *less* of the excitatory glutamate to get that "Aha." That synapse has just learned something! Neuroscientists say it has "potentiated" or strengthened. How this potentiation works long-term is one of the most exciting findings that neuroscientists are now investigating.

When a long-term potentiation has been made and used repeatedly in the early years, it becomes permanent. In contrast, a long-term potentiation that is not used at all, or often enough, is unlikely

Keeping your students engaged helps them achieve understanding sooner.

to survive. A study by Janellen Huttenlocker of the University of Chicago showed that when socioeconomic factors were controlled, babies whose mothers talked to them more had a bigger vocabulary. At twenty months, babies of talkative mothers knew 131 more words then infants of less talkative mothers and at twenty-four months, the difference was 295 words (Kotulak, 1997). Children who are rarely spoken to or read to in the early years may have more difficulty mastering vocabulary and language skills later on. A child who is rarely played with may have difficulty with social adjustment as he or she grows to adolescence (Levine, 2002).

Men Are on Testosterone, Women Are on Estrogen

To understand how men and women are different, one might look at our human ancestors from the past fifty thousand years. Our brains are remarkably like those of the humans we have followed. We can gain some insight into sex differences by studying the roles men and women have played during the time when human cultures were dominated by hunter-gatherer societies. The roles played by men included hunting and defending the tribe against predators and enemies with handmade weapons. Women stayed near the home, tending children, gathering food, and preparing food and clothing for the tribe. These two specializations would have put different selection pressures on men and women. Successful members survived to reproduce and pass on their genes to the next generation's gene pool. From an evolutionary understanding it would seem logical that sex differences would have accumulated in brain structure and function. But questions remain regarding how hormones act on human brain systems to produce the sex differences. Data from laboratory animals have helped us understand this process, and brain-imaging technology has increased our knowledge of hormonal influences and the impact on behavior.

Certainly, even the most ardent of critics would agree that men and women look at life differently. Neuroscientists would go further: There are significant differences in the anatomy and physiology of the brains of the two sexes. As long as the brain has been examined, scientists have been looking for differences between the sexes. "At least one hundred sex differences in male and female brains have been described so far," said Nancy Forger from the University of Massachusetts.

Neuroscientists are now able to look carefully at the living brain as it functions and grows. The deeper the probe, the more information begins to grow— suggesting that in most cases men and women do not behave, feel, think, or respond in the same ways, either on the inside or on the outside. A summary of some of this research includes some interesting findings:

Women seem to have better connections between the two brain hemispheres. This may be attributed to the corpus callosum, a bundle of nerve fibers that connects the two hemispheres of the brain. About twenty years ago, research suggested it is about 20 percent larger in women (Carter, 1999). That would explain why the emotional right side of women's brains is more in touch with the analytical left side, albeit the old theories on the functions of left and right sides of the brain are now completely revised. Perhaps the enhanced corpus callosum might explain quite a few things. Dave Barry, the well-known columnist from the *Miami Herald*, wrote an article that include the differences between the way men and women look at cleanliness:

> *Men—because of a tragic genetic flaw—cannot see dirt until there is enough of it to support agriculture. This puts men at a huge disadvantage against women, who can detect a single dirt molecule twenty feet away.*

> *This is why a man and a woman can both be looking at the same bathroom commode, and the man—hindered by Male Genetic Dirt Blindness (MGDB)— will perceive the commode surface as being clean enough for heart surgery or even meat slicing; whereas the woman can't even see the commode, only a teeming, commode-shaped swarm of bacteria. A woman can spend two hours cleaning a toothbrush holder and still not be totally satisfied; whereas if you ask a man to clean the entire New York City subway system, he'll go down there with a bottle of Windex and a single paper towel, then emerge twenty-five minutes later, weary but satisfied with a job well done.[1]*

While Mr. Barry may not be scientifically accurate, he does have a point. Typically, men and women view the world differently. Women are credited with sensitivity while men appear to be more pragmatic and have a harder time looking beyond the surface of a situation. The theory of a larger corpus callosum has since been discredited by some workers, however, and scientists are still searching for the answers. Some research suggests that the apparent superiority of the use of the corpus callosum in females may be due to the structures that tend it (Geyer, 2003).

In certain areas the brain of the female is more densely packed with neurons. Women are better at multitasking and tend to use more parts of their brain to

---

[1] Reprinted with permission of Dave Barry. Further duplication is not permitted without his express permission.

accomplish certain tasks. That might explain why they often recover better from a stroke, since the healthy parts of their mind compensate for the injured regions. The female brain is more diffused and utilizes significant portions of

both hemispheres for a variety of tasks. Women naturally see everyday things from a broader, "big-picture" vantage point (Ripley, 2005). In a recent study, women reported more feelings of worry than men. Women also reported a more negative problem orientation (Dugas, 2003).

The male brain appears to be highly specialized, using specific parts of one hemisphere or the other to accomplish specific tasks. This allows men to focus on narrow issues and block out unrelated information and distractions for long periods of time without tiring. Men are able to separate

Female vs. Male: Their brains are truly different.

information, stimulus, emotions, and relationships into separate compartments in their brains, while women tend to link everything together. Men have as much as twenty times more testosterone in their systems than do women (Kastleman, 2001). Testosterone levels correlate several behaviors such as competition, self-assertion, and self-reliance. This makes men typically more aggressive and dominant, although the effects of testosterone are not fully understood.

In men, the dominant perceptual sense is vision, which is typically not the case with women. All of a woman's senses are, in some respects, more finely tuned than those of a man. Females hear and retain hearing better. At 85 decibels they hear two times more loudness than males. They learn to speak earlier and learn languages more quickly. Women excel at verbal memory and process language more quickly.

Indeed, men and women seem to handle emotions quite differently. While both sexes use the amygdala, women seem to have stronger connections between the amygdala and regions of the brain that handle language and other higher-level functions. That may explain why women are, on average, more likely to talk about their emotions and men tend to compartmentalize their worries and carry on, according to Dr. Richard Haier, psychology professor from UC Irvine (Carey, 2005).

Regarding vision, males have better distance vision while women excel at peripheral vision. Males see brighter light; females have superior night vision and excel at visual memory, facial clues, and context. Considering touch, females have a more diffused and sensitive touch; they react to pain more acutely and more quickly, but females are superior in fine motor dexterity. A significant advantage goes to females regarding smell and taste. Females have a stronger sense of smell and are more responsive to aromas, odors, and subtle changes in smell (Klutky, 1990). This continues throughout adulthood and has been demonstrated many times in the laboratory.

When it comes to activity, just observe children of upper elementary and middle school on the playground. Boys tend to run, kick, and wrestle with each other in what appears to be a way to release excess energy while girls tend to form small groups and talk to each other. Girls are wired to talk; boys are wired to do (Sylwester, 2003)!

From research it appears that the brains of males and females grow differently and also decay differently. It's been reported that the degeneration of nerve cells in the male brain proceeds much faster than in the female brain (Kimura, 1992).

THE EDUCATIONAL CONNECTION

What does this mean? What are the implications for middle and high schools? We know there are real differences in the sexes. One of the outcomes of this is to think of how different sexes respond to different teaching strategies. Knowing this can help teachers become more sensitive to the learning styles of the two sexes. In middle school, as the bodies of boys and girls change due to puberty, teachers need to be aware that every day, every hour, every minute brings about changes in behavior. Expressed more overtly by boys, this has been the undoing of many new teachers. More than anything else, it requires the patience of Job! Middle-school teachers are a unique breed that if successful, have learned that boys and girls will be different almost every day of this period of their lives.

Managing boredom seems easier for girls. Boys are easily distracted and want to spread out with their more spatial brains searching for space. Try to give boys more space to operate in and find ways to allow boys to move. All children need movement and exercise; think about how students can be allowed to move about. Using movement to introduce lessons is essential to reducing the "seat snoring" so frequently observed in middle- and high-school classes (see Chapter 7).

Novelty is crucial for all students but is particularly important for boys. They respond to humor of almost any sort, the cornier the better! If you ask a middle-school boy why he likes a teacher, he will almost always say it's because the teacher is funny (see Chapter 7).

Since girls generally have better language and writing skills, their writing tends to be more effective, and often they will score much higher on assignments. When compared to girls, boys often fall short because they either use too few words developed poorly or they find jargon and coded language to communicate (Gurian, 2003). Teachers need to be aware of how boys often fall behind because of poor writing skills when compared to girls. Given more variation in assessment tools, which include verbal and kinesthetic options, may help boys function on par with girls during the middle- and early high-school years.

Right Brain/Left Brain?

If you want to know how each half of the brain operates, just sever the corpus callosum that connects the left and right cerebral cortex. The split brain now separates the two hemispheres, and they operate independently from each other. Roger Sperry in 1981 won a Nobel Prize for this work; however, twenty-seven years later, much of this work is used metaphorically or has been updated. The anatomy of the brain was far easier than the interpretations of the findings, yet much of what Sperry inferred has been written into popular books—including school textbooks—suggesting children should complete activities based on whether they are left- or right-brained. In fact, it's very likely that both sides of the brain are involved with nearly every human activity (Jensen, 2000).

Our present understanding of early brain plasticity has explained why the brain is not so compartmentalized as we might have thought a quarter century ago. The evidence has come from children who have had severe injury to the right or left side of the brain. After undergoing a hemispherectomy, where one half of the brain is removed, almost all of these children have slowly regained functions lost to that half of the brain by the use of the remaining side (PBS Series, *The Brain*, 2000). In other words, some of their left-brain functions might have moved over into their right brain during childhood or vice versa. Millions of adults who lose their speech through a stroke will testify that this degree of plasticity is probably lost with age. Research suggests that the ability to move functions stored in one side of the brain to the other is probably mostly confined to the preschool years.

The work of Gregory Hickok at the University of California at Irvine illustrates how much we have progressed since Sperry's time. Presenting at the *Learning Brain Expo* in San Diego, Dr. Hickok shared research conducted on processing music in the brain. Using fMRI brain imaging, his group found that music, as well as language, is processed in both hemispheres of the brain (Hickok, 2005).

THE EDUCATIONAL CONNECTION

Those educators who advocate for right-brain thinking or left-brain thinking would benefit from reading updates on the research. Unfortunately, we are still seeing textbook publishers selling books based on this concept and others administering assessments to children for the purpose of determining whether they are left- or right-brained. It's important that we not take the simplified explanation of left/right brain dominance into the classroom, and, more important, that we help validate all children as "whole-brained."

Summary of Chapter 2

- The progress in neuroscience is largely due to the development and continued progress of imaging technology that safely provides detailed and accurate information about the living brain.

- The development of functional MRI has allowed researchers to study the impact of neurotransmitters, drugs, and other influential factors on the brain in real time.

- The process of forming new connections between neurons (synaptic connections) is involved with cellular memory.

- Research suggests that the brains of men and women have distinctive differences. Those differences appear to have significance in how the sexes interpret the environment.

- Earlier ideas about right- and left-brain functions have been modified. It is now understood that the brain isn't as compartmentalized as was previously thought.

ENGAGING THE BRAIN THROUGH ACTIVITIES

Activity #1

Viewing the Effects of a Stroke
For more information on the impact of strokes on the brain, view an interactive video clip from the PBS series—*The Secret Life of the Brain*.
http://www.pbs.org/wnet/brain/episode4/video.html

Activity#2

The Cerebrospinal Fluid: A Comforting Solution
Background: As a visual activity, try showing adolescents how important the skull is for protecting the brain. Risk taking on motorcycles, all-terrain vehicles, skateboards, and other equipment has increased the number of head injuries in adolescent populations.

The cerebrospinal fluid has several functions. One of these functions is to protect the brain from sudden impacts. To demonstrate how this works, take a raw egg with a drawn-on face. The inside of the egg represents the brain, and the eggshell represents the pia mater (the innermost layer of the meninges, or coverings, of the brain).

Put the egg in a container (Tupperware works fine) that is a bit larger than the egg. The container represents the skull. Now put a tight top on the container and shake it. You should observe that shaking the "brain" (the egg) in this situation results in damage (a broken egg).

Now repeat the experiment with a new egg, except this time fill the container with water. The water represents the cerebrospinal fluid. Note that shaking the container does not cause the "brain damage" as before because the fluid has cushioned the brain from injury.

This activity could be the start of a science fair project: Test the hypothesis that "the cerebrospinal fluid and skull protect the brain from impact injury." Possible procedure: Drop an egg from a standard height (or heights) in different conditions: (1) with fluid in the container, (2) without fluid in the container, (3) with different fluids or materials (sand, rocks), or (4) in differently shaped containers. Make sure you keep notes to record your observations!

Materials:
* Eggs (at least two)
* Markers to draw on a face (waterproof ink)
* Plastic container with top
* Water (to fill the container)

This activity has been modified with permission from Dr. Eric Chudler's Neuroscience for Kids Web site:
http://faculty.washington.edu/chudler/neurok.html

A variation of this activity uses hard-boiled eggs. Place a large clean piece of butcher paper on the floor and let hard-boiled eggs roll off a table to drop onto the paper placed on the floor. Pick the cracked eggs and their shells up carefully. Provide groups of students with white glue and toothpicks to return all of the cracked pieces back on the shell. After students have struggled with the process, ask questions about how this might be compared to cracking a skull in an accident and how difficult it might be to piece it all together.

Activity #3

Simulate Penfield's Experiments

Wilder Penfield mapped the brain's motor cortex—the area that controls the movement of the body's muscles. He did this by applying mild electric currents to the exposed brains of patients while they were in surgery. His work was pivotal for the entry of technology to study parts of the brain in living people. You can simulate his experiments by going to this site and probing the brain:
http://www.pbs.org/wgbh/aso/tryit/brain/

Activity #4

Facilitating Discussions

Background: In the classroom, teachers should develop activities that encourage students to talk about their emotions, listen to their classmates' opinions, and think about the motivations of people who are outside the classroom. Using one carefully chosen question or activity for discussion makes it possible for students to make judgments or propose courses of action and report their reasons. As effective discussion leaders, we need to establish and maintain a nonjudgmental environment that encourages open, reasonable communication with other students.

Preparation for the Discussion

Set Your Objective
Design the learning objective for your open-ended discussion by referring to the curriculum lesson or by answering, "What do I want students to understand, explore, or conclude as a result of this discussion? How can I keep it simplistic and based on the information I have already taught them?"

Select Questions

Choose questions that have two legitimate points of view. The brain responds to a dilemma with solvable solutions. The questions should be selected to elicit higher-order thinking skills. Use questions like: "How do you feel about . . ." "What should be done about . . ." or "What should [name of person in story] do?"

Discussion Steps

A. Review What Is Known
Try an engaging scenario to make the subject interesting and relevant to students (you might use an article, a story, or a video clip). Have information that is critical to the discussion.

B. Present One Question
Present one question for discussion. Create a nonjudgmental environment that allows all students to participate. When you feel that students are finished with the question, suggest another question or conclude the lesson.

C. Facilitate the Discussion
Students should be able to formulate and express their own opinions, hear responses or reactions from their peers, and become more effective in interacting with others. When appropriate, ask students if they would like to "conference." Allow all students to talk to each other for a designated time, and then call students back and remind students of the ground rules. Remain

neutral; do not influence student response or communicate your opinion about the discussion question. Clarify or paraphrase student comments to promote or deepen understanding. Provide additional information only if requested by students.

D. Student Reflections

When first participating in these types of discussions a teacher may want to ask students questions about the discussion like: How do you feel about this discussion? How do you feel about the way we have been working? How is this type of discussion different from others you have participated in? What do you do when someone disagrees with you? What are some ways you can express your disagreement with someone's ideas?

Allow students to internalize the lesson by asking them to quietly reflect on how the discussion has influenced their thinking.

Selected Books for Enhancing This Chapter

Carter, Rita	*Mapping the Mind.* University of California Press: Berkeley, CA, 1998 This is a wonderfully illustrated story of brain exploration. Carter invites readers to join her to look at the social implications of the discoveries of neuroscience. She addresses questions regarding the meaning of the mind as well as the creation of memory, the development of language, the complexities of sensations, the genesis of emotions, and the occurrence of behavioral eccentricities.
Levine, Mel	*A Mind at a Time.* Simon and Schuster: New York, 2002 Probably one of the most influential educators in this field today, Levine's books read like he speaks. Brimming with intelligence, humor, wit, and originality, this book is useful to every educator on the planet.
Sylwester, Robert	*A Celebration of Neurons: An Educator's Guide to the Brain.* ASCD: Alexandria, VA, 1995 Sylwester provides a comprehensive and well-written overview of the research in neuroscience. Using lots of metaphors, he helps the reader understand the implications of the research for education.

3

Environmental and Genetic Effects on the Developing Brain

Chapter 3
Environmental and Genetic Effects on the Developing Brain

Brain wiring involves an intricate dance between nature and nurture.
—Lise Elliot, neuroscientist and author

The debate between nature and nurture is age-old but was significantly revised in the past decade when the disciples of genetics and behavioral science began to look at how the two forces may work together. We know that the genetic material a child brings to this life is greatly influenced by the experiential part of life, even before birth. If a child doesn't receive a caregiver's love, touch, and attention early in life, the sectors of the brain responsible for behavioral and social acceptance may not be formed sufficiently to assure good mental health later in life. Fortunately, the plasticity of the young brain is so powerful that there is hope for children from mentally impoverished homes when given the right ingredients.

The concept of emotional intelligence has gained strength since it became popularized ten years ago. While not an exact science, it seems to present a better representation than what it means to be "smart" using only the intelligence quotient (IQ).

Early Exposure to Violence and Its Effect on One Man

How ironic that it should have come to this. . . . He began life in a mud hut in a small village in 1937, born to a poor peasant family, some 100 miles north of an Old World city. His father died of an "internal disease" while his mother was pregnant with him. A few months later, during his mother's eighth month of pregnancy, his twelve-year-old brother died of childhood cancer. Devastated and destitute, his mother attempted suicide. A Jewish family saved her. Then she tried to self-abort but was again prevented by her Jewish benefactors.

After he was born, his mother did not wish to see him, which strongly suggests that she was suffering from major depression. His care was relegated to her brother, in whose home he spent much of his early childhood. At age three, he was reunited with his mother, who had married a distant relative. His stepfather reportedly was abusive psychologically and physically with the young boy.

The first several years of life are crucial to the development of healthy self-esteem, and so his inability to bond with his mother and the subsequent abuse at the hands of his stepfather would have profoundly wounded his emerging self-esteem, impairing his capacity for empathy with others. One course in the face of such traumatizing experiences is to sink into despair, passivity, and hopelessness. But another is to etch a psychological template of compensatory grandiosity, as if to vow, "Never again shall I submit to superior force." This was the developmental psychological path he followed.

From his early years, he charted his own course and would not accept limits. According to his semiofficial biography, when he was ten, he was impressed by a visit from his cousin who knew how to read and write. He confronted his family with his wish to become educated, and when they turned him down because there was no school in his parents' village, he left home in the middle of the night, making his way to his maternal uncle's home in the city to study there.

His uncle tutored his young charge in his view of history and the ideology of nationalism, eventually facilitating his secondary schooling at a school known for teaching an inflammatory brand of nationalism. He inspired his young charge with dreams of glory, telling him that he was destined to play an important role in his country's history, following the path of heroic relatives and heroes of the world he was learning about.

When he attended high school, the streets were aflame with revolutionary fervor. After joining the party at twenty, he had ambitions to rise, and he did, moving from street thug to strategist to the leader of a pivotal country in world history.

But no matter how grandiose a life a person like this constructs—and he built for himself as lavish a life as is possible, creating a cult of personality in his country, dotting the landscape with opulent palaces—the well of pain and insecurity caused by early wounds can never be filled. In his case, his strong desire to never again be humiliated and abused fueled an intense rage. The stories of his cruelty are legendary.

But his actions also deprived him of the check of wise counsel. When his minister of health criticized a decision made by this leader, he was sent home in a body bag, chopped into pieces. This combination of limited international perspective and a flattering leadership circle led him repeatedly to miscalculate and ultimately led to his downfall.

The man who emerged from the "spider hole" during his capture in December of 2003 was shorn of his defensive defiance, revealing the emptiness beneath his facade. This was Saddam Hussein.

These destructive experiences described in Saddam Hussein's life and the remarkable similarities in the early lives of Joseph Stalin and Adolf Hitler provide a glimpse of how the impact of violence on the developing child increases risk for emotional, behavioral, social, and physical problems throughout life. How can these experiences result in influencing the development and functioning of the child's brain?

SOURCE: Adapted with permission from Post, J. M. (2003, December 21). Rathole Under the Palace. *Los Angeles Times*.

Traumatic Experiences, Development, and Malleability

Animal and human research suggests that under favorable experiences, the brain develops healthy, flexible, and diverse capabilities. When there is disruption of the timing and intensity of normal developmental experiences, however, it may have a devastating impact on neurodevelopment (Diamond & Hobson, 1998). Children who are neglected or traumatized may experience incidents that influence the development of their brains. During the traumatic experience, the brain is racked with fear-related activation. This activation of key neural systems in the brain leads to adaptive changes in emotional, behavioral, and cognitive functioning to promote survival. Continued traumatic events can lead to increased muscle tone, a focus on threat-related cues (typically nonverbal), anxiety, and behavioral impulsivity—all of which make their lives difficult (Perry, 2002).

The brain of a young child is very malleable. It is capable of changing in response to experiences, especially repetitive and patterned experiences. "It's clear that the brain is far from immutable," writes Marian Diamond of the University of California. One of the pioneers in neurological research, Dr. Diamond found that young rats raised in impoverished environments had changes in their brains that indicated less development when compared with young rats in enriched environments. Sensory areas in the enriched-environment rats were thicker and other layers heavier (Diamond & Hobson, 1998).

Evidence from many laboratories clearly shows that the blueprint for developing a brain is not just the genes but also the experiences children have that decide when and how to sculpt the growing brain.

Dr. Diamond and other researchers have found similar patterns in children. When the environment is changed for abused and traumatized children the brains of these youngsters will recover in proportion to their age. The younger the child is when the environment improves, the less damage is recorded. When aggressive, early identification and intervention of abused and neglected children takes place, they have a greater capacity to respond and be influenced in positive ways (Siegel, 1999).

One of the most exciting areas of neuroscience today is that of neural plasticity, according to Megan Gunnar from the University of Minnesota. Neural plasticity refers to the capacity of the brain to change with experience. Evidence from many laboratories clearly shows that the blueprint for developing a brain is not just the genes but also the experiences children have that decide when and how to sculpt the growing brain.

The flexibility of brain areas is different. The cortex, the most complex area, possesses the greatest flexibility or plasticity, the brain stem the least. We can continue to modify the cortex throughout our lives, albeit it takes more effort when you reach old age. Try teaching an eighty-year-old how to program their VCR or TiVo and see how receptive the cortex is. In contrast, try the same experiment with a five-year-old, and it's obvious whose brain is more malleable!

For survival reasons, the brain stem and diencephalon are not very plastic. The life-sustaining functions are critically regulated there and must remain turned on to maintain circulation, heartbeat, and breathing.

As we progress upward toward the neocortex, the level of plasticity increases in proportion to the level of complexity. In other words, as the areas of the brain increase in complexity, they become more plastic. One of the key issues to understand is that under threat, the brain is less capable of abstract thought, concrete thought, and emotional reactivity. Consequently, a brain under threat has less capacity for plasticity.

The Brain Is Dependent on Being Used

In order to gain cognitive learning, emotional learning, motor-vestibular functioning, and state regulation, we must use that part of our brain that "learns" the particular lesson. For instance, if you don't get on a bicycle, your motor-vestibular system will never be challenged to learn how to balance on a bicycle. You can read all about how to ride a bike, watch video footage of people riding bikes, and talk to people who ride bikes, but you will never learn to ride a bike unless your motor-vestibular structures experience riding a bike. In order to learn—to change the brain—the experience has to activate the part of the brain that mediates the function. Interestingly, the part of your brain designed to keep the information on riding a bike never loses it unless brain trauma or injury blocks it out.

The "use it or lose it" principle can be strengthened by what we have found from studies of the migration of neurons to their final places in the brain. Once they find their "homes" they start to grow dendrites and axons to communicate with other dendrites and axons. When a given neuron doesn't receive specific chemical signals from experiences, i.e., never riding a bike, it will be eliminated and pruned from the neural network of communicating neurons. In other words, if the neuron is not stimulated by experience, it doesn't appear to make the vital connections with other neurons designated to carry out that function (Ratey, 2001).

The Early Brain

Not all of the brain's areas are organized and fully functional in the infant. The lower regions of the brain and the parts that act as regulators are the first to develop, followed in sequence by adjacent but higher, more complex regions. The brain is organized so that the lower structures go online first, allowing simple functions such as respiration, heart rate, and blood pressure regulation. The higher structures that control more complex functions such as thinking and regulating emotions come online later. Only a small amount of mylenation of the neurons has taken place at birth compared to what will happen in the first two years. If we were to look at the newborn baby's brain using imaging technology, we would note high activity in the sectors of the brain that control the sucking motion but little else in the those higher regions.

It is during childhood that the brain begins to mature and the whole set of brain-related capabilities develop with a predetermined order dictated by genes. We crawl before we can walk upright, and we must babble before turning language into polished patter.

The concept of nature versus nurture is so ingrained in our thinking, says Sharon Ramey, formerly professor of neurobiology at the University of Alabama, that "it's almost impossible to get beyond." The debate between nature and nurture was significantly influenced in the past decade, when the disciplines of genetics and behavioral science began to study how the two forces may work together (Ramey, 1999).

External influences start to affect the genetic component from conception onward. Even in the confines of its mother, each child is impacted by the environment. If the mother experiences high levels of stress, smokes, or abuses alcohol and drugs, these threatening environmental influences can trigger brain chemicals and determine how genes are expressed. Early experiences before and after birth can lay down a biochemical foundation for the intellectual, emotional, and social functioning of a life ahead . . . very powerful stuff!

Some children by their very nature or genetic makeup are more vulnerable to stress during intrauterine or postpartum development. Stress caused by abuse, poverty, neglect, or sensory deprivation can affect the genetic makeup of the child. It can switch brain development sectors on or off at the wrong times, sometimes making individuals more aggressive, violent, or depressed (Lally, 1997).

Sequential Brain Development

The process of sequential development is guided by experience and genetic signals. The key finding that gives "nurture" its due is that the brain develops and modifies itself in response to experience. Neurons and synapses change in an activity-dependent fashion. This developmental dependence of the brain seems to help us understand that if the "nurture" of the brain is not favorable (neglect and trauma) the impact can be severe on the development of critical areas of the brain (Perry, 2005).

The more a certain neural system is activated, the more it will build neural connections at that site. What occurs in this process is an internal representation of the experience corresponding to the neural activation. In other words, the brain of the individual is being shaped by its experience with the outside world.

THE EDUCATIONAL CONNECTION

How receptive youth are to what you teach them is often mismatched with the receptive portions of the individual's brain. If the teenager has been traumatized or is in a persistent state of anxiety due to factors in his or her personal life, it becomes very difficult to be receptive to the demands of a teacher. When middle- and high-school students flow in and out of classrooms we assume that they are capable of learning as we use the teaching styles familiar to us. However, when in a state of anxiety, the key parts of the cortex are not receptive to cognitive information that isn't relevant to survival. "The traumatized child's brain is essentially unavailable to process efficiently the complex cognitive information being conveyed by the teacher" (Perry, 2002).

The first step in understanding why some students act out in class is to appreciate the fact that you are probably not the causative agent. It's very likely that the student's state of anxiety has prevented him or her from being receptive in your class. You can, however, ask, "How can I engage the student? What can I do to encourage more learning and cooperation?"

A New Window Into Brain Development

Nitin Gogtay and his colleagues at the National Institutes of Mental Health have reported a powerful new technique for creating maps of growth patterns in the brains of children (Gogtay, et al., 2004). This strategy offers a new window into brain development that reveals the patterns of brain tissue growth and loss. Using MRI technology, they were able to show how the development of gray matter in the cortex matured in subjects between four and twenty-one years of age. This resulted in the ability to track local changes in growth throughout the brains of these individuals over time.

The studies were accomplished by scanning the brains of thirteen healthy children for whom MRI scans were obtained every two years for eight to ten years. Recent studies using similar technology were led by Paul Thompson of the University of California, Los Angeles. Some remarkable findings have led to broad implications for educators. First, the team found that brain systems specializing in learning language grew rapidly from age six through puberty in both sexes. The linguistic brain areas experienced a shutting down of growth around ages eleven through fifteen (Thompson, et al., 2000). Earlier, using PET scans, neurologist Harry Chugani scanned the brains of children to follow the consumption of sugar, which is the energy the brain uses to carry out its work.

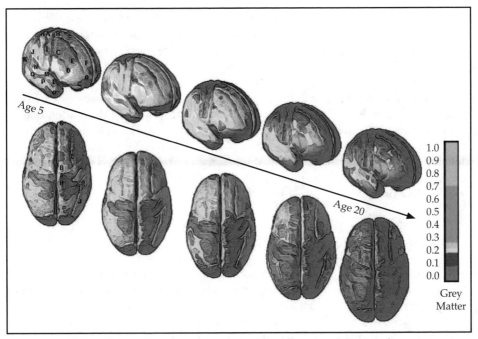

These brain scans were digitally enhanced to help differentiate the activated areas.
(Used with permission of Nitin Gogtay.)

What he found several years ago supports the Thompson team's findings: Beyond the age of twelve, learning language is more difficult because the brain must tear down old connections and build new ones. "Who was the idiot who decided that youngsters learn foreign languages in high school?" Chugani asks. "We are not paying attention to the biological principles of education" (Kotulak, 1997).

Thompson and his team at UCLA detected massive growth spurts from ages three to six in the frontal areas of the brain that specialize in organizing and planning new behaviors. During this period, children learn a great many new behaviors.

The simple and unavoidable result of this sequential neurodevelopment is that the organizing of an infant or young child's brain is more malleable to experience than is the case with a mature brain. While experience may change the functioning of an adult, experience literally provides the organizing framework for an infant and child.

The key finding from studying brains is that they are most receptive to environmental input in early childhood. The consequence of sequential development is that as different regions of the brain are organizing, they require specific kinds of experience targeting the region's specific function. Research suggests that there are critical developmental periods for particular functions such as vision and hearing. In other words, the brain "expects" certain visual images and patterns once the eyes are exposed to light. The developing neural system "expects" to hear sound in order for the auditory system to develop effectively. For certain functions, neurologists have found that if the particular stimuli (e.g., exposure to light in the development of vision) is not present at that time of early development, the window closes and the opportunity is lost forever. These times during development are called critical or sensitive periods.

One of the best examples of this discovery was a famous experiment by David Hubel and Torten Wiesel. They found that if they temporarily blindfolded one eye of a kitten at a crucial developmental period, the kitten would never recover its sight in that eye even when the blindfold was taken off. It would never develop binocular vision. Apparently, when the neurons devoted to developing vision in the eye did not receive sensory input (light), they never are able to carry out that function.

The Third Factor

If we consider the debate between factor one: nature, and factor two: nurture, one could argue that a third factor plays a major role in shaping the development of an individual's brain: experience-dependent mechanisms. These refer to lessons children receive that are not unique to humans but to the individual (Spinks, 2002). For instance, a child born in the mountains of Lima, Peru, will

THE EDUCATIONAL CONNECTION

In the public school classrooms of America, we are dealt the students that reach us much like being dealt a hand of cards: randomly! In middle- and high-school, children bring to the classroom neural networks that are well on their way toward being established. While we can make a great deal of difference in shaping the neural networks or templates that will serve these children for a lifetime (see Chapter 5), the most important intervention needs to come before children reach school age. Research on the effects of exposure to violence and maltreatment on young children show that they suffer from long-term consequences such as increased depression, anxiety, post-traumatic stress, anger, alcohol and drug abuse, and lower academic achievement (Perry, 2002). "The findings also confirm that these children are more likely to become juvenile and adult offenders. In 2001, 671,000 children were reported to child abuse agencies in California," says Bill Lockyer, Attorney General for California. If you extrapolate even a small portion of this population to adult offenders of the law, you have huge costs. Lockyer says the expenditure that California has is about two million dollars for the court costs, care, and feeding for each career criminal (Lockyer, 2001).

learn to herd llamas, live in family groups of forty to fifty people, weave intricate patterns in wool fabrics, and know how to raise crops. Meanwhile a young child in Peoria, Illinois, might develop good hand-eye coordination from manipulating a PlayStation, riding a bike, and learning to catch a baseball. The brain develops neural connections and networks specific to what is learned by the individual. What a child learns is specifically dependent on a particular environment and is therefore experience-dependent. But whether it's Peru or Peoria, a child's brain would still expect to find spoken language, visual and auditory stimuli, and motor input.

The implications of this third factor are great. If an adolescent is studying music, for instance, those cells and connections associated with learning music will become hardwired. If an adolescent concentrates on learning auto mechanics, those are the cells and connections that will be hardwired. If, however, the adolescent is lying on a couch all day and continuously watching MTV, those are the cells and connections that are going to survive. In other words, if an adolescent formed neural networks from specific experiences, the chances of developing those later in life are lessened. It's certainly possible, but the brain loses some of its plasticity as it matures into adulthood, thus making it more difficult to benefit from learning experiences usually associated with youth.

THE EDUCATIONAL CONNECTION

These findings may help educators develop better curricular choices in the future for children. While the size of the brain isn't changing that dramatically after four or five years, its intricate structure continues to unfold for the next decade or so. With a better understanding of how the brain architecture develops, educators should teach language, math, and other specific skills at the most advantageous times.

Attachment: Forming and Maintaining Emotional Relationships

The umbilical cord provides the last physical link between mother and child until, after the birthing process is reaching completion, it is unceremoniously severed. From that moment, the newborn does not yet have strong connections to another human. It takes months for myelination of the infant's brain to allow the beginning of the next kind of attachment to take place. During the next few years of life, a second attachment will replace the first attachment (the umbilical cord) and serve the growing child with the required nutrients of social and emotional health. This attachment will improve the child's chances of social survival, just as the umbilical attachment meant survival inside the womb.

A human baby requires constant attention and care from another person or persons in order to survive. The love from a caregiver is transformed by the child's sensory intake and then sent to the brain. This reaction influences the infant's development in positive ways. While the immediate response from a parent to a child's stress signals can serve to amplify the child's positive emotional state in the short term, the signals being sent to the brain serve as the templates for attachment, which will shape the personality and social interactions throughout the child's life. It is in this dependent relationship between the primary caregivers and the infant that the new social attachment grows. This attachment or emotional relationship is not as easy to see or document, yet it is very important to the continued development of the biological brain. As dependent as it will ever be on caregivers, an infant requires constant attention and care from another human being in order to survive and to thrive.

If we consider the debate between factor one: nature, and factor two: nurture, one could argue that a third factor plays a major role in shaping the development of an individual's brain: experience-dependent mechanisms.

The capacity to create these special relationships begins in early childhood. According to Daniel Siegel of UCLA, there are several characteristic factors that describe attachment: The earliest attachments are usually formed by the age of seven months—nearly all infants become attached, attachments are formed to only a few persons, those selective attachments appear to be derived from social interactions with the attachment figures, and they lead to specific organizational changes in an infant's behavior and brain function.

Attachment serves many functions, including being protected from harm, starvation, and separation from the caregiver. The capacity to form and maintain healthy emotional relationships is dependent on this relationship. It is these experiences of infancy and early childhood that create the roots of attachment. Most people are born with the genetic capability to form and maintain healthy emotional relationships. When the infant has attentive, responsive, and loving caregivers, this genetic potential is expressed. As the infant becomes a toddler and more people enter his or her life, the child will continue to develop this capacity to have healthy and strong emotional relationships (Perry, 2005). Our brain is designed to allow us to get pleasure from positive human interactions. The systems in the brain that mediate pleasure appear to be closely connected to the systems that mediate emotional relationships (Siegel, 1999).

If a child has had a negative start due to a primary caregiver who hasn't been able to attach to the child during infancy, the child is at risk for harm in the future. "In a very real sense, the glue of normal human interactions is gone," says Bruce Perry, the noted child psychiatrist from Baylor University. "A child with poor attachment capacity is much harder to 'shape' and teach. This child will feel little pleasure from the teacher's smile or approving words. And he does not feel bad disappointing, angering, or upsetting a parent or teacher. Without the capacity to use human interactions to 'reward' and 'punish,' the teacher and parent often are confused and frustrated in their attempts to promote appropriate social behavior."

Some of the most significant findings connected with a lack of attachment to a caregiver came out of the Romanian orphanages in the early nineties. Western visitors found overcrowded and understaffed institutions where hundreds of swaddled babies in cribs were never touched. Some of the babies lived this way for two years (Rutner & O'Connor, 1999). This provided shocking evidence illustrating children who had been deprived of caregiver attachment. These children were stunted, acted less mature then most children of their chronological age, and had abnormal levels of stress-fighting hormones in their blood (Rutner & O'Connor, 1999). The orphans tested showed that there was considerable dysfunction of some brain regions. This may have resulted from the stress of early deprivation and could account for the long-term cognitive and behavioral deficits displayed by some Romanian orphans (Chugani, 2001).

Insecure Romanian orphans who were later adopted into families had more behavior problems, scored lower on the Stanford-Binet Intelligence Scale, and had parents who reported significantly more parenting stress than Romanian orphan children classified as secure (Rutter & O'Connor, 1999).

Emotional Intelligence: The Early Signs of Success and Struggle

It has been at least 15 years since research first linked "emotional intelligence" to education. Peter Salovey of Yale and John Mayer of the University of New Hampshire were considered the primary researchers in this field and coined the term "emotional intelligence." They outlined five abilities that have been considered "key traits" for success. In other words, they believed that people born with, or who had acquired, these capacities were healthier, had better personal relationships, and were more employable than people that didn't have these capacities. Like so many discoveries that become popular with the media, their preliminary findings in the early 1990s became popularized and exploited by popular authors.

If there is anything close to a consensus in the understanding of intelligence, it is that the intelligence quotient (IQ) does not completely account for an individual's success or failure in the world. In 1995, Daniel Goleman, who wrote the enormously popular book *Emotional Intelligence: Why It Can Matter More Than IQ*, wrote, "One of psychology's open

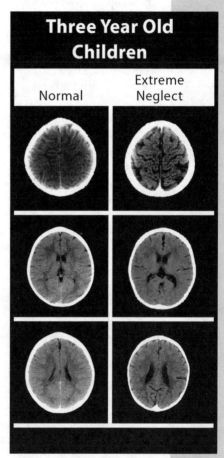

Three Year Old Children

Normal	Extreme Neglect

These images illustrate the negative impact of neglect on the developing brain. The CT scans on the left are from healthy three-year-old children with an average head size (50th percentile).

The image on the right is from a a series of three three-year-old children following severe sensory-deprivation neglect in early childhood.

Each child's brain is significantly smaller than average, and each has abnormal development of cortex (cortical atrophy) and other abnormalities suggesting abnormal development of the brain.

SOURCE: From studies conducted by researchers from the ChildTrauma Academy (www.childtrauma.org) led by Bruce Perry, MD, PhD. Used with permission.

secrets is the relative inability of grades, IQ, or SAT scores, despite their popular mystique, to predict unerringly who will succeed in life. At best, IQ contributes about 20 percent to the factors that determine life success. Emotional intelligence includes abilities such as being able to motivate oneself and persist in the face of frustrations; to control impulse and delay gratification; to regulate one's moods and keep distress from swamping the ability to think; to empathize and to hope."

Research in brain-compatible learning suggests that emotional health is fundamental to effective learning. According to a report from the National Center for Clinical Infant Programs, the most critical element for a student's success in school is an understanding of how to learn (Goleman, 1995).

The concept of emotional intelligence has inspired research and curriculum development throughout corporations, universities, and schools nationwide. Researchers have concluded that people who manage their own feelings well and deal effectively with others are more likely to live content lives. Plus, happy people are more apt to retain information and do so more effectively than dissatisfied people.

Parents and schools have been concerned about how to deal with the rising numbers of conflict in young schoolchildren. Issues like depression, drug

THE EDUCATIONAL CONNECTION

Researchers and clinicians report that children with poor attachment capacity often demonstrate no remorse when harming others and risk developing further antisocial or even violent behaviors. Studies of Romanian orphans clearly illustrate what can happen to populations of children who are deprived of attachment with other human beings. The most needy adolescents often have parents who are emotionally unavailable to them and are not able to perceive their needs. Although removed from the initial damage done to these infants, we are the recipients in secondary schools of some of the negative behavior that can be attributed to their unfortunate early brain development. One has to wonder how many of our high-school students have suffered from poor attachment relationships as infants.

It's important for teachers to understand that healthy early brain development is critical for laying down the templates needed to develop an emotionally well-developed child.

abuse, and low self-esteem can be addressed by teaching children how to ameliorate their negative behaviors and understanding how they can improve their emotional intelligence.

Emotional intelligence has an impact long after the brain matures from adolescence. Corporations are beginning to realize that many of their training programs of the past are not reducing negative behavior in the workplace. Consequently, the inclusion of emotional intelligence in training programs is helping employees cooperate better and work as teams more effectively. The results are increased productivity and profits for the companies (Goleman, 1995).

Perhaps one of the most interesting and identifiable cases for educators is the study done by Stanford University psychologist Walter Mischel, who invented the marshmallow test. Researchers watched four-year-old children interact with marshmallows. Each child went into a plain room and was told that he or she could have one marshmallow immediately, but if the child waited until the researcher returned from an errand in fifteen to twenty minutes, the child could have two marshmallows.

Some children grabbed for the treat the minute the researcher was out the door. Some lasted a few minutes before they gave in. But others were determined to wait. They covered their eyes, they put their heads down, they sang to themselves, they tried to play games or even fall asleep. When the researcher returned, he gave these children their hard-earned marshmallows. Mischel studied these children through their high-school graduation (Goleman, 1995).

By the time the children reached high school, something remarkable had happened. A survey of the children's parents and teachers found that those who as four-year-olds had the fortitude to hold out for the second marshmallow generally grew up to be better adjusted, more popular, adventurous, confident, and dependable teenagers. The children who gave in to temptation early on were more likely to be lonely, easily frustrated, and stubborn. They buckled under stress and shied away from challenges. And when some of the students in the two groups took

Peter Salovey and John Mayer expand emotional intelligences as abilities that fit into five categories:

1. Self-Awareness
   a. recognizing a feeling as it happens
   b. ability to monitor feelings from moment to moment
   c. results in self-understanding

2. Managing Emotions
   a. handling feelings
   b. impulse control
   c. ability to bounce back from life's setbacks and upsets

3. Motivation
   a. hope, optimism
   b. emotional self-control, delayed gratification
   c. highly productive, whatever the undertaking

4. Recognizing Emotions in Others— Empathy
   a. fundamental "people skills"
   b. sensitive to others
   c. more attuned to social signals indicating what others need

5. Handling Relationships— Social Skills
   a. interpersonal effectiveness
   b. abilities that are the basis of popularity, leadership
   c. social stars

The key traits of confidence, curiosity, intentionality, self-control, relatedness, capacity to communicate, and the ability to cooperate are all aspects of emotional intelligence, according to Daniel Goleman.

the Scholastic Aptitude Test, the kids who had held out longer scored an average of 210 points higher (Gibbs, 1995).

The marshmallow test has since been validated with middle- and high-school kids. Edelgard Wulfert and her colleagues studied the reactions of high-school students who were offered a monetary incentive for participating in research. They were given a choice between a smaller fee immediately or a larger fee one week later. Compared to students who delayed gratification, those who chose the immediate fee showed less self-regulatory behavior and greater involvement with cigarettes, alcohol, and marijuana. They exhibited a poorer self-concept and underperformed academically. Younger adolescents who chose the immediate monetary incentive showed a pattern of problem behaviors similar to the high-school students. The findings indicate that this simple choice-delay procedure yields an unobtrusive behavioral measure of self-regulation and offers a developmentally appropriate extension of the delay-of-gratification paradigm for use with older children and adolescents (Wulfert, et al., 2002).

This suggests the possibility that for most, not only will they not grow out of it or get treatment, but that they will miss out on many of the rewards in life that depend on some deferred gratification. The ability to control one's mental state appears to be paramount in long-term rewards.

Goleman's book and his follow-up book, *Working With Emotional Intelligence*, have impacted how we look at education and corporate structure. This work has made educators reevaluate how we should assess students and how—and if—we can teach the elements of emotional intelligence. Can we teach children to delay gratification? To have empathy for others? To channel their anger into more productive states? To handle emotional relationships better? If so, does this make them better students, more responsible, and more capable as citizens? Educators in the last ten years have begin to think so. The work of the Search Institute (Developmental Assets) and hundreds of communities throughout the United States are determined to change the norm by increasing the number of developmental assets each child needs to have (see www.search-institute.org).

The Critics

Some researchers have been concerned that schools are now treating the elements of emotional intelligence like a universal remedy for the ills of the past century of teaching. In a 1995 *TIME* magazine article, Jerome Kagan said, "You don't want to take an average of your emotional skill. That's what's wrong with the concept of intelligence for mental skills, too. Some people handle anger well but can't handle fear. Some people can't take joy. So each emotion has to be viewed differently." In an article appearing in *Educational Psychologist* in the fall of 2002, a review shows that most intervention programs were not specifically designed to change emotional intelligence, and very few systematic interventions meet the standards of internal and external validity. Consequently, little objective evidence attesting to the useful role of emotional intelligence as a predictor of school success and adjustment exists beyond that predicted by intelligence and personality factors (Zeidner, et al., 2002).

Another criticism of emotional intelligence is that it presumes that you can correct a child's deficiency in one of the domains of emotional intelligence. For instance, if teachers emphasize how to handle feelings with classes, their students will be able to handle emotions more effectively. Goleman would argue and say that children have the ability to marshal their emotional impulses; they have the self-awareness to know what they are feeling, and are able to think about and express those things; they have empathy for the feelings of others

THE EDUCATIONAL CONNECTION

The advice to parents and teachers could include encouragement to start working on delayed gratification early in life, and the earlier the better. Students need to have guided feedback activities that can help them develop better focus and delayed feedback capacity. Unless we start early, we may lose a student's interest or engagement from a lack of that skill and the corresponding self-concept. Even preschool teachers should focus on developing these skills. Activities for elementary school include slower, more focusing strategies. Introduce games to children that will develop their delay skills. Games such as chess, Clue, Monopoly, Scrabble, and other slow-moving board games may help offset the rapid-reward-based electronic games so available to children today. Developing a love of reading, working with clay, building blocks, and play dough can be beneficial for young children.

For middle- and high-school students, youth development projects have provided some excellent opportunities to help build the skills of delayed gratification. Community-service projects like working with the elderly and the very young have provided some remarkable results (Scales, 2004).

A wide variety of research has found positive associations between community-service projects and other academic and social outcomes. Because it provides real-world relevance, it is seen as an "authentic" form of learning, and it may be of much greater value to those students who are the least engaged with traditional curriculum.

and insight into how others think; they can do things like delay gratification; they are optimistic and generally positive; they understand easily the dynamics of a given group, and, most important, where they fit inside that group. Promoters of emotional intelligence do not assert that this is a completely learned phenomenon or that it is independent from heredity. Based on what we know of the way the brain develops in the first two decades, it seems that in some ways the neurological wiring that helps you read the emotions of others is not so different from the wiring that controls your fingers and arms as you play violin: The neural pathways that last are the ones we use, the ones we need to get on in the world (Goleman, 1998).

Summary of Chapter 3

- Neural plasticity refers to the capacity of the brain to change with experience.

- The brains of young children are very malleable.

- External forces start to affect the genetic component from conception onward.

- The brain develops neural connections and networks specific to what is learned by the individual.

- Nearly all infants become "attached" to adult caregivers. Attachment serves many functions and appears to be required by the brain to form and maintain healthy emotional relationships.

- Possessing the key elements of emotional intelligence may be more important to the social adjustment and success in life than intelligence quotient.

ENGAGING THE BRAIN THROUGH ACTIVITIES

Activity: Storytelling

Background
The story, a powerful teaching tool, engages the brain in many more ways than simple memory or repetition. Stories transport us to other worlds, other lives, and into situations that students might never experience in real life. Stories often appear to be little more than fairy tales or folktales, but they are designed to teach morals with their characters, plots, and imagery. A good story is universal and appeals to all kinds of brains with an intense engagement far beyond what many other methods of teaching provide.

Storytelling is probably the oldest method of teaching. Today with all of the visual and auditory input available, from MTV to PlayStations, storytelling is still unparalleled when integrated into a lesson effectively.

Oral traditions passed along in families and stories told by elementary teachers have provided the teen brain with a familiarity and comfortableness with this art form. However, when students reach middle and high school, the time for storytelling is often reduced or forgotten as a teaching strategy altogether (Laursen, 2003).

How Do Stories Impact the Brain?
Patterns and relationships that nurture a part of the brain that is unreachable in more direct ways are activated, thus increasing our understanding and increasing the ability to think critically. "These stories, with improbable events that lead the reader's mind into new and unexplored venues, allow her or him

to develop more flexibility and to understand this complex world better," says Robert Ornstein, who has taught at Stanford, Harvard, and the University of California, San Francisco. According to Ornstein, psychologists have found that reading stories activates the right side of the brain much more than does reading normal prose.

When to Use Them

Stories may be used as part of an introduction or as a "hook" to entice students to get into the lesson. Several justifications for using stories are as follows:

• To emphasize important points

• To capture student interest

• To make difficult concepts easier to grasp

• To add emotional appeal to otherwise less interesting material

Delivering a Good Story

It's important to select a story that has the elements of emotion and action. Good stories can be found everywhere: Think about the story at the beginning of this chapter about Saddam Hussein. It builds into a mystery, and told orally, keeps the learner in suspense till the very end. To tell a story effectively, the teacher should use all of the elements of a good storyteller:

• Dramatic use of the voice that includes pauses and voice variations where applicable

• Movement of the body, including hands and arms

• Eye contact with individuals and movement of the head from side to side in an attempt to gain visual contact with all of the audience

Enhancing a Story With Music

One of the ways to increase interest in the story and to add dramatic flair is to add selected music to a story while telling it. It becomes critical to find just the right selection(s) of music to use with the story. With some practice a teacher can become very proficient in selecting and using music to enrich almost any story. Using the Saddam Hussein story as an example, try adding the following selection and start the music a few seconds before beginning to tell the story. The song needs to be repeated due to its length; the story takes from four to five minutes to tell effectively.

Recording Artist: Enya
Song: "Boadicea"
Album: *Paint the Sky With Stars*

Selected Books for Enhancing This Chapter

Diamond, Marian Hopson, Janet	*Magic Trees of the Mind: How to Nurture Your Child's Intelligence, Creatively, and Healthy Emotions From Birth Through Adolescence.* Dutton: New York, 1998 This book highlights the development of a child's brain from birth to the teenage years and shows parents how they can take a positive hands-on role in their children's mental growth. Very well written, and parents of young children will identify with it easily.
Goleman, Daniel	*Emotional Intelligence: Why It Can Matter More Than IQ.* Bantam Books: New York, 1995 Drawing on brain and behavioral research, Goleman shows the factors at work when people of high IQ flounder and those with modest IQ do well. He summarizes the research on emotional intelligence from a perspective that is easy to read and understand.
Goleman, Daniel	*Working With Emotional Intelligence.* Bantam Books: New York, 1998 The author uses brain science and human behavior studies to help reshape how business organizations and their leaders need to change leadership strategies. While the target audience is the business world, there are many applications that educators will find appropriate.
Eliot, Lise	*What's Going on in There? How the Brain and Mind Develop in the First Five Years of Life.* Bantam Books: New York, 1999 Dr. Eliot charts brain development from conception through the first five years. It is written for parents and caregivers and is very readable and well researched.
Jensen, Eric	*Enriching the Brain.* Jossey-Bass: San Francisco, CA, 2006 This powerful book reveals the new science of how our brain changes and how teachers and parents can get the best out of any brain.

The Brain During Adolescence:
Making Sense of Technology, Media,
Social Status, and Education

Chapter 4
The Brain During Adolescence: Making Sense of Technology, Media, Social Status, and Education

The brain you have when you enter your teen years is not the brain you have when you grow out of them...Thank Goodness!
                                                     —Stuart Zola, neuroscientist

There are more than twenty-nine million teenagers in the United States today. They are the risk-taking, creative, impressionable, and rich brains that face the daunting array of challenges called adolescence. Adolescence is a busy time for the human brain; it's a time of transition as the teenager shifts into adulthood. The brain's gray matter absorbs stimuli uniquely attached to the teenage years: high school, peer pressure, sexuality, vulnerability to poor self-concept, mood swings, and a great deal of additional input that previous generations have never seen. The amygdala and the prefrontal cortex begin to switch roles in governance of the brain during adolescence, affecting a teen's decision-making process.

The thundering spread of technological gadgetry giving access to music, communication, and games has changed the brain forever. Sleep cycles are different, too. Adolescents need more sleep to effectively function in the classroom than many of them allow for each night. How does this deprivation impact their studies?

In about 90 percent of adolescents, the brain thrives; however for some 10 percent, brain changes cause such severe stress that recovery may not be possible in adulthood. Current research on the dramatic brain changes taking place in the teen brain is adding remarkably to the growing database. This, it is hoped, will lead to helping teenagers deal with the most turbulent period in their lives. Parents and teachers are beginning to understand the underlying causes of risk taking, erratic behavior patterns, and personality shifts. Parents and teachers also need to be sensitive to teenagers who are not socially adept and realize the daily trauma that many of these children go through. From these new findings a greater understanding will emerge of how to work with the adolescent brain and to get teenagers through these tumultuous years.

A Sinkhole Salad Bar

When science writer Tom Hollon recently went digging for bones of Columbian mammoths on Earthwatch's Mammoth Graveyard project, he found himself re-membering what it was like to feel young and invulnerable....

Hot Springs, South Dakota—What would I do if I were a young Columbian mammoth here in the first snow of winter, 26,000 years ago? Turn my tusks into snow shovels, pushing snow aside so I could eat something underneath, or waltz over to the edge of the dangerous sinkhole, where heat from a thermal spring below melted the snow to reveal all my favorites—grass, pigweed, and ragweed? Would I be wise or lazy? With thousands of years of paleontological hindsight, I know lazy is the wrong answer. But back then, mighty as I would have been, I would have sauntered toward that pit like it was my personal salad bar. Snow shoveling was for squares and squirts—females and infants. The sinkhole—the deathtrap—would hold no fear.

In my mind's eye I see how the pit would become my grave. Grazing near the edge, suddenly the ground gives way under my weight, or I slip on snow, and in I go, my fate sealed. Wet winter weather has turned the clay walls of the pit slippery, impossible to climb. Swallowed by the sinkhole, I will starve or drown.

As I dig in the pit where the remains of fifty-two mammoths have been found, I realize that thousands of mammoths must have grazed near this hole without harm. This thought underscores one astounding fact: *Every mammoth that fell into this pit was male.* Teeth measurements revealing their age show they mostly died young.

The Columbian Mammoth and paleontologist Larry Agenbroad at dig site. (Photo by Tom Hollon.)

Thousands of towns have some sort of Dead Man's Curve. In evolutionary terms, these asphalt death-traps "select" certain drivers. Most "selectees" are teenage boys and young men, the ones most likely to ignore the message that speed kills, to hear but not heed warnings about drinking and driving.

When I was a teenager, I had a heavy foot on the accelerator. One rainy Sunday afternoon I drove a '66 Ford Fairlane around a sharp curve at seventy miles an hour. From out of nowhere a stop sign appeared. Slamming on the brake with everything I had, I stopped, but not without spinning the car completely around. Here in Dead Mammoth's Pit this dredged-up memory gives me a sense of kinship to these awesome animals.

I was lucky only to suffer embarrassment that day—my cousin, brother, and I could have been killed. I'd like to tell you that I learned my lesson, but the truth is that years passed before I finally eased off the gas. Today it comforts me to hear my daughter complain that I drive like an old man. I just want to get there in one piece, I reply.

I did not expect to be moved when I came here, but I am. I am moved by the shared weakness—call it stupidity—of being young and male. A once-young human fool empathizes with once-young fools of the Ice Age. Amidst the bones of fallen giants, I reflect anew how lucky I was to learn about my own mortality without paying with my life.

An interview with the principal investigator at Mammoth Cave, Dr. Larry Agenbroad, further suggests that young mammoths were risk takers:

"I think this is a behavior pattern for teenage and young adult male mammoths much like our own species. Once they reach puberty, they are driven out of the matriarchal family group. Unless they are dumb, sloppy, or lucky, they don't have much success in the mating game until they are older than thirty years.

As a result, the 'teenybopper' and adolescent males have no supervision and wander as isolates or in small gangs. With no supervision or protection, they do dumb things and get into dangerous places. I think they went to the sinkhole, occupied by a thermal spring and pool, in the first big snow of winter. They had the choice of sweeping snow off last year's dead grass or going for the 'salad bar' of green vegetation around the edge of the thermal pond like bison do in Yellowstone winters. I used to watch them with my introductory level classes. We would classify the young males and say, 'Yep, if you were a mammoth, you would be in the sinkhole!'"

Risk taking appears to be synonymous with young Columbian Mammoths and today's teenagers. Does it mean that human youth can identify with the behavior of those once-young fools of the Ice Age who seemed to share a weakness for risk taking?

SOURCE: Tom Hollon, reprinted with permission.

Is Human Teenagers' Behavior Comparable to That of a Pleistocene Mammal?

Some researchers have argued that adolescence is uniquely human and therefore cannot be modeled in animals (Bogin, 1994). For example, Barry Bogin maintains that only humans undergo adolescence based on the conclusion that only human adolescents show a growth spurt, yet common markers of such a growth spurt, such as developmental overeating and accelerated growth rates, are found even in adolescent rodents. Other investigators have concluded that pubertal growth spurts are common across mammalian species, but argue that it is the relatively long period of slowed growth during the preadolescent childhood/early juvenile period that is unique to humans and other primates (Weisfeld & Billings, 1988).

The kinds of risks that human adolescents take include not only behaving recklessly, acting out in school, and behaving antisocially (fighting, stealing, trespassing, and damaging property) but also using alcohol or other drugs. Shedler and Block (1990) have proposed that modest amounts of risk taking may represent "developmentally appropriate experimentation." According to the researchers' findings, adolescents who engaged in moderate amounts of risk taking were found to be more socially competent in both childhood and adolescence than were abstainers or more frequent risk takers. Risk-taking behavior may have a constructive role if accomplished without damage to the individual or the environs. Within human adolescence, excess risk taking may be disadvantageous, if not life-threatening— both for the adolescent and for other people affected by the adolescent's behavior. It's interesting to speculate how the young Columbian Mammoths' adolescent brain may have led to their demise in the same way that teenagers take risks today.

Forced to Be a Generalist

Believe it or not, the real world is actually kinder to the adolescent than the world of school. The real world allows for specialization. It's very unlikely that you would ask your mechanic questions about biology or your supermarket-checker how to treat a serious illness. In high school, we expect children to become generalists and learn everything equally well. For many youth, adolescence is the worst time of their lives because it is the one time that you are expected to excel at everything, from algebra to art.

The need to be good at everything becomes a significant issue during adolescence. It's not surprising that some teenagers drop out of school or have a great deal of difficulty meeting expectations. Noted child psychiatrist Mel Levine says, "I really believe that some mentally challenged teenagers who drop out of school may not have true learning disorders but may have something called 'highly specialized minds' that are going to thrive when allowed to practice their specialties."

It's safe to assume that this example could be applicable to adolescents that seemingly have no apparent learning problems: Larry enrolled in sixth-period biology during his junior year. It seemed to his teacher, Tom Carpenter, that Larry was a total waste of space and had received failing grades each term to date. If he wasn't sleeping during one of Mr. Carpenter's frequent and animated lectures, he was uninterested in every aspect of the course.

We expect every adolescent to be successful in our classes, yet as hard as we try, it's improbable to think that teenagers will succeed in all of the classes they are required to take.

One day late into the first semester, Mr. Carpenter ran an errand during his prep period to the animation class. Even being aware that the class was well liked by students, he was surprised to observe a totally active and committed Larry working on a Claymation project. "Is this the same Larry I teach in period six? How could this be?" Energized by his work in the animation class, Larry later admitted to Mr. Carpenter that the animation class "just flies by" while the sixth-period biology class seems to drag on forever.

The point here is that we expect every adolescent to be successful in our classes, yet as hard as we try, it's improbable to think that teenagers will succeed in all of the classes they are required to take. It was a blow to Mr. Carpenter's ego that he wasn't able to convince Larry that doing well in biology should be important. It was only when he observed Larry thriving in the animation class that he realized however hard he tried to entice Larry into liking biology, it wasn't going to happen.

THE EDUCATIONAL CONNECTION

Robert Brooks of Harvard Medical School says that it becomes our responsibility as important adults in adolescents' lives to find things that they do well in school. He suggests that we ask our students what types of things they enjoy, when they feel successful, what makes them happy, and then do everything we can to take that and work that into curriculum and class offerings. He says, "Give a child a taste of success and build on that."

Think about how you felt when learning to hit a baseball, the first time you hit the ball out of the infield and felt that solid contact with the bat. "Okay, that's what it feels like . . . that is what my coach has been telling me to work toward." Until you've experienced success, you really have no goal to work toward. As teachers sometimes we need to contrive situations where adolescents can have a feeling of what it means to succeed.

The antithesis of this happens when we overload classes with the anticipation of "weeding out" those who can't make it according to our standards. "Some teachers feel that their goal is to weed out everyone but the very best," Says Alfie Kohn, noted author and educator. The common practice in high school and college suggests that setting up failure for students who believe they will fail can have a lasting impact on the long-term success in that content area.

The overriding problem, however, lies in the fact that many adolescents actually believe that failure in a class labels them accurately. They don't have enough life experience yet to know that the diagnosis of failure in a math class is not indicative of how much they can accomplish using math skills in the future.

For affirmation that this problem exists, ask elementary-teacher candidates how they feel about teaching science and math. Many of them have a poor self-image of their abilities in science and math because of debilitating experiences in high school and undergraduate coursework in those subjects. When given an opportunity to develop and share enriched lessons in science and math during their teacher preparation, these people start to develop a confidence that overshadows those earlier self-images of defeat.

Failed a Test, but Succeeded at Life

Dan was like many kids in his high school: just scraping by. Interested in cars and girls, he had fallen in with older boys. After one particularly raucous Friday night football game, his parents were called to pick him up from the police station. Spending a few grueling hours in the holding tank made Dan think about his future.

After making a few well-placed calls to relatives living on a ranch in Colorado, Dan's parents shipped him off to spend the remainder of his sophomore year attending a small country school. It was a life-changing experience for him.

"High-stakes testing" was a term not to enter the educational vocabulary for another forty years, but Dan was still subjected to the state testing of the day. This consisted of a variety of mental activities, including putting round pegs in round holes and square pegs in square holes during timed intervals. Oblivious to what was going on around him, the retired teacher-proctor didn't notice the flying projectiles, but Dan did. He participated willingly in a game of throwing the pegs, thus scoring fewer points in that part of the test. A few weeks later, Dan's principal called him in to review the test results. The first part of the conversation went something like this: "Well, Dan, what do you want to do when you graduate from high school?" asked the principal. "I really don't know, but I like cars and trucks. I also like working on my uncle's ranch!" said Dan.

Remind your students that doing well on tests isn't the only way to succeed in life.

He never forgot the principal's next comment: "Well, that's good because your test scores and grades indicate that you shouldn't probably try to go to college. I think you might be best to think of a career driving a truck and working on the ranch. My advice to you is not to consider higher education."

Interestingly, Dan used this advice in quite a different way than the principal might have expected him to. From that day forward, he used the principal's opinion as a lynchpin for achievement, always thinking, "I'll prove you wrong." Teaching for more than forty years, Dan counseled many adolescents along the way who possessed a poor self-concept based on what authority figures had implied incorrectly about their abilities. Obviously, the results of one test in high school are not good predictors for success in life.

THE EDUCATIONAL CONNECTION

Neuroscientists have known for a long time that the brain is remarkably pliable and remains plastic-like for many years. In terms of cognitive systems and intellectual and emotional abilities, there seems to be a much longer period of time than the narrow windows of developing eyesight, speech, or language. The ability to modify one's intellectual potential and one's emotional feelings most likely remains pliable well beyond the teenage years. This should be conveyed to teenagers along with their SAT and standardized-test scores.

Approaching Adolescence

During the past ten years researchers have focused on brain development in young children. Recent findings by Jay Giedd and other researchers illustrate how many changes are taking place in the adolescent brain and how difficult it is for adolescents themselves and those who have dedicated their professional lives to working with teenagers. It's a most troubling time for all of us! "Now that we can observe these changes, we may be able to influence them," says Giedd, chief of child psychiatry at the National Institutes of Mental Health.

What has surprised Giedd, Paul Thompson from the University of California, Los Angeles, and other researchers is how much the teen brain is changing. The frontal lobes, or "executive center," of the brain are involved in judgment, organization, planning, and strategizing. As pubescent boys and girls begin to mature, their frontal lobes begin to thicken with gray matter.

After a peak at eleven or twelve years of age, the gray matter thins as the excess connections are eliminated or pruned, according to Giedd. His research has focused on trying to understand what influences or guides the building-up stage when the gray matter is growing extra branches and connections, and what guides the thinning or pruning phase when the excess connections are eliminated.

Giedd suggests that exuberant growth during the pre-puberty years gives the brain enormous potential. The capacity to be skilled in many different areas is building up during those times. He indicates that the powerful influences of parenting, teachers, society, nutrition, and infections on this building-up phase, are just now being understood. After this buildup, if the adolescent doesn't make connections and neural networks through exposure to new experiences, those cells will die. In other words, if the adolescents don't use it, they lose it (Giedd, 2002).

THE EDUCATIONAL CONNECTION

What is so astounding from this research is the impact of activities on the teenage brain. For instance, if a teen learns a musical instrument, learns how to repair a car, or is active on the water polo team, the neural networks associated with these tasks become "hardwired" in the brain. Contrastingly, a teenager deprived of effective brain stimulation—or worse, having to rely solely on other teenagers for influence—may be compared to those Columbian Mammoths, which were isolated and wandered about, getting into trouble. Giedd believes that what teens do during their adolescent years, whether it's playing sports or playing video games, can affect how their brains develop.

As teachers of adolescents we can help provide this neural networking more effectively than anyone thought in the past. This equates to a chance to influence with our enthusiasm and excitement about learning. It's certainly true that many of our "clients" don't want what we have to sell, but our task is to package it so more of them will be enticed to love the subject as we do. Now that we know how much the kind of hardwiring can make a difference in how the brain develops, it behooves us to make that much more of an effort to influence positively.

The Sculpted Brain

Puberty and on into the adult years is a particularly critical time for the brain sculpting to take place. Think of the brain at the beginning of puberty as a piece of raw pottery clay. A vase is shaped by the hands of the potter as liquefied clay spins off and is tooled into a recognizable pattern. The vase is also influenced by the characteristics of the clay much in the way the brain influences itself. The shape of the vase advances from removing slippery clay much as the brain is pruned of certain connections. The potter must have an "eye" for how the vase will look after glazes and firing; however, someone observing the process wouldn't necessarily have the same "eye" for the vase in its present state of completion. Nor should the buyer of the vase expect it to hold and pour water at this stage of development.

Comparably, it's not really fair for us to judge teens as capable of adult levels of organizational skills or decision making before their brains are finished being built. Just as water pours from a finished vase, the brain of an adult can be expected to perform more effectively than the teen brain because the maturity of the frontal lobe, often called the executive of the brain. It's involved in things like planning and strategizing and organizing, initiating attention and stopping and shifting attention. It's the part of the brain that has changed most in our human evolution and the part of the brain that allows us to conduct philosophy and to think about thinking and to think about our place in life.

THE EDUCATIONAL CONNECTION

The challenge is to bridge the gap between neuroscience and practical advice for parents, teachers, and society. Neuroscientists and educators are talking about this issue more intensely than ever before. Are we recognizing that the educational environment can guide this sculpting? Are schools doing a good job? How do we optimize the brain's ability to learn as children reach puberty? As brain research translator Bob Sylwester says, "It's all happening on our watch." The next step will be, what can we do to help people? What can we do to help teens optimize the development of their own brains?

The more technical and more advanced the science becomes, often the more it leads us back to some very basic tenets. The brain is largely wired for social interaction and for bonding with caretakers (see Chapter 3). With all the neuroscience and writings in education, the best advice we may want to give to parents is what our own grandparents might have told us: to spend loving, quality time with our adolescents. Teenagers desperately need contact with their parents. They need to be involved in their families just at a time when they are trying to separate themselves from the family.

As teachers, we know how crucial it is to guide them, influence them, and mold them. As much as they resist being molded and influenced, the fact is, they still need it. We know that if adolescents are left to their own devices without parental support they will rely unwittingly on the advice of their peers. Social research on risk and protective factors suggests strongly that adolescents will rely much heavier on their parents for advice when it is available and in a context that they understand. They only revert to the strong influences of their peer groups when effective parenting isn't available (Hawkins & Catalano, 1992). Just as the young male Columbian mammoths used faulty judgment in advancing to unstable ground for better food, so will our adolescents increase risky behavior without parent and teacher intervention.

Why Can't I Program the DVR as Easily as My Son Can?

If experience sculpts the brain, how are we dealing with the impact of the digital age on the teenage brain? Everything has changed in this generation. Access to training the brain to think in newer ways is upon us. One of the key problems in today's educational settings is how to accommodate a brain that grows up with PlayStations and surfing the Internet. Peter Moore, editor of the human resources newsletter *Inferential Focus* says, "Linear thought processes that dominate educational systems today now can actually retard learning for brains developed by playing electronic games and the Internet." This may help explain the attitude of the high-school student who complains that "every time I go to school I have to power down." Moore reports that teenagers use different parts of their brains and think differently than adults when at the computer. He suggests that their brains are physiologically different as a result of the stimuli provided by electronic media. Do children raised with the computer think differently from the rest of us? "They develop hypertext minds. They leap around. It's as though their cognitive structures were parallel, not sequential" (Prensky, 2001).

Patricia Marks Greenfield, professor of psychology at the University of California, has been studying the effects of media on cognitive development for some time. Her findings include some interesting discoveries: Playing video games augments skills in reading visual images. The combination of using the joystick, working in real time, and viewing multidimensional visual-spatial skills all have improved perception of three-dimensional space. It's interesting that Larry Lowry, also from University of California, some years ago reported research that children who watched a great deal of TV may have problems with representations of three-dimensional space; passively watching TV can hurt a teenager's perceptions, yet playing video games can improve them. Professor Greenfield also suggests that playing video games enhances players' skills at divided-attention tasks such as monitoring multiple locations simultaneously. Players get faster at responding to expected and unexpected stimuli.

With high-speed Internet access available to more teenagers either at home or at schools, adolescent Internet use grew exponentially in the last decade. According to research conducted by Elisheva F. Gross from the Department of Psychology, University of California, Los Angeles, teenage boys spend more time online surfing the Web and playing violent games, while girls chat or shop online. One of the findings she reports that may have profound effects on the teenage brain is that Internet use can cause social isolation and depression. Can this lead to more torment as the adolescent brain prunes itself drastically during this period?

Cell Phones, Instant Messaging, and Socialization

Adolescents are growing up in an age of cheap mobile phones and fast Internet connections—the gadgetry found in the bedrooms of many teenagers would impress the most ardent techie. Video-supported cell phones, iPods, digital cameras, and handheld organizers are "must-have" tools for the savvy sixteen-year-old.

"Teenagers have adopted this technology very aggressively, in part because it's inexpensive now, and it's mobile. Everything a teenager does is about being mobile and untethered," said David Greenfield, a professor of clinical psychiatry at the University of Connecticut. "With the complexity of our world and the scheduling kids have compared with twenty-five, thirty years ago, it's a newer way of connecting socially."

Instant messaging is now very trendy with teenagers. With the popularity of America Online's instant messaging access, adolescents are able to see who among their friends is online, and can send messages that pop up on the recipient's screen instantaneously, often while completing homework assignments. The size of these groups may grow to large numbers of adolescents chatting many hours. The Internet can also be an escapist way for youths to experiment with different images, a kind of self-voyeurism to escape from the image they perceive to have at school and at home.

"A teen may be a biology and ballet student offline, but online she becomes 'darkgirl92,' and goes to Goth blogs to experiment with that kind of personality, but not be seen that way by her ballet friends," said Amanda Lenhart of the Pew Internet & American Life Project.

If the computer isn't available because of their location or they want the emotional connection of dialoguing, talking on a cell phone for lengthy conversations is typical. They switch devices

Cell phones and other technologies are now an integral part of a teen's lifestyle.

depending on the complexity or emotional level of the conversation, their location, or the availability of a computer. Different messages fit different methods of delivery. Teens who want an immediate response say the cell phone is best. E-mail is old school: It can be a day or two before someone replies, an eternity in the frenetic lives of today's teens, although acceptable in certain contexts (Kaiser Family Foundation, 2005).

More than a quarter of fifteen- to eighteen-year-olds in the United States can send instant messages from their bedrooms, according to a March 2005 survey by the Kaiser Family Foundation, who published an extensive study on Internet use by eight- to eighteen-year-olds.

The study points to the rapid expansion of access and the use of computers and the Internet. According to the study, the number of homes with children in the United States with access to computers now tops out at 86 percent compared to 25 percent in 1999.

THE EDUCATIONAL CONNECTION

I t should come as no surprise to educators regarding the speed at which children have accessed computers and adapted the Internet for their own uses and interests. Now teenagers who know each other can be separated by miles but can communicate instantly over the Internet. As educators, we have to wonder whether this behavior indicates changes in the brain. The biological evidence for experience determining which neurons are pruned and which become hardwired neural networks provides a fairly persuasive argument. If that is so, today's access to technology will change the brain. We now know that brains that undergo different developmental experiences develop differently, and that people who undergo different inputs from the culture that surrounds them think differently.

At this point in time, we haven't yet directly observed a teenage brain that has been "digitally marked" by experience to see whether it is physically different. The indirect evidence for this is extremely strong. However, brains and thinking patterns do not just change overnight. A key question to be answered is this: Does the brain reorganize differently as a result of the digital age and the impact of technology?

The Cultural Gap

Whose voice captures this generation? What personality will hijack the adolescents of 2010? It will be a voice that captures the spirit and anguish of youth, a voice that bodes well against convention, against adult culture. The last decade heard Kurt Cobain's Nirvana. The song "Smells Like Teen Spirit" made millions and for millions of teenagers echoed the confusion, complexity, alienation, and torment of adolescence. Cobain's words are hard to understand. That was part of the point but they also became a hymn of sorts for huge numbers of teenagers that believed that Cobain understood them. He later allegedly committed suicide, which cemented his place in history in a James Dean sort of way. He become a folk hero, and movies and legends are being made of him now.

Today it's 50 Cent, following in the footsteps of Ice Cube, 2Pac, and Eminem. The pop culture story of 50 Cent was shaped by gunfire. As Madonna was to sex, 50 Cent is now to violence; she performed concerts in lacy lingerie while he prowls the stage with ribs wrapped in Kevlar. As with the Material Girl in her heyday, much of America's teenage population will pay to see what happens next. In concert, 50 Cent moves with the sculpted body of an athlete and reminds one of an in-shape Mike Tyson. Many of his lyrics suggest that degrading women is okay and that violence is an acceptable way of life. One of his songs, "Heat," captures his view of society and entices adolescents to understand his feeling about rebellion.

When you consider that more than 85 percent of teenagers listen to music, these kinds of lyrics are heard often (Kaiser Family Foundation, 2005). For some adolescents, the Internet is the way to expand their access to music. In the Kaiser Survey, 64 percent reportedly downloaded music online, and almost half (48 percent) have listened to the radio though the Internet.

A Teen Combo: Music and Visualization

One factor that distinguishes today's generation from previous ones is a preference for visual stimuli to accompany music. MTV has been available to teens for more than two decades and has made a great impact on how teenagers experience most of their music: now intertwined with a visual element of some kind, either a music video, a TV show, or a movie. The research in this area suggests that when most people close their eyes to listen to music, they normally see images of some kind and in some cases complete picture shows (Lynch, 1999). We're so visually oriented as a culture, we can't shut down our visual mechanisms even when they are not needed. Music can be combined very effectively with visuals in movies and TV. If done well, they can produce a powerful emotional impact. The technology has notched up to do this more effectively with the advent of the new video iPods. It doesn't take a brain surgeon to figure out who Apple will market this invention to. It's interesting to speculate that music used with movies and TV targeted to a teenage audience might be influencing changes in the brains of adolescents.

Tomorrow's music is out there, yet to be discovered in a more accessible format and by a larger audience through the advancements of technology. It may not be hip-hop, but it will be profound to the next generation of adolescents, and it will carry their emotional brains to rebel against the norm (see Chapter 8 for more on music).

THE EDUCATIONAL CONNECTION

The impact of digital learning and music on the teenage brain should be addressed as we plan our lessons and conduct the daily business of running middle- and high-school classrooms. Instant messaging and common home-work assignments make for instant plagiarism and answer sharing. While the sharing of responses can be a desirable component in some classes, teachers need to be aware that rapid technology has allowed our students to communicate much more efficiently with speeds unheard of a few years ago. More teachers every year are developing their own class-room Web sites and requiring students to interact in and out of class electronically. In less than five years, we can expect it to be a requirement for all teachers to have a Web site. Reviewing the day's homework, for instance, eliminates the forgetful teenagers' avenue of avoidance because they hadn't written the assignment down. Communicating online with teenagers will be as important as face-to-face conversations and in many cases the preferred form of contact.

If you hang around the staff room long enough, you will hear teachers complain about the attention spans of teenagers. "He has the attention span of a fig tree," said one colleague about a particularly troublesome sophomore. But is it really true? We now have a new generation with a very different blend of cognitive skills from its predecessors. "Sure they have short attention spans—for the old ways of learning," says one teacher. "Their attention spans are not short for games, for example, or for anything else that actually interests them."

We as teachers should look at how classes and school compare to their digital world. Is much of what we do aimed at the passive learner? Mark Prensky says, "Traditional schooling provides very little of this compared to the rest of their world (one study showed that students in class get to ask a question every ten hours). So it generally isn't that today's teen can't pay attention, it's that they choose not to."

The impact of today's music on teenage brains needs to be studied and monitored. Teachers should be aware of what their students enjoy listening to and what their favorite artists are saying to teenagers. Admittedly this concern goes back further than the debut of Elvis or the Beatles; however, it may have more impact now because we understand so much more about brain development.

Interpreting Differently

Now brain researchers are beginning to understand why adolescents act the way they do. Neurologists are embracing the idea that for teenagers, torment is something very real. "It is in the age of adolescence that they're preoccupied with, 'How am I accepted by my peers?'" says Sal Levine, professor and director of Child and Adolescent Psychiatry at the University of California, San Diego. "How am I accepted by authority figures, how do I stack up against the kid next door, down the aisle, across the classroom, why is everybody else so much more popular than I am?" (Levine, 2005).

THE EDUCATIONAL CONNECTION

This data does suggest that adolescents are more likely to follow their initial response or have gut reactions to stimuli. With increasing age and more frontal cortex, adults are more able to modulate, inhibit, or understand their behavior so they'll be more cautious. This seems to imply that adults are less predisposed to succumbing to the anxiety and stress that can preoccupy teenagers. By understanding the implication of this research, teachers of adolescents may better serve them. This would explain so much of the behavior we see in middle- and high-school classes. A teenager might be perfectly happy one moment and then turn around and be absolutely miserable and under the breath say, "I hate this class!" Today a disruptive student in class, the next, easygoing and eager to learn. That liability is probably because the frontal cortex is not adequately overseeing the amygdala that gives rise to emotion.

The part of the adolescent brain that interprets what we say may not function as well as later in life. If teens can't correctly read emotion, can they hear what we say? Does this mean that they can misinterpret what teachers are saying?

When you understand something about the teenage brain it's a wonder that only about 10 percent of adolescents experience what Sal Levine calls a "disruptive adolescence"—who have brains clouded by clinical disorders such as depression, violence, or risky behaviors. Dr. Levine points out that once we get past adolescence, adulthood surely will shield us from some of the stress and anxiety. The adult brain, however, confronts its own array of emotional challenges: careers, marriage, illness, and aging.

Debra Yurgelan-Todd is Director of Neuropsychology and Cognitive Neuro-Imaging at the McClain Hospital. She says that if you want to see how well people can respond to emotions, the amygdala is a good place to look. It is the amygdala, she says, that may help explain teenage anguish. The amygdala is the part of the brain that is essential for conditioning or learning new ways to respond to emotional stimuli, or to anything that has emotional importance to us. Yurgelan-Todd wondered whether there's something special about the adolescent amygdala and the way it handles emotions—something that distinguishes it from its adult counterpart, something that might explain why teenagers act the way they do. She studied a group of adolescents, from age eleven to young adults. She showed them pictures of different individuals who had the same facial affect, mainly fear, and asked them to look at these faces while she imaged their brain.

She put them in the MRI machine and then had them look at the faces of people designed to trigger an emotional response. When she compared the imaging results of the teens and adults, she found that the brains of adults and the brains of teenagers behaved differently. Adults used their frontal lobes more to process this task, whereas the younger adolescents processed more heavily in the amygdala and less with the frontal region.

This might help explain the different behaviors of teens and adults. The frontal cortex is the area of the brain that tempers emotional response. It's the gray matter that imparts insight, reason, and judgment—the thing that helps us act like adults. The frontal lobes of teenagers are not fully developed, according to Yurgelan-Todd. This means that in adolescence, the amygdala is especially active.

She also found that the adolescents were not very good at reading the emotion expressed on the faces. Pat Wolfe suggests that this research may lend credence to understanding why they tend to misinterpret what adults are saying (Wolfe, 2001). These findings suggest not only the basis for the emotional turbulence of adolescence but the misunderstandings that sometimes separate the generations. "These studies probably mean that we need to assume that they are not always understanding what we are telling them verbally and they may not even understand the consequences of their behavior," says Yurgelan-Todd.

A True Life Example

During a conversation with her counselor, Molly, a frustrated fourteen-year-old high-school sophomore, says, "Sometimes I'm, like, happy, like sometimes I get to the point where I'm not too happy, and then, like, sometimes I go to stay home, like, totally depressed, and then sometimes, I don't know, I just get to the point where I feel like I'm so sick and tired of it, you know, it was just over, I would just be, like, fine, you know. Right now, I mean, all I know is today. Today is very stressful, you know. There's, like, days when, like, my emotions just flip. Like, I'll be talking to someone and then I'll just be like, why did you do something like that and I would just start getting like real edgy. I mean, that's the point where, like, when I see that happening, that's the point where I just tell people I need to be by myself, just go away. My parents can't understand this . . . or me, for that matter. They keep talking about the good ol' days when I was twelve years old and wanted to do stuff with them. My mother can't understand why I feel awful having her hug me on impulse like she used to."

It's Time to Get Up!

Classes start at 7:30 AM. After school there are extracurricular activities or jobs for high-school students that run into the night, then homework . . . typical of the day for adolescents. They are often the last to bed in the home and the first to rise. Some experts say there's a crisis of sleep deprivation among adolescents. Researchers say part of the problem is the change in the brain that occurs during adolescence that causes teens to fall asleep later at night.

For years, people have assumed that teenagers went to bed at increasingly later times and slept in later because of psychological and social changes associated with adolescence: Teens feel pressured to stay up later whether they need to study or because their social lives are more active, or to assert their autonomy, but scientists now believe differently. Adolescents may give in to these factors more readily because of changes in the brain's biological timing system that governs their sleep and wakefulness.

"Older adolescents have a shift in the timing of their biological clocks so that they're unable to fall asleep as early as they could when they were in junior high school and therefore, should be sleeping later in order to awaken rested and restored," says Mary Carskadon, professor of Psychiatry at Brown University and director of the Biological Rhythms and Sleep Research Laboratory at Bradley Hospital in Providence, Rhode Island. The biological clock is actually a set of neurons in the brain, and these neurons send signals out to every part of your body. They control virtually all of the body's internal processes and their timing, and one of the things that biological clock is involved in controlling is sleep (Carskadon, 2002).

When the biological clock, or circadian timing system, tells the body it's time for sleep, the body secretes a hormone called melatonin. Melatonin production is prompted by the light/dark cycle. It occurs during nighttime hours and is detectable in saliva. In a study of teenagers in various stages of adolescence it has been found that the further along the teens were in puberty, the later at night their melatonin was secreted (Carskadon, 2002).

Studies indicate teenagers need nine and a quarter hours of sleep a night to be adequately rested the next day. If a student goes to bed at 11:30 or midnight because of a delay in the sleep cycle and has to wake up at 6:00 or earlier to get to school at 7:30, he or she accumulates a significant sleep debt by the end of the week (Hobson, 2003).

Despite the scientific facts that we know about adolescents, virtually all school systems in this country begin with the high-school students going first, which is in essence sending the students to school in the last third of their sleep period. The research suggests that the teenage brains at 8:30 in the morning should be in bed gaining valuable sleep time. How much effort does a first-period teacher pour into the system to get the attention of these brains that really should be home in bed? Sleep experts say there are also health issues to consider when adolescents are sleep deprived. Sleepy teens are more inclined to use stimulant drugs or nicotine for a boost, and according to the National Sleep Foundation in Washington, young people are the largest at risk group for drowsy driving and fall-asleep car accidents.

Another True Life Example

The Roberts Military Academy prides itself on discipline and polish as about five hundred high school students each year prepare for careers in the military. Established in 1887, the academy has traditions that date back to its founding fathers. This includes when cadets rise and when they go to bed. Because it has always been so, the academy buglers play reveille at 5:30 AM. Breakfast is finished by 7:00 AM, and classes start at 7:30 AM. In Professor Hall's first-period senior psychology class, half of the students exhibit signs of narcolepsy, an affliction that causes sufferers to spontaneously fall asleep against their will. Try as they may, most of the students in class just can't concentrate.

THE EDUCATIONAL CONNECTION

Some high schools report success with a later start time, but despite all the research on the adolescent sleep delay, the vast majority of school districts across the country are hesitant to make the shift. Many districts contend that one of the primary barriers is the difficulty in changing bus schedules, but sleep experts like Mary Carskadn say that if the primary mission of schools is education, then the districts are failing if they're sending kids to school too tired to learn.

As teachers we need to recognize that it's not a social or psychological problem with sleep deprivation but a biological one. Too many teachers find it easy to teach a first period because of reduced behavioral problems. Often those students less self-disciplined will not attend early classes, and those that do try, often fail to be as alert as they will be following the class. One course of action is to request having a first-period preparation where it is possible to avoid the problem of teaching a lethargic section due to sleep deprivation.

THE EDUCATIONAL CONNECTION

Parents and schools should monitor the social successes and failures of adolescents. Teachers whom youth have confidence in can act as counselors and mentors, but it's more often up to the parents for adolescents to confide in about social setbacks endured during the school day. Such adults need to be very good listeners and resist the impulse to preach a sermon.

More than anything, kids with social difficulties need adults who can be sympathetic to their situations and who are able to offer practical advice. Learning the best ways to function in our social world is a critical skill for the brains of all students.

Professor Hall had tried to enliven class by inviting guest speakers and involving students with cooperative-learning groups. After a year of low levels of participation from his first-period class he started interviewing his students to find out what was wrong. In one interview, John L. (one of the top-producing members of the senior class with acceptance to West Point) said, "I will hit the bed at like 10:30 PM when lights are out, and I can't fall asleep. I'm just awake, and I don't know why it is. It's like I'm physically exhausted but I'm not tired enough to just fall asleep. I end up just laying in bed for forty-five minutes, and I can't sleep, and then I finally just, you know, doze off because my body is ready to and that's just the way it is. When reveille sounds off in the morning, I am dead to the world and have to struggle, almost painfully, to rise and dress. During first period, what little energy I had from 5:30 to 7:30 AM is gone, and I can't help but doze in your class. I am sorry about that, but from what I can see, lots of other students are suffering for sleep in the morning, too."

Why Learning Is Ranked #2

Which has more potential for creating unhappiness among students, the social world or their learning world in school? You can probably answer that one without thinking much about it. All day, teens are faced with pressure to create a space for themselves without embarrassment and to form friendships for protection and support. The social realm is definitely #1 when it comes to importance in the life of a teenager.

For some, the social dilemma is awful from the moment they arrive at school to the moment they step back into the sanctity of their homes. Even there, they aren't free of harassment, depending on who their parents are. Often these kids have social dysfunctions. They simply lack the brain wiring needed for social success. We are seeing a trend in this country that says many parents realize how difficult this time is for youth. While home-schooling has become a more popular option for K–6 students, we are also seeing a surge in the number of secondary students who have chosen to stay out of our comprehensive high schools, too (U.S. Dept. of Education, 2004).

It's probable that movies like *Napoleon Dynamite* have become popular because they feature teenagers with social dysfunction. The unexpected popularity of the 2004 movie about a quirky, dancing teen and his sleepy Idaho town drives home the message that school is very painful for many teenagers. Adolescents like the one portrayed by actor Jon Heder in the film have social language dysfunctions and talk about the wrong things at the wrong time. They may sound angry when they're not angry. They may have trouble reading other peoples' feelings from the way they speak or sound. Socially rejected students are often boastful or verbally abrasive. When they try to converse with peers, their choice of language may make them sound too old or too young. In essence, they may be totally ineffective at using language as an instrument for social success (Levine, 2002).

Summary of Chapter 4

- One of the last areas of the brain to fully mature is the prefrontal cortex, which is responsible for such skills as setting priorities, organizing plans and ideas, forming strategies, controlling impulses, and allocating attention.

- Between childhood and adulthood the brain's neural networks become more complex, especially in the prefrontal cortex.

- Since the prefrontal cortex in the adolescent brain is not completely developed, the amygdala becomes more dominant until the prefrontal cortex matures. The data suggest that when the amygdala plays a larger role in decision making, risk taking is increased.

- During middle and high school, adolescents are expected to do well in many learning situations. They lack enough life experience to shield themselves against poor self-esteem.

- The great advances in communication technology have changed the way teens socialize and correspond. Educators are concerned about how these experiences will change the developing brain if the cultural gap increases even more.

- Researchers have found that not only do teenagers process emotion more intensely than adults but their brains may interpret differently, causing misunderstandings with adults.

- Research suggests that middle- and high-school schedules be adjusted to accommodate what we know about teen sleep patterns.

- Teens with social dysfunctions are more likely to suffer in school from unhappiness than those who have mastered social interaction with peers and teachers. They need assurance and confidence building from all adult role models.

ENGAGING THE BRAIN THROUGH ACTIVITIES

Activity #1

The Scissors Game

This game is allows teenagers to determine why it's important to be a good observer and how we often make judgments before we see the entire picture. Teens' brains (and adults') tend to become focused on what they think they should see, rather than the entire scene because the brain seeks order and pattern. We want to discover how each piece of the puzzle is part of something larger and how it's related to the whole.

Caution: This activity works best with classes where the teacher senses some bonding and fellowship with all members of the class. It wouldn't be an activity that one might use until class members have familiarity and confidence in each other.

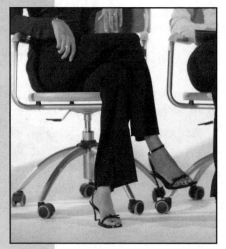

Paying attention to the big picture is critical in this game!

This activity requires students to think "outside the box" and can become emotionally challenging for students who experience frustration when some of their peers get it while they are still struggling.

You will need only one pair of large scissors and chairs arranged in a circle so every participant can see the legs of every other participant.

Say, "Why is it important to have an open mind when you observe a situation or a behavior by a person?" Students will respond with a variety of answers. Tell students that this exercise will test their powers of observation. Ask students to think about the whole picture as they observe the following interaction.

Tell participants that they are going to partake in a game called "passing the scissors." Their task is to receive the scissors from the leader in the proper position and to pass the scissors in the proper position. If they fail to pass or receive the scissors in the correct position then they will be asked to get up from their chair and allow the others in the circle to move one space closer to the leader. The participant who failed to receive or pass the scissors in the proper position will then sit next to the leader opposite the direction that the scissors were passed.

Participants will demonstrate the ability to become more effective observers by looking beyond what seems obvious at first.

Begin with your legs together and uncrossed. Say, "The scissors will appear to be crossed or uncrossed as they are passed to participants. Look studiously at the scissors as you pass them crossed or uncrossed to the first participant." When you pass the scissors to the next person, cross your legs.

Participants will be looking for a pattern, i.e., scissors closed or open. **The real object to the game is to observe whether a person's legs are crossed or uncrossed when they receive and pass the scissors!** The more participants focus in on a pattern of crossing and uncrossing the scissors, the less likely they are to realize the scissors are not the focus for change—it's the legs that are crossed or uncrossed as a person receives and passes the scissors to the next person. Participants will tend to fixate on a pattern that can be enhanced by participants who have figured out that the scissors have nothing to do with the problem.

Note: You might clue in a few students who will be good "actors" to sit directly to your left or right, whichever direction you start the scissors going.

Continue to play the game until the majority of the participants figure out that the legs are crossed and uncrossed. Continue to emphasize that participants must look at the entire picture. If participants are having a hard time figuring out that the legs are the key, exaggerate the crossing of the legs when receiving and passing the scissors. Finish by making sure that all participants figure out the answer.

Follow-up Discussion With Students

Ask participants to think about the game they have just completed. Focus discussion on the following questions:

1. How did it feel when someone else figured out the problem and you couldn't?

2. How did it feel when you figured out the problem?

3. Why is it important to focus on the big picture? What does this game suggest about how your brain works?

4. How can this experience be compared to judging people when you first meet them?

Activity #2

Labels Game
The brain tends to look for patterns. When we get visual and verbal clues about a person, our brains tend to rely on our experience; we tend to make judgments about that person based on inadequate information. Often these judgments are overriding and can prevent us from treating a person with fairness.

This activity is designed to help students see how first impressions can determine the way we treat teenagers we meet. It allows students to see and feel how it is to be identified by the subgroup they are associated with. When students are given an opportunity to mingle with other students at a school function represented by different groups, they begin to realize how the first impressions overshadow all interactions and prevent communication between groups of students.

In order to complete this activity with your students, the following equipment is needed:

1. About eight Velcro headbands that will stretch large enough to fit around the student's head. A small piece of Velcro should be attached to the front of the headband. If Velcro isn't available, any strapping material can be used that will fit comfortably around students' heads.

2. 3" x 5" cards with labels on the front and a small piece of Velcro on the back to attach to the headband. Students should not see the card they are assigned

until after the activity. The labels will be different for each card. The set of cards should include the following labels: *Jock, Nerd, Leader, Brain, Gang-Banger, Artist, Stoner, Clown.*

3. Pick eight students who will be at ease in front of the groups and will be willing to speak during the role-play.

4. Protecting the labeled student from seeing his or her card, place the card on the Velcro directly over the forehead and out of the individual's visual sight.

The object of the game is to have students interact at a school function with kids they normally do not hang around with. The students will be informed that they are to treat the "card holder" in the same manner they might if the person wearing the card actually fit the description. Again, it's very important that the students do not see their own cards until the end of the game.

Say, "Today I have brought you together as a group to discuss whether you think our school should have metal detectors at the entrances. It will be your job to make a recommendation to the school board as student representatives. This is why we have asked students representing different groups on campus to assist in this task."

It's likely that students will begin to treat some of the students with respect and ignore or give little credence to others because of their labels. Since students do not know what role they are playing, it will be confusing because of the verbal treatment they are receiving from other students.

Continue to play the game until the students have had several rounds of discussion. Some participants will become frustrated with the role they are perceived to play while others may figure it out from cues provided during the discussion or comments from the students observing the process.

Follow-up Discussion With Students

Ask participants to take off the cards from their foreheads and think about how they were treated. Focus discussion on the following questions:

1. How did it feel when someone treated you in a different way than you are usually perceived?

2. What did you learn from judging people based on their appearance?

3. Why is it important to treat every comment with respect even if it appears that the person making the comment isn't serious?

4. How can this experience be compared to judging people when you first meet them?

5. What implications does this game have for how we relate to each other in school?

Selected Books for Enhancing This Chapter

Feinstein, Sheryl	*Secrets of the Teenage Brain: Research-Based Strategies for Reaching and Teaching Today's Adolescents.* Corwin Press: Thousand Oaks, CA, 2004 An excellently written book recently published. Ideal for the teacher or parent who works with adolescents and needs the latest background research on adolescent brains. Feinstein provides applications and teaching strategies for every topic.
Jensen, Eric	*Arts with the Brain in Mind.* ASCD: Alexandria, VA, 2001 In another book from ASCD, Jensen makes an important point for reviving and improving art and music in the curriculum. He passionately pleads the case for what the arts do in learning development and what happens when schools reduce or eliminate art and music programs.

5

Making Material Meaningful:
Connecting Emotions and Learning

Chapter 5
Making Material Meaningful:
Connecting Emotions and Learning

I'm tryin' to think, but nothin's happening!

—Curly from *The Three Stooges*

Neuroscientists have discovered that regions of the brain such as the thalamus, amygdala, the hippocampus, and the hypothalamus are critical switchboards that take memories, emotions, and biochemicals and then mix them up as if in a blender. The brain then uses this special cocktail to make some sense out of neural networks that shape the ways that happiness, fear, panic, and social pressure influence the choices people make.

Positively Fearless

Donald awoke early one morning with the uncertainty that comes with a first-time public speaker. At nine-thirty on this morning he would give his first presentation as a Positive Speaker. Positively Speaking is a statewide organization that trains persons infected with HIV to tell their stories in middle- and high-school classrooms.

He wondered if the tenth graders at Garfield High would know what stress this put on his already taxed system, and what strength that it would take to just get up in front of them and hold himself together, let alone teach them anything. Could he remember his well-rehearsed tri-part presentation—life before, diagnosis, and life after? Oh yes, he had glided through the training and felt buoyed by the reception given him from the trainers. But now the real test was here. Could he hold up without emotionally showing how he really feels? Wait. What was that bit about how people learn? How it's important to show your emotions…

Donald couldn't remember how he got to Mrs. Laver's classroom or how he even reached Garfield High. All he recalled was seeing hostile males in baggy pants and heavy black satin Raiders jackets. The staring glances from young toughs who made him feel as if he were eyeing their girlfriends or invading their turf on the street.

The time it took for the kids to get settled in class seemed to go on forever. Both boys and girls seemed to have total disregard for anything the classroom had to offer. They seemed like aliens from a different place and time. Donald contemplated just walking out the door, getting into his car, and leaving this awful place, but from somewhere in the deep recesses of his uncontrollable memory, out came the first words.

He remembered standing there and in his mind, rehearsing a scenario to flee while talking about life before his HIV-positive diagnosis. He thought, "I don't think I can get through this without breaking down!" Then he suddenly let himself get into the presentation, and that's when he started to show some emotion. He felt his voice quiver—surprisingly, it felt right! After he was well into the first part of his story, he found that he could recall with laughter how his older brother tossed him around. It made all the kids laugh. He had evoked joy and happiness in his audience. Because the events associated with diagnosis were so entrenched in his long-term memory, it was easy to re-create the scene where he was told of his HIV-positive status. This is called episodic memory, and the brain, without any rehearsal, can aggregate it. The story immediately turned from being lighthearted to extremely sad.

Suddenly these kids were transformed from alien beings into people who seemed interested in what he had to say! It was as if a 180-degree shift had taken place. He felt their embrace—a breakthrough! Perhaps they weren't as bad as he had surmised? Maybe they were willing to listen?

With the recognition of the change in receptivity, Donald was able to concentrate on telling his story, and it was a good one—one that brought them through a cycle of emotions. With this newfound roller-coaster approach, he let himself become real to them. Spacing smiles and jokes between tears and compassion, he understood they were capable of all the emotions he was trying to evoke. He thought, "Thank goodness I allowed myself to show emotion!"

The next day he received a call from Mrs. Laver, who told him how much the kids received from his presentation and expressed her gratitude for making the effort to speak. Later she sent him the reflections her students had written and talked of her amazement about how much compassion and understanding the kids' expressed in their writing. All year long she had tried pulling written work from them, and never had the class performed like this! Reading the kids' reflections made Donald feel great about expressing his emotions while speaking. He was convinced that showing emotion helped develop his audience and led to a more effective presentation. He felt that by telling his story he had helped the students think twice about their own risky behavior. He knew he had done his best and felt exhilarated by his success. His next speaking assignment was scheduled for next week, and he couldn't wait to get to campus.

Emotions and Learning

What Donald may not have realized is what that research suggests about how controlling the students' emotional state affects their learning. Here is a case for what we know from brain research: When strong feelings of happiness and sadness are engaged, they flavor the human experience such that the learner is unable to bring anything else to conscious attention at the time. This phenomenon is probably what Donald sensed as he observed the student reaction to his joy and tears just minutes after smiling broadly. The students, drawn in by his stirring story, were now poised to learn, incapable of resisting the important message that Donald had to offer. Further, "Emotion drives attention, which drives learning, memory, problem solving, and almost everything else we do," according to Bob Sylwester, professor from the University of Oregon.

Our emotional system informs us that something important has occurred; the students in just this fashion perceived Donald's emotions. This arousal allowed the students to quickly reduce sensory intake (the environment around them) and focus on what Donald was saying. What researchers are saying now is that in order to get anything into long-term memory, there must be an emotional component. Think about it: What events do you remember in the classroom? When have your students really keyed into what you were trying to teach them? Almost everyone will recall an event that is tied to an emotion if that emotion is felt at the right intensity.

Dr. James McGaugh, pyschobiologist at UC Irvine, says that when emotions are engaged, the brain is activated. Emotional arousal causes all the chemical cocktails, the neurohormones, to enter the nervous system. We think those chemicals are memory fixatives. This is important, says McGaugh, because "The emotional components in learning can and do enhance retention."

When strong feelings of happiness and sadness are engaged, they flavor the human experience such that the learner is unable to bring anything else to conscious attention at the time.

There is much we do not yet know about how emotion affects learning or how learning affects emotion. Often events that trigger moderate to strong positive emotions (joy, happiness, relief) or negative emotions (pain, fear, disgust, sadness) improve learning and memory. The brain keeps track of what is important, whether it's from a strong positive emotion or a strong negative emotion. We know that learning and memory are complex and are influenced by other factors (McGaugh, 2003). Emotions often let us know what things or thoughts are "good" or "bad" and the degree of each. The effects on learning and memory of events that trigger extremely strong emotions may sometimes have contradictory effects. For example, an extremely traumatic event (or series of events) can sometimes disrupt learning or memory.

Larry Cahill of the University of California, Irvine speaks of interesting animal research in his lab that assists in understanding how emotion intersects with learning. He indicates that it is important to study rats and mice to understand humans. "When you put a rat in the middle of a tub of water he will swim to the edge even though he has never swum before. Put him in once and he will swim desperately. Each day the animal will get a little better at swimming the course, but if you inject the animal's brain with adrenaline (which increases the emotional input) the animal learns to swim better than his counterpart who received a saline injection in the brain. The findings suggest that hormones like adrenaline increase memory storage."

THE EDUCATIONAL CONNECTION

Teachers need to be aware that some students entering their classrooms are belabored with extremely emotional issues. For teachers, the message is clear: If we want the students to retain the learning that we bring to class, we must appeal to their positive emotions. Using just the right amount of emotion during a presentation can be the key to delivering the message we want to offer.

A Structure to Remember

A great deal of the brain is designed to remember and to piece together events that are real or imagined, autonomic or conscious, short-term or long-term.

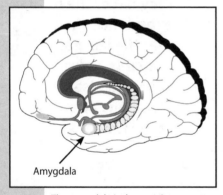

Amygdala

The amygdala is the emotion processing center of the brain.
(Used with permission of Eric Jensen.)

One structure stands out in the processing of emotional memory: The almond-shaped amygdala located on both hemispheres of the brain is buried deep within the temporal region. The emotional connections from outside stimuli are probably funneled through this structure.

Its primary function is to figure out all incoming information for surviving and emotion. When it interprets the data received, it helps initiate the correct responses. For an example of how the amygdala functions, think of what it might feel like if Ed McMahon were to ring your doorbell. He announces to you that you have just won a million dollars. While having your photo taken with a huge cardboard check, first shock, then a feeling of euphoria surrounds you! Researchers would suggest that your amygdala is highly involved with processing the pleasurable stimuli received when you realized that you were getting a Publisher's Clearinghouse check for one million dollars.

Contrastingly, stepping on an object like a rattlesnake while hiking in the mountains would induce an aversive reaction in the amygdala that would trigger a survival atmosphere in that part of the brain. Without much consultation from the "higher brain," the amygdala would start the process of initiating alertness, directing your body to move out of the way and quickly react to the imminent danger.

Joseph LeDoux, a neuroscientist at the Center for Neural Science at New York University, writes in his 1996 book, *The Emotional Brain: The Mysterious Underpinnings of Emotional Life*, about the relationship and interaction of the emotional and thinking brains. His research suggests there are specific neural pathways bringing information to the brain through the senses. The information received by the eye or ear goes first to the thalamus. The thalamus acts as a sorter that decides which parts of the brain to send the information to. If the incoming information, for instance, is emotional, the thalamus sends out two signals—the first to the amygdala and the second to the neocortex. What this means is that the emotional brain has the information first, and in the event of a crisis can react before the thinking brain has even received the information or had a chance to weigh the options.

An example to illustrate the thalamus-amygdala reaction might include the story of having a brick thrown at you. If you see it coming, your neocortex might analyze the structure. "It's about four inches by eight inches, red, rough texture, and hurtling along in a tumbling direction toward me at about five feet per second!" Of course, that wouldn't happen because your thalamus has given directions to your amygdala. This would be pressed into service immediately and tell you to "duck!" This would all take place without consulting the neocortex. You have just experienced an "amygdala response" (AR). Although the brick is a bit more of an extreme example than most ARs, we all have them. Think of the last time that you reacted without thinking through a situation clearly. At the same time or miniseconds later, areas of the cortex are involved and evaluate incoming data. Guidance from the cortex would tell us to "back off" or "cool it" before inadvisably acting out. Have you ever reacted anyway? Yes, it happens to all of us, albeit not advisedly. We think later that the decision we made was not the one we would have made if we had allowed ourselves a chance to think about it and not had an AR. In Chapter 5, we will explore this very problem in adolescents who, by the lack of myelination in that juncture between the neocortex and the amygdala, let the limbic system make their decisions more frequently than not.

Remembering hearing Ed McMahon ringing your doorbell, stepping on a rattlesnake, or seeing a brick thrown at you brings emotional memories to your consciousness after the events. There is substantial evidence in support of the amygdala as the critical player in the brain in processing emotional events (Bechara, et al., 2003). Interestingly, it seems to take in all kinds of information and helps consolidate those memories briefly. When you look at the remaining key memory-related structures in the temporal region and beyond into the cortex, you would find that the amygdala is directly connected to many of them. This might explain why the amygdala is so involved with memory consolidation (McGaugh, 2003).

Molecules and Emotion

In 1997, the work that Candace Pert reported in *Molecules of Emotion* was a landmark for lay readers. In understandable terms, she described the present thinking of integrated body/brain system. In other words, the emotional system can be viewed as an integrated system including the brain, the endocrine system, and immune system. She also indicated that emotion affects all other organs and that our emotions are the glue that ensures that our body and brain work together. Mix in peptide molecules, and we have the soup that concocts emotion! Peptide molecules are the messengers of our emotional system. A peptide

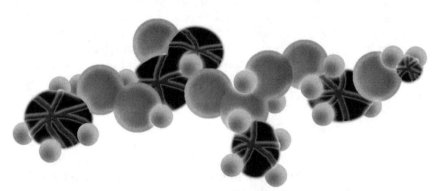

Rendition of a peptide molecule

molecule is a chain of amino acids much shorter than a protein. About sixty known peptides are involved in processing emotions (Pert, 1997). Peptides developed within body/brain cells are called hormones and neuropeptides. To experience pleasure and pain, peptides travel throughout our body/brain via our neural networks, circulatory system, and air passages. A peptide's message can impact structures in the body differently and vary the way they modulate individuals.

Our emotional decision-making process is affected by these powerful yet tiny forces. In effect, the shifts in the body/brain levels of these molecules allocate our emotional energy—what we do, when we do it, and how much energy we expend (Sylwester, 2001).

The endorphins are a class of opiate peptides that affect our emotions within our pain-pleasure continuum. Remember the last time you stubbed your foot while getting out of bed? The intense pain you suffered at first probably caused you to shout out loud, grab your foot, and hop about until the pain started to subside. It's likely that your brain was squeezing out molecules of endorphins to ease the pain shortly after you stubbed your toe. Contrastingly, when we experience pleasure, the endorphins are partly responsible.

What is remarkable is that certain behaviors can raise the level of endorphins in the brain. Exercising and positive social contacts can increase levels (Ratey, 2001). Think about the times when students have indicated either directly or indirectly that they liked your class. Surely, your levels of endorphins increased proportionately as you felt good from the comment.

The glucocorticoids provide another powerful example of a peptide molecule that can affect students' behavior in the classroom. As a secondary reaction to stress (the first being the release of adrenaline), the glucocorticoids are a group of steroid compounds released by our adrenal glands. They activate important body/brain defensive responses that vary the intensity of what makes us stress. In Chapter 6, a more in-depth discussion of their impact on the classroom will assist you in understanding why continued stress is so damaging to the brain.

THE EDUCATIONAL CONNECTION

Studies that explore the effects of attitudes and emotions on learning indicate that negative emotions such as stress and constant fear can circumvent the brain's normal circuits. A student's physical and emotional well-being is closely linked to the ability to think and to learn effectively. While schools cannot control all the influences that invade a student's sense of safety and well-being, classrooms and schools that build an atmosphere of trust and intellectual safety will enhance learning. Finding ways to vent emotions productively can help students deal with inevitable instances of anger, fear, hurt, and tension in daily life.

Our Biological Brains

Talk to teachers of high-school seniors, and to the person they will say, "These kids just seem to check out after their first semester." It's apparent that as high-school seniors, these young people are waking up to the realization that most of the unwanted shepherding from parents, significant adults, and teachers is going to be a lesser factor in their lives from now on. School is the only time in their lives where they have interacted with people all at the same developmental stage, and they are more than ready to leave that familiar situation.

What's happened to all the information that our educational culture has pumped into their brains during the last thirteen years? There has been lots of it, but how much has the biological brain found to be important? While our society has concentrated on the social and cultural brain awareness that graduating seniors must have for success in an adult world, what about the biological brain?

The biological brain seeks out what is important, sheds much of what educators have deemed important, and favors a survival mentality. Now that we know more about how the brain operates, teachers are starting to understand why the priorities set by the teenage brain may be quite different from those perceived by educators. Neuroscientists are starting to answer some of the problems that have bewildered us for years about the brain. We need to add dimensions to our classrooms that recognize the understanding of the biological brain.

Some of those dimensions include developing qualities in our students that can't readily be measured. Schools have become more efficient, run more economically, and above all, assess everything under the guise of high-stakes testing. If it's not measurable, we don't have time to teach it. Bob Sylwester of the University of Oregon says, "The notion is that we need to measure everything. All of our values came from this notion."

How do we measure things like love, acceptance, and compassion? How are we going to melt these together with the social and the biological brain? Measurement isn't nearly as important to the biological brain as survival. This means being able to adapt to new situations. As we recognize what research says about how adolescents process emotion there will be a need to reevaluate our educational goals and the way we program student schedules.

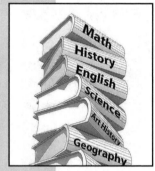

The biological brain has difficulty remembering things with little real-life application.

The Search for Meaning Is Instinctive

Think about how we program a high-school sophomore's typical day: Any given tenth grader may have a random schedule that starts with U.S. history, followed by biology, then physical education. After a short break, geometry, then English II and finish the day's classes with an elective in art. Isolated homework assignments from many classes add to the difficulty. One wonders how an adult's brain might perceive a schedule like this and how much sense it makes to the adolescent brain for this hodgepodge of classes and their sequence.

Research tells us that what the brain wants is a meaningful organization and categorization of information. The brain is designed to perceive and generate patterns, and it resists having meaningless patterns imposed on it (Caine, 1998). Trained to respond in a follower's role, the great majority of middle- and high-school students will do what they can to learn under conditions available to them. Surprisingly, many of them do fairly well.

The problem is that with a typical random sequence of unrelated coursework, the adolescent brain translates the day's classes as meaningless. We hope they identify with at least one of those isolated classes and its teacher. Isolated pieces of information unrelated to anything that makes sense to a student have little impact on the long-term memory systems of the student. Just ask a high-school student after school, "What did you learn today?" Most of the time an honest answer is given: "Nothing!" For teaching to be effective, a learner must be able to create and understand relevant patterns.

All learners are trying to make sense out of what is happening at all times. There are several elements that significantly strengthen the ability of the brain to learn, changing meaningless information into sustained memories.

Emotion affects learning; in fact, emotion, thinking, and learning all seem to be tied together (LeDoux, 1996). When the learner's emotions are engaged, the brain "codes" the content by triggering the release of chemicals that single out and mark the experiences as important and meaningful. This may give meaning to something without a student even understanding it (Jensen, 1998). A key point for teachers to remember is that too much emotion or too little emotion can impede learning (Cahill, 2004).

At the level of the neurons, relevance is the activation of existing connections in neural networks. It relates new knowledge to something the learner already knows. The more relevance this has to the learner, the greater the meaning (Jensen, 1998). The practical application for teachers is to connect classroom teaching with real-life experiences.

The brain seeks patterns. Patterns of shape, size, color, texture, sound, and many others determine meaning and memory. Isolated information has little meaning. Subjects that can be presented to help students understand the meaning of life have an advantage; it's hard for students to understand the value of algebra, for instance. It takes an effective teacher to help students seek patterns in higher mathematics.

A True Life Story: Emotions, Relevance, and Pattern Making

Mr. Curry was a good teacher, always understanding to students who didn't get it the first time, and often trying new strategies that might appeal to different learning styles brought to class in the brains of his biology students. There were some topics in biology, however, that "you just have to wade through!" He placed the teaching of photosynthesis in that category. Try as he would, the subject of photosynthesis left his students bored and lethargic as he methodically explained the steps of photosynthesis, time and time again. He had a difficult time making the subject relevant to his students. The use of fairly concise readings, interesting lab activities, and the ubiquitous review sheets didn't seem to prevent him from thinking himself as a "droner" when it came to this subject. The looks on the students' faces during his lessons let him know just how bored they were with this subject.

Emotions are crucial to memory because they facilitate the storage and recall of information.

The coinciding of Halloween and the week devoted to studying photosynthesis proved to be an awakening for Mr. Curry and his students. Like the more popular teachers in his high school, Ed Curry always dressed up for Halloween. This particular year, as he thought about his costume, he decided to dress up as a chloroplast, the key component of his teachings about photosynthesis.

"Why don't I teach my photosynthesis lesson dressed up in costume this year?" he thought. Slipping on a Kelly green ski suit, an orange wig, and green facial makeup, he didn't look like the tweedy old science teacher anymore. Ed taped on labels that stuck out like barbs all over front and back of the ski suit. Each label named the major chemical components found in the chloroplast.

After first roaring with laughter at this normally reserved teacher's costume, his students settled back into their chairs, pencils poised, waiting for the photosynthesis lesson to begin. What happened next was powerful and a breakthrough in the teaching of photosynthesis for Ed Curry.

As his lesson progressed, Ed experienced a change in the attentiveness in his students. They were intrigued with what he was saying! As he turned his head back from writing the equations and symbols on the whiteboard, he felt almost uncomfortable from their smiling faces, so intent on what he was saying and how he was referring to each tag on his ski suit. His students had found a connection to the learning process! He discovered that his students were having fun learning as a result of his antics and laughter while in the ski suit. Reciprocally, Ed was more animated and creative in his teaching of this previously boring subject. The students discovered a pattern because Ed, more confident than ever, was able to validate the reason for learning about photosynthesis.

What we know from science is that emotions (in this case, humor) influence receptivity for learning. Good teachers have always known that you can't separate the cognitive from the affective domains for learning. Emotions are crucial to memory because they facilitate the storage and recall of information (Caine, 1998). The students on that Halloween day found a pattern for learning and experienced the emotional input to help fix the otherwise boring process of learning the essentials of photosynthesis.

Postscript: Ed Curry taught high-school biology for more than twenty years at the same location. He used the ski suit to teach of photosynthesis for the

THE EDUCATIONAL CONNECTION

Our students are, by the very nature of their brains, looking for meaning and patterns in learning. Their perceptions of events will either create meaningful memories or toss them out. As educators we can influence the direction, but we cannot stop the process. Highly structured activities do not ensure appropriate patterning because the student may be engaged in busy work even though the brain is not engaged with the activity. Remember that emotion can actively engage students, which ensures that they will have a deeper understanding of the material. Ignoring emotions as part of the learning process isn't productive in the classroom. They are part of every learning experience, and neuroscience has shown us that emotions are essential in fixing memory.

One of the most effective on-screen performances of how a natural-born teacher can engage emotions was given by the late Richard Mulligan in Nick Nolte's 1984 movie *Teachers*. Mulligan, playing an outpatient from a mental hospital, mistakenly gets called in to substitute teach a high-school history class. He dresses up as George Washington crossing the Delaware and Buffalo Bill teaching westward movement. The scenes are hilarious and demonstrate very effectively how emotion can engage the learner.

last fifteen of those years, whether delivered on Halloween or not. Ed would often see students after graduation around town. After he asked how they were doing, he would almost always ask what they remembered most about his class. Invariably, the answer would be, "The field trips and the day you dressed up as a chloroplast!"

Talking About What They Have Learned

Creating a learning atmosphere that takes advantage of what we have learned about the brain isn't always easy. One strategy that is almost foolproof is based on the understanding so well stated by David Sousa, author of *How the Brain Learns*. Dr. Sousa says, "Learners must talk about the learning while they are learning it." Confirming David Sousa's statement are the findings reported in Rita Carter's book, *Mapping the Mind*.

Here is a brain scan showing relative activity during four real-time functions. When students talk about the learning they are activating considerably more of their brain than when just listening or reading.

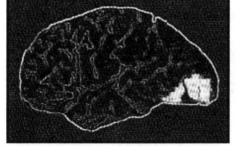

This scan shows the visual cortex activated when a person is reading.

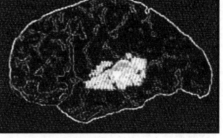

This scan shows the auditory cortex lighting up when a person is listening.

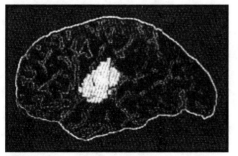

This scan shows what is happening when a person is thinking about words.

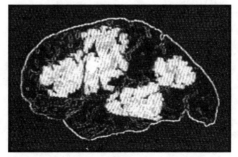

This scan shows what happens when a person thinks about words and speaking.

SOURCE: Used with permission of the Regents of the University of California.

Summary of Chapter 5

- Emotion is the driving force for attention and drives every other aspect of learning, memory, and problem solving.

- Processing emotional memories is a function of the amygdala and its surrounding structures.

- Peptide molecules (hormones and neuropeptides) are the messengers of our emotional system.

- The biological brain seeks its own priorities; survival is the most important dimension.

- The brain seeks patterns and discards isolated pieces of information.

ENGAGING THE BRAIN THROUGH ACTIVITIES

In middle and high schools, activities are less efficient than "covering the material" through more traditional methods of lecture and individual assignments. Although we've long known that activities are popular with elementary teachers, in secondary schools we tend to think of them as time wasters, considering the pressure for high-stakes testing. Thematic teaching, integration of the curriculum, and life-relevant approaches to learning are more ways teachers can tie in material with an emotional context. We know that memories are contextual and that activities can encourage emotional contexts.

Activity #1

Rituals

The brain loves rituals! So often the positive rituals elementary teachers instill in their classrooms dissolve into negative rituals in high school. The thinking is that kids are old enough to come in and settle down for class on their own. We know that the brain thrives on rituals, and if we make them positive, our classrooms are improved markedly.

Try posting a new affirmation on the board every day for students to see when they enter. Although the demands between periods are great, try greeting students personally as they enter the classroom. Play music between classes as students enter and leave (see Chapter 8 for more suggestions on the use of music).

A positive classroom atmosphere is one that encourages all students to interact and become comfortable. It doesn't happen without teacher intervention. It requires teachers to be aware of the social complexes of the students. Research suggests that when students feel comfortable upon entering a classroom and accepted in class, they produce internal chemical responses that make them more adept at solving problems in potentially stressful situations.

Activity #2

Games

Games help and encourage many secondary students to sustain their interest. Too often, games are associated with younger learners, and secondary teachers shun them for multiple reasons.

The brain is always seeking meaning, and games can provide that context whereas other teaching strategies may not. If they are amused, angered, intrigued, or surprised, the content is more meaningful to their brains. With the availability of thousands of free and inexpensive games on the Internet, teachers have a wide assortment to draw from in any subject.

Activity #3

Project-Based Learning

Project-based learning (PBL) occurs when students create their own projects, including the content, research, and project structures that really interest and engage them. The world and the universe are the curriculum, and projects and technology are tools for inquiry, exploration, creativity, and understanding.

Teachers who use PBL agree that one of the most interesting, efficient, and meaningful ways to uncover the curriculum, teach the standards, and address individual learning styles is through the use of integrated and authentic projects.

There are some wonderful Web sites concentrating on PBL that have projects and information to help teachers implement PBL in their classrooms. To get started, look at a few exemplary projects, representing the best practices of other teachers who use this exciting method of teaching. A good Web site to start with is sponsored by WestEd corporation: www.pblnet.org. The exemplary projects shown here were nominated and selected by an outstanding panel of experts, researchers, and experienced PBL teachers and practitioners.

PBL deserves more emphasis in secondary classrooms. Ideally suited to a brain looking for meaning, it's a unique way to engage emotions in students by connecting them in their own learning.

Activity #4

Field Trips

Without question, field trips provide students with memorable experiences they couldn't get with other activities in school. The emotional connections to locations, events, and real-world situations are unparalleled. If well planned and efficiently delivered, they can provide a connection between the curriculum and real experience. Unfortunately there is less money available for transportation costs, and there is greater pressure to directly pursue the core curriculum for high-stakes testing. The good side of this is that never have educators had such a plethora of virtual field trips to all kinds of environments. The Internet has changed everything! Virtual field trips can take a classroom Internet experience and provide context and focus, utilizing existing resources in a way that takes the best of the Web and makes it work for us. If you do a search on the Web for "virtual field trip," you will come up with a list of hundreds of thousands of possibilities.

Activity #5

Simulations and Role Playing

Role playing helps students use real-world scenarios to draw out and recall information and place it in context. The brain is designed to respond to social interaction (Sylwester, 2001). The key to developing this strategy for the students is to create dynamic scenarios that support what the teacher wants the students to learn. Several positive things happen when learners engage in role play: their motivation to participate increases, enthusiasm for the project enhances their memory of it, and physical motion strengthens learning by activating multiple neural pathways.

Selected Books for Enhancing This Chapter

LeDoux, Joseph	*The Emotional Brain: The Mysterious Underpinnings of Emotional Life.* Simon & Schuster: New York, 1996 LeDoux discusses the history of efforts to understand emotions and how they relate to cognition. He explores the origin of emotion in a readable fashion. Credited with discovering how the emotion of fear works in the brain, LeDoux provides an excellent reference for serious brain junkies and is quoted by many others.
Pert, Candice B.	*Molecules of Emotion: The Science Behind Mind-Body Medicine* Scribner: New York, 1997 This book describes a personal journey of professional obstacles encountered by Dr. Pert as she works on the discovery of the bio-molecular basis of our emotions. Seeking to find the link between body and mind, the author provides a vivid picture of the science community and how difficult it was to break the barriers of tradition.

6

Stress and the Brain-Body Connection: Restoring the Balance in the Classroom

Chapter 6
Stress and the Brain-Body Connection:
Restoring the Balance in the Classroom

When stress persists for too long or becomes severe, the normally protective mechanisms become overburdened and run amok, causing damage.

—Bruce McEwen, neuroendocrenologist

Today's meaning of stress refers to a state of complete overload. External events unite and exhaust both educators' and students' ability to cope with the routines of schools and learning. This affects our immune system and can eventually lead to serious health problems, including cardiovascular disease and obesity. Cognitive learning may also be impaired, and the susceptibility to a greater reliance on drugs and alcohol is a possibility. Teens are less resistant to stressful situations and less likely to use healthy coping mechanisms to deal with them. This requires an understanding by educators of how to reduce this problem in the classroom.

The Science Fair

Tom had taught from grades four through twelve in his long career with the school district. When the opportunity arose to be a full-time coordinator for science and math, he jumped at it. Providing teacher workshops, working with textbook section committees, and developing curricula were all part of the assignment, and he gave the same high level of energy he had in his classroom.

As a way to encourage more emphasis on science, he developed an idea for a district elementary science fair. A few schools had sponsored them, but they didn't provide a conduit to the county and state science fairs that winning projects could be fed into. Once he had drafted a plan, Tom met with the assistant superintendent and shared his ideas. While encouraging Tom to meet with the principals, he cautioned that they were on overload and faced high-stakes testing that spring, sprinkled among myriad other events. When the next principals' meeting took place, Tom was his usual enthusiastic self. A polished presenter, he walked into a gathering he would never forget.

He noticed a lavish buffet of snacks laid out in a wonderful presentation as the principals sat around a large boardroom table. They were just getting comfortable when Tom made the first presentation of the day. He started with a warm welcome and got everyone's attention by showing a short video clip of his former students performing at a previous science fair. Using charts, time lines, and directions, he carefully outlined the plan for each school to participate in the science fair.

About five minutes into his presentation, Tom noticed that room had become almost deathly silent. As he talked about the detailed time line, his attention was diverted from the screen displaying his presentation to the stunned principals. Almost on cue, every person close enough to reach for a snack on the table did so with gusto! If he hadn't known better, he might have thought the action was going to result in a food fight! On the contrary, the principals jammed the food down their mouths and came back for more.

Startled by this unexpected response to his presentation, Tom just froze in place and looked at the free-for-all. A few more moments elapsed before the assistant superintendent rose and said, "Tom, I think we all feel on overload and a little stressed out. I would suggest that the science fair idea be postponed until next year." His mouth full, one principal echoed the statement by spewing food and uttering, "Yes, postpone it! We have way too much to do this spring!"

What Was Happening in This Room?

Why did the stress of another spring task make these school leaders reach for food? What happened to the food they so ardently ate? As the principals reached for potato chips or other snack food, they provided a short-term source of energy or satisfaction, temporarily reducing the feeling caused by stress (McEwen, 2002).

The principals' emotional and physical responses to the stressor were set into motion by a series of chemical releases and reactions. A predictable response to the stressor was to grab food and eat with abandon. Even with food readily available as a deterrent, their body language as a group signaled that idea was going nowhere!

As science gains greater insight into the consequences of stress on the brain, the picture that emerges is not a pretty one. A chronic overreaction to stress overloads the brain with powerful hormones that are intended only for short-term duty in emergency situations. Their cumulative effect damages and kills brain cells, creates memory loss, and reduces receptivity to new ideas.

What Is Stress?

The term *stress* can be defined as a mental, emotional, or physical strain. In ancient times, the Romans used the term to mean "to draw or pull apart." When "stressed out," many of us would agree this is a better definition. The classical definition is as follows:

Stress: Any input, external or internal, which potentially is capable of driving a variable, whose stability is essential to life, outside the permissible bounds (Rogers, 1974).

It's likely that the technical definition does very little to help one understand what stress is and how to relate to it. The story that follows may help you understand how stress plays a role in almost everything we do.

Stress, Pain, and Basketball

By Eric Chudler, Research Associate Professor, Department of Bioengineering, University of Washington. Reprinted with permission.

Because I play basketball once or twice a week, I am used to the regular bumps and bruises that come with the game. Last month I experienced a common way that the body responds to stress: pain relief ("analgesia"). As I drove toward the basket, I was tripped and fell to the ground. I didn't think much of the foul and continued to play. A few minutes later, the player who was guarding me noticed some blood on my shirt. We stopped the game to find out who was bleeding. I was surprised to find out it was me! My knee was bleeding from a large cut that must have happened when I was fouled. The cut did not hurt until after we had stopped the game and someone pointed out that I was the one who was bleeding.

Our bodies release various chemicals to help us cope with stressful situations. Endorphins are among these chemicals. The word "endorphins" comes from two words meaning "endogenous" and "morphine." In other words, the endorphins are our own morphine-like drugs that reduce pain. Pain during times of stress may distract an animal and prevent it from dealing with the situation by escaping or fighting. The endorphins act to reduce pain until the stressful situation is over. That's what happened to me: even though I was injured, I continued playing the game and did not feel the cut. The cut did not hurt until I stopped playing.

Playing through pain is common in competitive sports.

An Adrenaline Rush

When something stressful happens, the brain decides what is threatening and what is not. When faced with the first class of students, the brain does a quick search and asks itself, Have I done this before? If so, how did it feel the last time? What was the outcome? Can I cope with addressing this class as a teacher?

If the brain has any doubt that we can successfully do this, the stress-response is set into gear. First, it signals the hypothalamus. This tiny structure secretes an array of hormones while kicking the pituitary gland into action. In turn, this tiny embedded brain structure releases a hormone into the bloodstream called ACTH. This hormone flows out of the brain into the bloodstream, then to the adrenal glands, which sit atop the kidneys.

Hormones vital to the stress response are now ready for release to do their job. The adrenal glands release adrenaline (also known as epinephrine) in seconds as well as other hormones that increase breathing, heart rate, and blood pressure. This moves more oxygen-rich blood faster to the brain and to the muscles needed for fighting or fleeing. Because adrenaline causes a rapid release of glucose and fatty acids into the bloodstream, a stressed person has a great deal of energy available at this point in time. Sweat is produced to cool the body. All of these physical changes prepare a person to react quickly and effectively to handle the pressure of the moment. The senses become keener, the memory sharper, and interestingly, the brain seems less sensitive to pain.

Growth, reproduction, and the immune system all go on hold as other hormones shut down unnecessary functions during the emergency. Blood flow to the skin is reduced. Adrenaline constricts the blood vessels and triggers a substance called fibrinogen that speeds up blood clotting.

Bruce McEwen, the famous neuroendocrinologist from Rockefeller University, says that as swordsmen battled in hand-to-hand combat, this restriction of blood flow to the skin and increased ability to clot blood would have been a decisive advantage should an opponent strike blows that opened the skin. During this stage of fight or flight response the brain releases natural painkillers called endorphins to keep the individual fighting.

A Word About the Autonomic Nervous System, Adrenals, and Stress

With the mind and body in this temporary state of heightened concentration, preparation to respond to a stressful situation has started. The autonomic nervous system now comes into play. One half of it, the sympathetic nervous system, turns on in emergency situations. If one is really terrified or excited about something, the result of this interplay from the sympathetic nervous system moves out from the spine to every blood vessel, sweat gland, and the muscles that regulate body hair under the skin. Getting "goose bumps" is the result. In contrast, the other half of the autonomic nervous system, the parasympathetic nervous system, promotes the relaxation response. It mediates all those nervous responses and brings about the opposite results.

Like two tug-of-war teams skillfully supporting their rope with a minimum of tension, the autonomic nervous system's two halves carefully maintain a balance by making adjustments whenever something disturbs this stability. "It's no surprise that it would be a disaster if both branches were very active at the same time—kind of like putting your foot on the gas and the brake simultaneously. Lots of safety features exist to make sure that doesn't happen," says Robert Sapolsky, professor of neurology and neurological sciences at Stanford University.

Another group of hormones that back up adrenaline in the course of minutes or hours are the steroid hormones called glucocorticoids. Like adrenaline, they flow out into the bloodstream from the adrenal glands and have a great impact on what happens next. First they start to replenish energy stores depleted by the adrenaline rush. The glucocorticoids prepare internal organs, shutting down systems that may not be needed and arousing others that are more critical. Glucose is produced and provided as energy, and blood pressure rises to help the body's muscles. The effects are evident almost every time a person is under stress. The heart races, palms sweat, pupils dilate, and breathing quickens. In a second phase, these hormones continue to circulate and keep the body on alert mode until the third phase, when the body reaches exhaustion and requires rest to refuel (McGaugh, 2003).

Too Much of a Good Thing

An appropriate stress response is a healthy and necessary part of life. One of the things it does is to release noradrenaline (norepinephrine), one of the principal excitatory neurotransmitters. Noradrenaline is needed to create new memories. Stress also improves mood (Sapolsky, 1999). Problems feel more like challenges, which encourages the creative thinking that stimulates the brain to grow new connections within itself. The stress response is critical during emergency situations. Avoiding an accident on the freeway by quickly looking in the rearview mirror while simultaneously pressing hard on the brake pedal is a good example of how stress improves one's alertness and response to danger. It can also be activated in a milder form at a time when the pressure's on but there's no actual danger. An example might be entering a class to take the final exam. A little of this stress can help increase sharpness and provide the feeling of being ready to rise to a challenge. Under these conditions, the nervous system quickly returns to its normal state, standing by to respond again when needed.

The problem with stress hormones is that they may remain active too long. This can injure the body and brain. Chronic oversecretion of stress hormones adversely affects many systems. There is a high price to pay for chronic emotional stress.

Research has shown that sustained stress can damage the hippocampus, the part of the limbic brain that is central to learning and memory. Damage to this structure can hinder the ability to distinguish between important and unimportant elements of a memorable event (Gazzaniga, 1992). The culprits are glucocorticoids. That's why people get befuddled and confused in a severe crisis. Their mind goes blank because the "lines are down." They can't remember what kind of a car hit the pedestrian or what the driver really looked like. Interestingly, "eyewitness" accounts are often inaccurate and can leave false impressions of the truth because the brain has been confused.

The Allostatic Load

In the 1980s, the term "allostasis" began to be used as a refinement for "homeostasis." A more familiar term, homeostasis means steady internal body control. Many bodily functions must remain within a narrow range of consistency. Body temperature, for instance, cannot fluctuate more than three or four degrees without doing great harm to the body and the brain. Blood chemistry, oxygen flow to the brain, and myriad other functions are rigidly controlled and function within a narrow range. The part of the brain that controls these functions is not very plastic. Automatic controls maintain the body's systems evenly and almost always without conscious awareness.

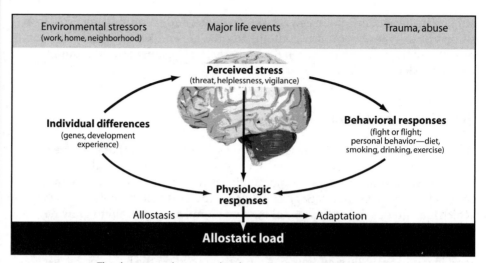

Environmental stressors (work, home, neighborhood)   Major life events   Trauma, abuse

Perceived stress
(threat, helplessness, vigilance)

Individual differences
(genes, development experience)

Behavioral responses
(fight or flight; personal behavior—diet, smoking, drinking, exercise)

Physiologic responses

Allostasis ———————→ Adaptation

Allostatic load

The elements and stressors that determine a person's allostatic load

Allostasis is a term that describes how the body systems maintain stability by adapting to new conditions and changing accordingly. Allostatic systems have a much broader range of boundaries and enable us to respond to our physical states (e.g., awake, asleep, supine, standing, exercising) and to cope with noise, crowding, isolation, hunger, extremes of temperature, danger, and some types of infection.

The stress response provides an excellent example of how the body adapts when stressors are present. In other words, the body is capable of changing when circumstances demand different set points. For instance, the ideal blood pressure when you are at rest is quite different from the ideal blood pressure when you are getting ready to bungee-jump. The heart rate of someone at rest would be around sixty beats per minute. That is normal. When a person is standing atop a bridge with bungee cords tied around the ankles, ready to make the plunge, we would expect the heart rate to be well over one hundred beats per minute. That would be a normal heart rate for this event. Allostasis describes how the body maintains whatever an optimal set point might typically at a given time (McEwen, 2002).

A stressor is anything that throws the body out of allostatic balance, such as an injury, an illness, or subjection to extreme heat or cold. The stress response in turn is the body's attempt to restore balance, and this is where the glucocorticoids come into play. Our complex lives and those of our students ignite the stress response for psychological stressors more often than any stress reaction to fight or flight. For example, even though you always allow ample time, you are stuck in a traffic jam one morning while driving to school. Knowing your first-period class will be waiting outside the classroom when you arrive late brings on a stress response that you can overcome. However, think about that event happening three or four times in a row. By the third day the levels of glucocorticoids that were helping you get through the stress response on the first two days are now starting to cause wear and tear. The very system that was protecting you is now beginning to work against you.

THE EDUCATIONAL CONNECTION

Have you ever forgotten something during a stressful situation that you should have remembered? Glucocorticoids also interfere with the function of neurotransmitters, the chemicals that brain cells use to communicate with each other. What about students in the classroom who are under severe stress? Can they be expected to accurately recall what they are taught?

Teens often feel that there are too many pressures and demands on them. Many students complain about losing sleep worrying about tests and schoolwork. Eating on the run because of a busy schedule is a chronic complaint. But under stressful conditions, the body needs its vitamins and minerals more than ever. Everyone experiences stress at times—adults, teens, and even young children. Some of the stressors that can overwhelm the teen brain and body's ability to cope if they continue for a long time include the following:

- being bullied
- relationship stress
- a broken heart
- violence or injury
- family conflicts
- the death of a loved one
- ongoing problems with schoolwork related to a learning disability or other problems, such as ADHD

All students experience stress a little differently. Some become angry and act out their stress or take it out on others. A few internalize it and develop eating disorders or substance-abuse problems. Some students who have a chronic illness may find that the symptoms of their illness flare up under an overload of stress.

But stress doesn't always happen in response to things that are immediate or that are over quickly. Adolescents may have ongoing or long-term events, like coping with moving to a new school, that can cause stress. Long-term stressful situations can produce a lasting, low-level stress that becomes toxic to the body and brain. The nervous system senses continued pressure and may remain slightly activated and pump out extra stress hormones over an extended period. This can wear out the body's reserves, leave a person feeling depleted or overwhelmed, and even weaken the body's immune system.

This type of stress can now be called an allostatic load. The concept was proposed to refer to the wear and tear that the body experiences due to repeated cycles of allostasis as well as the inefficient turning-on or shutting-off of these responses.

When the brain perceives an experience as stressful, physiologic and behavioral responses are initiated, leading to allostasis and adaptation. Over time, the allostatic load can accumulate, and the overexposure to the glucocorticoids can have adverse effects on various organ systems, leading to disease.

Our brain adapts:
The adaption to distress creates a new allostatic state

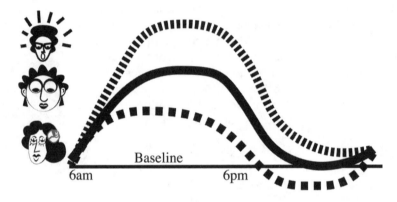

SOURCE: Adapted from Eric Jensen.

Wide Dashed Line (bottom) This represents baseline stress—a typical day when stress is managed effectively and the levels of glucocorticoids recede by evening.

Solid Line (middle) This now becomes the new adapted allostatic level. Teachers and students can be productive, but not at their best because levels of glucocorticoids are consistently too high. This level becomes the range for the body. In other words, the body has adapted to a new level of glucocorticoids.

Tight Dashed Line (top) This represents extreme stress where glucocorticoids levels are very high. Everyone has days like this, but if teachers or students are consistently reaching this level, it will change their allostatic load. Even when the stress is over, the systems are not able to recover and return to baseline.

The Long-Term Effects of the New Allostatic State

Students, teachers, and administrators can suffer from chronic stress. Once recognized, it can be moderated, but too often we see students and faculty members suffering from the effects of chronic stress, and little may be done about it.

Some of the impact of chronic stress on the brain and body includes the following:

1. Exposure to high levels of glucocorticoids over time accelerates the degeneration of the hippocampus (Sapolsky, 1999). Because the hippocampus is part of the feedback mechanism that signals when to stop glucocorticoid production, a damaged hippocampus causes glucocorticoids levels to get out of control—further compromising memory and cognitive function. The cycle of degeneration then continues.

2. An increase in blood pressure that can lead to cardiovascular disease. Arteries can become clogged and set the stage for serious damage. Chronic stress apparently aggravates the clogging process and increases the risk for arteriosclerosis.

3. Lowered resistance to illness can compromise the immune system through chronic stress. Interestingly, first-year teachers consistently report that they suffer from more cold and flu infections than they ever have and probably ever will. The stress associated with the beginning of a their first year coupled with the fact that many students attend school while sick makes the classroom a "germ factory" that may account for this unfortunate workplace hazard.

4. Some obesity and weight increases can be attributed to chronic stress. When secreted in large enough quantities, the major stress hormones, adrenaline and glucocorticoids, increase the fat available for accumulation. The two locations where fat is more likely to be stored is in the blood vessel walls and around the abdomen. According to Bruce McEwen, an increase in waist-to-hip ratio is a risk factor for cardiovascular disease. "If fat levels are high enough for the midriff to expand, then fat is probably building up in the blood vessels as well," says Dr. McEwen.

5. Stress can increase forgetfulness. People going onstage or taking an exam or finding themselves in similarly tough situations already know this, of course. But a team of researchers has found how it happens, a discovery that they say could point the way to better treatments for such illnesses as schizophrenia and bipolar disorder. Stressful situations in which the individual has no control were found to activate an enzyme in the brain called protein kinase C, which impairs the short-term memory and other functions in the prefrontal cortex, the executive-decision part of the brain (Arnsten, 1998). By affecting that part of the brain, researchers say, the prefrontal cortex could be a factor in the distractibility, impulsiveness, and impaired judgment that occur in those illnesses.

The Educational Connection

When teachers are suffering from chronic stress and their allostatic loads have changed, it is unlikely that they can work collegially or with the effectiveness they once enjoyed. It's more likely that they won't accept new ideas or be able to act as an agent of change in the classroom. We all see teachers that are overly concerned about such issues as high-stakes testing, student behavior problems, or administrative demands. With consistently high levels of the stress hormones driving the body to modify the allostatic state, a temporary change in behavior can be expected. In some cases the change may persist.

Students often suffer from chronic stress in our classrooms without our being aware of it. Previously mentioned are some of the factors that can cause chronic stress and allostatic changes in the teenager. Being aware is critical to understanding the subtle responses to this condition we receive from students each day in class.

Summary of Chapter 6

- The body releases a flood of hormones during stress that in the short term act to alert the brain-body and prepare it for the situation.

- Chronic overreaction to psychological stress overloads the brain with powerful hormones that can have a damaging cumulative effect.

- The two branches of the autonomic nervous system play a role during stressful situations.

- Some of the stressors that overwhelm the teen brain can have deleterious effects by changing the allostatic balance.

ENGAGING THE BRAIN THROUGH ACTIVITIES

Activity

Helping Students Deal With Stress

Teachers can provide good advice to students who show signs of chronic stress and allostatic state changes. Below are strategies that teens can use to minimize stress and manage the stress that's unavoidable:

1. Try to keep stress under control

What can you do to deal with stress overload or, better yet, avoid it in the first place? The most helpful method is to learn how to manage the stress that comes along with any new challenge—good or bad. Stress-management skills work best when used regularly, not just when the pressure's on. Knowing how to de-stress and doing it when things are relatively calm can help students get through challenging circumstances that may arise.

2. Take a stand against overscheduling

If a student is feeling stretched, consider advising him or her to cut out an activity or two, opting for just the ones that are most important the student.

3. Be realistic

Advise students to shun trying to be perfect. No one is perfect. Expecting perfection can add to their stress level as well (not to mention put a lot of pressure on them!). Advise students to ask for help when it is needed.

4. Get a good night's sleep

Getting enough sleep helps keep the body and mind in top shape, making the student better equipped to deal with any negative stressors. Because the biological sleep clock shifts during adolescence, many teens prefer staying up a little later at night and sleeping a little later in the morning. The dilemma is that by staying late and still needing to get up early for school, the student may not get all the hours of sleep he or she needs.

Teachers can help students understand the significance of getting enough sleep by sharing the research findings about teenage sleep requirements.

5. Learn to relax

The body's natural antidote to stress is called the relaxation response. It creates a sense of well-being and calm. The chemical benefits of the relaxation response can be activated simply by relaxing. Advise students to build time into their schedules for activities that are calming and pleasurable: reading a good book or making time for a hobby, spending time with a pet, or just taking a relaxing bath.

6. Deep breathing

The student can also trigger the relaxation response by learning simple breathing exercises and then using them when caught up in stressful situations. Do some deep-breathing exercises when your classes come in and see how it relaxes students.

7. Treat the body well

Experts agree that getting regular exercise helps people manage stress. Excessive or compulsive exercise can contribute to stress, though, so as in all things, use moderation.

8. Negative thinking hurts

Outlook, attitude, and thoughts influence the way people see things. Is the cup half full or half empty? A healthy dose of optimism can help make the best of stressful circumstances. Everyone can learn to think more optimistically and reap the benefits.

9. Solve the little problems

Learning to solve everyday problems can give a sense of control; avoiding them can leave students feeling that they have little control, and that just adds to stress. Help them develop skills to calmly look at a problem, figure out options, and take some action toward a solution. Feeling capable of solving little problems builds the inner confidence to move on to life's bigger ones.

10. Build resilience

Researchers have identified the qualities that make some people seem naturally resilient even when faced with high levels of stress. The Search Institute of Minneapolis suggests that to improve resilience, a student should work to develop these attitudes and behaviors:

- Think of change as a challenging and normal part of life
- See setbacks and problems as temporary and solvable
- Believe that you will succeed if you keep working toward your goals
- Take action to solve problems that crop up
- Build strong relationships and keep commitments to family and friends
- Have a support system and ask for help
- Participate regularly in activities for relaxation and fun

SOURCE: This information was provided by KidsHealth, one of the largest online resources for medically reviewed health information written for parents, kids, and teens. For more articles like this one, visit www .KidsHealth.org or www.TeensHealth.org. Copyright 1995–2006 The Nemours Foundation

Selected Books for Enhancing This Chapter

Sapolsky, Robert M.	*Why Zebras Don't Get Ulcers: An Updated Guide to Stress, Stress-Related Diseases and Coping*. W.H. Freeman and Co.: New York, 1998 A witty lecturer as well as writer, Sapolsky entertains the reader with theories on how prolonged stress causes a range of physical and mental afflictions. Wonderful anecdotes and stories about classic and contemporary studies. A great read!
McEwen, Bruce	*The End of Stress As We Know It*. Joseph Henry Press: Washington, DC, 2002 A great book for those interested in following up on the work of Robert Sapolsky. Excellent explanations of how stress leads to systematic loss of health, and the concept of allostatic load is explained and interpreted. A very easy read.

7

Managing Students'
Physiological States
for Engaged Learning

Chapter 7
Managing Students' Physiological States for Engaged Learning

I have come to believe that a great teacher is a great artist and there are as few as there are any of the great artists since the medium is the human mind and spirit.

—John Steinbeck, author

If there is one skill that could be considered the most important for educators to know and practice, it would be managing the physiological state of the learner. This chapter provides the background and three categories of practical methodology critical for teaching educators how to control the learner's state. Research from the animal work of Eric Kandel provides an excellent neuronal example of how this process works; the range of learning states that students need to shift into are also discussed.

Brain Breaks

Sandy Mahan had been a math teacher at Grover Middle School for about five years. Everyone at Grover had great respect for her and her capacity for teaching with enthusiasm. In spite of this sterling reputation, Sandy knew that she could get better. There were class periods that seemed to drag on forever, especially when she introduced new math concepts that were difficult for her students to relate to in a practical sense. Although she was good at "reading" kids' faces for boredom, she often found herself prioritizing the coverage of the content higher than their disinterest because she felt very pressured to get them ready for the state tests.

During a summer break, she decided to attend a local workshop offered on brain-compatible learning. It was free, and she received a stipend for attending. "It can't be all that bad," she thought. Little did she know that it would change the way she would teach her classes. Sandy returned to Grover that following September with a great deal of enthusiasm and a new understanding for managing the physiological state of her students. She introduced a whole new approach to teaching as a result of what she learned and loved it.

Ms. Mahan introduced "brain breaks" to her students on the first day of school. She told the kids that when they exercise their muscles by riding their bikes or playing soccer they must rest them by stretching or relaxing. She explained that as they are learning new information, their brains were working hard to absorb all of the new material, just like their muscles when exercising. They must rest their brains by giving them more oxygen just as they would after muscles were strained from exercising. She told them that if they fed their brains more oxygen, it would be easier to learn.

"I asked the students if they wanted to try an experiment. Of course they were all willing specimens. I told them that first we would have to work really hard and focus on math. We worked through some algebra problems until I could see their eyes start to glaze over. Then when I knew they couldn't sit for another minute, I told them to stand up and push their chairs in, extend their arms out to their sides to find their boundaries. Then I walked over to my CD player that had the theme song to 'Hawaii Five-O' cued up. I told the kids to get their surfboards out because surf's up! I fired up the music, and like magic, we were at the beach! We surfed for about three minutes dodging waves, hanging ten, and avoiding dangerous jellyfish. As the song came to an end, I made sure they ended up in their chairs for the finale. Their ability to concentrate and learn new material was amazing!"

Throughout the school year, Sandy found other ways to take brain breaks. What she realized was that her primary function as a teacher was to manage her students' physiological states. If her students were in a positive state, where their brains were fresh, learning became much easier, and her class period was devoid of the dreaded boredom of the former years. She devised all kinds of successful brain breaks, and found that TV theme songs, particularly from old shows such as *Batman* or popular cartoons, worked well. On the last day of school, Sandy told them that she wanted to do one more brain break with them as seventh graders. "I played 'Who Let the Dogs Out?' at full volume as we danced in a conga line out the door into summer vacation!"

"I really have fun with this….I do it every day, and my students have responded much better than I could have imagined," said Sandy.

Modified from a story by Sandy Rowlett, teacher, Conejo Valley School Unified District

What Are States?

Our behavior is a manifestation of what occurs in the brain. In other words, all external behaviors somehow correlate to the brain processes that take place internally. This includes millions of neurons hooking up with other neurons to form neural networks that determine the quality of a physiological state. J. Allen Hobson describes the amount of electrochemical reactions going on at any one time as "100,000 billion neurons in the brain and they are sending messages at the rate of 2 to 16 per second. That turns out to be about 10 X 27th power bits of information processed per second. This only requires about 20 watts of power, which is equivalent to a refrigerator light bulb! Pretty efficient if I must say!"

Think of your classroom when the students first enter and before the bell rings. Imagine that you freeze-frame this procession and examine the state of your students. Teenagers are coming in from the previous classes ranging from band to biology. You see and hear some individuals coming in without their assignments. It's just dawning on them that the homework you assigned is due and they have forgotten to do it. This recall will likely affect their physiological state negatively. Enter the student who hates school today and doesn't like your class any better. Now arriving is the girl that aces your exams and provides you with the affirmation that you are a good teacher. Young people are changing continuously from one recognizable physiological state to another.

Coming to class, each person brings a physiological state that represents how he or she feels at this given moment of the day. The brain and the body become entwined in this display of biochemistry and neurological circuitry that governs how they act at a particular time. The routes of information to the brain come from the sensory and peripheral nerves through the bloodstream, which carries the chemical signals, including hormones, neurotransmitters, and modulators, all working together to form a given physiological state at a given time. The brain now receives additional input from hundreds of stimuli from all over the classroom, including the students sitting near each other, the interrelationships that are opaque to the teacher, the condition of the classroom, and the odors detected upon entry to this particular classroom. The pungency of a dirty carpet to the faint, but prevailing smell of animal preservative solutions that have lingered in the room since the last decade provide input to the brain and affect the student's state subconsciously. Fortunately, the brain discounts the majority of this kind of chemical stimuli and quickly concentrates on more important issues.

A physiological state is simply the mind-body moment made up of an individual's thoughts and physiology. Emotion plays a huge role in the process because as brain research translator Eric Jensen says, "What we feel is what is real—it's the link to how we think. If a student isn't in a receptive state for learning, the chances are very good that learning will not take place."

Perceptive teachers are aware of, and are able to manage, the physiological states of their students.

There are many internal factors that keep students' physiological states changing all the time. Students get messages from their stomachs signaling hunger, from their muscles triggering pain from inactivity, and hundreds of other internal regulators. When a teacher looks at all the distracting factors, both internal and external, it's rather amazing that students can be in an effective state for learning any more than a fraction of the time they are in your class.

How Do States Affect Our Teaching?

In a sense, a physiological state for our purposes can be referred to a "learning state." Since all behavior is state-dependent, it is very important that we understand what state our students are in and, more important, how to change the state if it's not what we want. It's our primary task to orchestrate the conditions that place our students in effective learning states.

As teachers we are most concerned with the collective learning state of our students. Individual temperament is controlled by myriad factors and often out of the teacher's domain of influence during an instructional period. Some of those issues become behavioral problems and must be dealt with. The skill possessed by the teacher who deals with these individuals determines how successfully the secondary goals are reached. Unfortunately, all learning goals are secondary when compared to behavioral issues that need to be solved first.

The brains of our students are open to many learning states or "degrees of openness" to the world as they enter our classroom. States are always changing because the internal brain shifts them around constantly. These mind-body moments dominate the lives of our students and produce great joy at one end of the spectrum and great sadness or misery at the other.

What states do you want your students in to learn? How receptive are their learning states to what you want to teach them? These are probably some of the most important questions that you can ask yourself with regard to effective teaching.

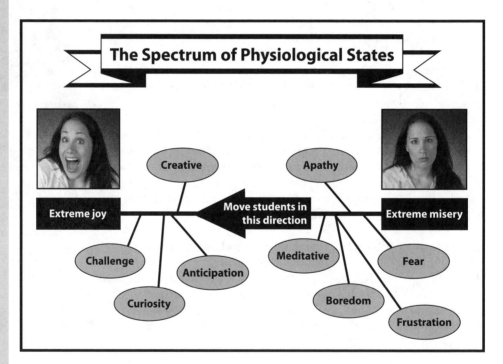

Any teacher who has ever seen the movie *Ferris Bueller's Day Off* will probably not forget the scenes that show high-school students totally uninterested in what is being taught. Ben Stein, the actor playing the part of the history teacher, virtually talks to himself as the camera captures the faces and expressions of students totally uninvolved with the learning as Stein softly says, "Anybody? Anybody?" then answers the questions himself. If you can identify with those actors as examples of your students and have seen those blank expressions in your classroom, please read further!

A Most Amazing Slug

Perhaps one of the most bizarre and least likely candidates for many experimental procedures on the nervous system, memory, and behavior is the gigantic California sea slug, *Aplysia californica*. This slimy purple creature is naturally found in the deeper tide pools off the coast of California and has been successfully raised in the laboratory for all phases of its life.

Aplysia have shown to be particularly useful in brain research because they have a relatively simple nervous system that is easy to access in the living animals with just minor dissection. Another reason they are so useful is that, as in many primitive sea slugs, the individual nerve cells are very large and brightly colored. The brain is also split into eleven ganglia, separated from each other by nerve cords (Sossin, 1997). This means that individual cells can be mapped and their functions isolated. This feature makes them particularly useful for brain research.

Aplysia californica—The California sea slug (photo courtesy of Caroline Schooley).

This big (average weight of about ten pounds) creature has provided scientists like Eric Kandel of Baylor University with an effective laboratory animal. He won the 2000 Nobel Prize in Medicine and Physiology for his study on learning and memory.

One of Kandel's studies has important implications for understanding how the brain responds to stimuli:

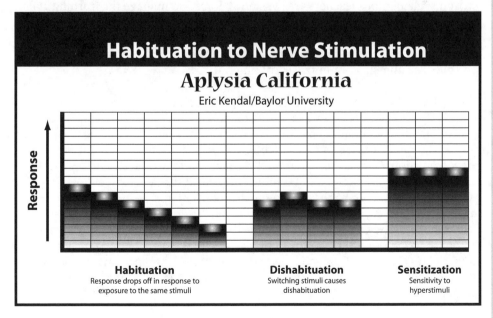

Habituation to Nerve Stimulation

Aplysia California

Eric Kendal/Baylor University

Response

Habituation
Response drops off in response to exposure to the same stimuli

Dishabituation
Switching stimuli causes dishabituation

Sensitization
Sensitivity to hyperstimuli

SOURCE: Adapted from J. David Sweatt, Baylor University.

This graphic is drawn from information about the neuron response to electrical stimuli. Neurons from Aplysia were subjected to the same electrical stimuli over a period of time. Over time, the level of response dropped off as a result of using the same stimuli to trigger a response. Kandel calls this habituation. When the electrical stimuli are switched, dis-habituation is noted. In other words, when the stimuli were changed, the response was much higher than if the same stimuli were used on Aplysia neurons continuously (Sweatt, 2002).

Combat Learning Fatigue With the "The Twenty Minute Rule"

The single most important thing a teacher must do is to manage the learning state of his or her students. Twenty minutes is probably the maximum time that most people can stay in a positive learning state without a change of stimulus (Grieco, 1986). Most students may not even be aware that they have moved down the spectrum from a positive learning state to a feeling of the brain being out to lunch! Effective teachers are aware of the looks on the faces of students, the squirming, and general disinterest. These teachers are always scanning the class for signs of learning fatigue and know what to do to ameliorate the problem.

For middle school, the rule could easily be reduced to "The Fifteen Minute Rule." Teachers cannot expect middle-school students to stay in a favorable learning state for more than fifteen minutes without intervention. A maximum of twenty minutes for high-school students and probably most adult learners, including those in graduate school, is appropriate.

We could learn from observing how lower elementary teachers handle learning fatigue. Since students in the early grades generally have a limited attention span and suffer from learning fatigue in a more demonstrative way than older students, elementary teachers are constantly forced to manage the learning state more acutely than teachers of middle and high school. Visiting a good teacher of second graders, for instance, would provide an opportunity to see a master of state management since most second graders are able to stay continuously in a positive learning state for only a short time.

Visit college classes, particularly graduate education courses, and you will frequently observe a professor lecturing on and on and on. The concept overriding almost all other objectives is to cover the material. The most expedient way to do this, of course, is to teach didactic lessons. Creative teaching strategies are talked about but because of limited class time and a great deal of material to cover are seldom demonstrated fully. Students at this level know how to play the game and are habituated to the didactic lesson. The eyes make contact, the pencil is poised, the laptop is humming, but after about twenty minutes without a learning-state change, even the brains of these high achievers are on autopilot with very little learning taking place. As we see a higher percentage of courses taught online, the challenge to demonstrate the management of learning states becomes even greater. These classes now become the models for teacher preparation.

The most effective teachers know intuitively how to read their students and have almost a built-in clock that reminds them that middle- and high-school students need to have their learning states adjusted about every twenty minutes.

Naturally gifted teachers and speakers change the learning states smoothly and without even their own awareness at times. As you experience an outstanding presentation from a gifted speaker, make mental notes to see how often the speaker changes the learning state. It may be a change of voice, a joke, gesture, a story telling, or a relocation of the speaker. Anything that allows the participants to change their state!

In classrooms where teachers are effective learning-state managers, students know what to expect and often look forward to getting out of their seats periodically and interacting with others, ultimately refreshing their learning states. Some teachers say that once they get the students settled into their seats, they want to retain that structure for the remainder of the class period if possible. The problem isn't as critical when students are involved with cooperative learning, project learning, or other activities that require students to move around and be involved in hands-on learning and discussions with other students. The bottom line is that students need to have their learning states changed frequently.

THE EDUCATIONAL CONNECTION

I f we expect our students to stay in the same learning state (stimuli) for a long period, then we can expect that their receptivity to learning the material to drop off much like the neural experiments on Aplysia (habituation). However, if we change the learning state then we can hope to place students in a more favorable state and increase the stimuli (dishabituation). In other words, if the teacher doesn't recognize the need to change the state of the learner's brain, learning fatigue sets in over a very short time period.

State Changers

State changers can be placed into three categories. Those designed to "process the learning" have a double objective. Processing the learning involves getting students out of their seats and involved plus getting feedback on the learning by processing it. This is a very effective way to provide students with feedback on their learning. The second category is "teacher directed." These are state-changers that involve the teacher performing the process. This category requires the teacher to perform. The third category involves "student-directed" activities. Although the teacher provides direction and guidance, the students actively engage in the process.

State Changers to Manage Your Students

Process the Learning	Teacher Directed	Student Directed
Partner Reteach Select partners, find creative ways for teams to pick a teacher and a student. Assume the roles and re-teach concepts.	**Use music** Learn how to use music to change and manage the learning states. See Chapter 8	**Cross-Laterals** Have students alternately move one arm and its opposite leg. This accesses both hemispheres of the brain simultaneously.
Think, Pair, Share Students reflect on a question or problem. They then turn to a partner and share ideas. Finally, have them write down new ideas generated from partner discussion.	**Change where you stand in the room** Without fanfare go to another position that you normally do not stand in. Continue the lesson from this point. Try establishing a position among the students.	**Invent ways to shake hands** Encourage students to be innovative and come up with an unusual handshake. Demonstrate to the class.
Snowballs Give a half sheet of paper to each student. Have each student write one concept they have learned today. Wrinkle up the sheets, and have them throw snowballs at each other. Each student collects one and reads it to the class.	**Turn your back on the group** Continue to provide a didactic lesson, but turn your back on the class for a few minutes while continuing with the lesson.	**Kinesthetic learning** Find some 80 beat/minute music with a solid beat. Ask students to kinesthetically review what you have learned. Use an overhead or chart to direct students to move their whole bodies while acting out the word. Example: Word–Movement Dendrites–Move fingers.
Jot thoughts Name a topic and set a time limit. Students write as many ideas as they can in the allotted time.	**Wear special clothes or hat** Keep a box of hats and special clothes that help place emotional emphasis in lesson topics. Use at critical times to set the stage.	**Brain breaks** Every twenty minutes ask students to get up and walk around or conduct stretching exercises. Limit the walk/stretch to two minutes or so and teach students why you are doing this.

Process the Learning	Teacher Directed	Student Directed
Note taking/note making This strategy requires students to divide pages in their notebooks in half vertically, writing Note Taking on the left half and Note Making on the right. After instructing the students to take notes on the left side, start a didactic lesson and proceed talking and having students take notes for about eight minutes. Then ask students to write their responses under the Note Making side to what has been said. They can read aloud their Note Making to a partner. After a time, proceed with another cycle.	**Tell a story or tell a joke** Tell students a story that ties into the subject or share a metaphor to help them understand the material you are teaching. Try using appropriate background music to enhance the story. (See activities in this chapter for laughter and the brain)	**Seat changes** Give students one minute to gather their books and find a new seat within the same row or column. Have students shift seats to different quadrants in the room so they have a different perspective of the environment from where they have been sitting.
Frisbee or ball toss review While students are in their seats, toss a ball or Frisbee to any student. That student is required to answer a question, then toss the ball to another student.	**Do a magic trick** Learn a magic trick and use it to make a point or teach it to the class.	**Ball toss** Have groups of 6–8 stand in a circle facing each other. One person has a ball and tosses to another student while doing a Q-and-A from what is being studied. The ball is then thrown to the next person, and the process is repeated.
Brainstorming Generate many ideas for discussions or evaluation. This is nonthreatening if accomplished correctly.	**Bring in snacks** For special occasions bring healthful snacks for student celebrations—or for any time the class might need a pick-me-up!	**Have students stand to learn** Have students process with each other while standing. While reading have students stand for every other page.

The Punctuated Lesson

What impact does the punctuated lesson have on retention, and is it practical to consider it as a strategy for learning? In a study of college students by K. Ruhl and others, a teacher paused frequently during a series of lectures. The intervals ranged from twelve to eighteen minutes. During the pauses, while students worked in pairs to discuss and rework their notes from the lesson, no interaction occurred between the teacher and the students. Students hearing the lectures while the instructor paused did significantly better on the free recall and a comprehensive test. The experimental group did much better on the subsequent test than the group who were subjected to the typical sixty- to ninety-minute lecture.

The implication of this research is staggering—it essentially suggests that if we talk less, students learn more. These results are consistent with other studies and support the research on learning-state management. This study seems to

Teach like Abe: short and sweet, and to the point.

verify what we know about learning: (1) that short lessons (twelve to eighteen minutes) are consistent with the research suggesting students' ability to retain information falls off substantially after ten to twenty minutes; and (2) by engaging in an activity that reinforces the information presented, student learning should increase (Ruhl, et al., 1987).

Think about a speech in history that had a profound impact on our nation since it was delivered about 150 years ago. You probably guessed that it was Lincoln's Gettysburg Address. Did you know there was another speech given that day? Two speeches were given in Gettysburg on November 19, 1863, and the contrast between them is remarkable. Edward Everett, who had been a president of Harvard, a congressman, a senator, and a governor of Massachusetts as well as a secretary of state and a minister to England, was chosen to deliver the principal address at the dedication of the new national cemetery on the battlefield at Gettysburg. Lincoln was invited almost as an afterthought. Everett spoke for two hours, his speech was printed, distributed in advance, and has rarely been read since. Lincoln's speech lasted two minutes (234 words) and is arguably the most famous composition in American history.

The message is clear: Short, succinct lessons punctuated by activities that allow students to process the learning are critical for success. Lincoln knew it; Edward Everett did not. As a middle- and high-school teacher, consider the priorities for delivering a lesson. Managing the learning state is truly the number-one priority of the teacher.

Summary of Chapter 7

• All behavior is a manifestation of what is happening in the brain.

• A physiological state is a mind-body moment made up of an individual's thoughts and feelings.

• All behavior is state-dependent; we need to know what states our students are in and change them if they are not what we want.

• Students in class need to be in a receptive state; it is up to the teacher to modify the learning state to a receptive one.

• The single most important thing a teacher does is to manage the state of the learner.

ENGAGING THE BRAIN THROUGH ACTIVITIES

Activity

Laughter

Background: In recent years, scientists have started to take laughter and humor much more seriously. Their investigations are shedding light on how the brain processes humor and prompts laughter. Researchers believe that uncovering the brain and body's specific response to positive stimuli like humor and laughter may lead to new therapies.

Using fMRI, neuroscientists have found that increased blood flow to the nucleus accumbens occurred when subjects found cartoons funny (Wild, et al., 2003). Studies suggest that the complex process involves three main brain components. One component, a cognitive thinking part, helps a person get the joke. A second component helps move the muscles of the face to smile and laugh. And a third emotional component helps produce the happy feelings that accompany a jovial experience.

Laughing in the classroom: There is probably no better way to maintain and direct the learning state of a classroom of any age than laughter. When learners laugh together, they learn together. Laughing with a class of adolescents is a great gift and an important skill to model. There are so many attributes to laughing in the classroom. A few of them include:

• Increasing a feeling of hope—taking the drudgery out of the time in class.

• Increasing retention—the research on this is extensive and includes examples from traffic school to airline attendant preflight messages.

- Building rapport—nothing works like humor or adds so much credibility to a teacher at any level. The first thing kids will remember is, "She was funny!"

- Relieving stress—when a teacher can become humorous, even poor attempts will reduce the amount of tension in the classroom. This works particularly well before a test.

Post a Joke

For fun and an attention grabber each morning, post one of these clever sayings on a designated bulletin board. The students may groan at them, but if you forget to change the board, they will ask you if you forgot. After several weeks of changing the joke, ask students to bring in sayings, jokes, and quotes to post each day. If you have a homeroom or students who could be responsible to post a joke for each day for the week, they can keep you well supplied.

Try these word plays as a start:

Those who jump off a bridge in Paris are in Seine.

A man's home is his castle, in a manor of speaking.

Dijon vu: the same mustard as before.

A hangover is the wrath of grapes.

Does the name Pavlov ring a bell?

Reading while sunbathing makes you well red.

When two egotists meet, it's an I for an I.

A bicycle can't stand on its own because it is two tired.

What's the definition of a will? (It's a dead giveaway.)

In democracy your vote counts. In feudalism your count votes.

A chicken crossing the road is poultry in motion.

If you don't pay your exorcist, you get repossessed.

When a clock is hungry, it goes back four seconds.

The man who fell into an upholstery machine is fully recovered.

Every calendar's days are numbered.

A boiled egg in the morning is hard to beat.

A plateau is a high form of flattery.

Those who get too big for their britches will be exposed in the end.

Once you've seen one shopping center, you've seen a mall.

Bakers trade bread recipes on a knead-to-know basis.

Acupuncture is a jab well done.

Here are a few of our favorite one-liners for verbalization that might work well for middle-school adolescents:

How do crazy people go through the forest? They take the psycho-path.

What do prisoners use to call each other? Cell phones.

What do you call a boomerang that doesn't work? A stick.

What do you call Santa's helpers? Subordinate Clauses.

What do you get from a pampered cow? Spoiled milk.

What do you get when you cross a snowman with a vampire? Frostbite.

What lies at the bottom of the ocean and twitches? A nervous wreck.

What's the difference between roast beef and pea soup? Anyone can roast beef.

What do you get if you cross a student with an alien? Something from another universe-ity!

Where do large animals go to school? The hippocampus!

Why do bagpipers walk when they play? They're trying to get away from the noise.

What is a zebra? 25 sizes larger than an "A" bra.

What kind of coffee was served on the *Titanic*? Sanka!

Delivery: Many new teachers who are not at ease with their students require confidence to let go and become humorous. You must convince yourself that humor is fun for you as a teacher. What makes you laugh will probably work with them. Just try it. You will find that students will give you more license than you think they will because of the universal wish to laugh and have fun in class.

Types of jokes to use: There are wonderful resources such as viewing cartoons from *The New Yorker* magazine as well as Gary Larson's "The Far Side" and listening to digital recordings of jokes. With the Internet virtually exploding the joke world, an endless supply is available at little or no cost. Nothing compares to storytelling or joke telling. Start building a repertoire and bring your collection of jokes out for the state changes you wish to make. Remember, timing is everything, and practice improves the timing greatly . . . Seinfeld wasn't great at first!

Selected Books for Enhancing This Chapter

Jensen, Eric	*Tools for Engagement: Managing Emotional States for Learner Success.* Corwin Press: Thousand Oaks, CA, 2003 Finally, a book on the importance of managing the physiological state of the learner. Many applications to learning from the brain research on emotional states. Theory and practical ideas abound in this exceptional work.
Evanski, Jerry	*Classroom Activators: 64 Novel Ways to Energize Learners.* Corwin Press: Thousand Oaks, CA, 2004 This little book is full of classroom activators and state changers. A wonderful reference to have at hand to help spark student interest during lessons.

8

*Using Music Effectively
to Enhance Learning*

Chapter 8
Using Music Effectively to Enhance Learning

Music's impact on your mind and body begins with the physiological process of hearing. The ear is the first sensory organ to develop in the womb, preceding even the nervous system, so sound is your first source of information about the world.

— Elizabeth Miles, enthnomusicologist

Everyone thinks music is important, but few understand why. Maybe it's been that philosophy that has persuaded school districts to trade in their music programs for more high-stakes-testing prep time. Regardless, many educators have been convinced that learning to use music in classroom management strategy has promise. With the new technology, selecting music to use in the classroom is much easier then ever before. This chapter will provide teachers and presenters with justification for using music and some strategies for using it more effectively with their students.

A Dedicated Teacher

Typical of dedicated high-school biology teachers, John Kiefer always expended a great deal of energy trying to get his classes to clean up after a lab activity. About five minutes before the end of each period, he resorted to yelling at the top of his lungs, "Clean up!" Rushing to see that all the thermometers were back in their cases, glassware cleaned for the next class, reagents capped, and lab tables swabbed down with disinfectant, a tired teacher prepared for the onslaught of the next class.

After a few years of frustration he decided on a whim one day to pick out a favorite instrumental song on the stereo as a signal for cleaning up, carefully instructing his classes that when they heard a particular song begin, they were to stop working on the lab activity and clean up. Pushing the play button to start Ray Lynch's "Celestial Soda Pop," the students started to clean up. This process took more training and patience than he first thought. After one week, they still needed reminding; two weeks passed with very little success, but after the third week, he noticed that the students begin reminding each other that it was time to clean up as the song played on. It finally worked!

What John found out was that he could manage the learning state of his students with music. It sure beats yelling and coercing students to clean up! Elementary teachers have known for a long time that habituating their students in response to music for initiating tasks works well. Given what he found out about controlling the learner's state, John realized that using music in the classroom helped students transition from one activity to another.

How Music Affects How Our Body Functions

Music affects many functions of the body with its rhythmic pattern and vibratory rate. Music affects the nervous system from the moment our auditory nerves start to distribute the effects of music to many functions such as internal secretions, circulation, and respiration. Rhythm in music exerts a strong influence on the heartbeat and can raise and lower blood pressure (Miles, 1997). Who can doubt that music influences our emotions? Researchers just now are beginning to understand this phenomenon. It appears that listening to music stimulates the release of endorphins that are produced by the brain. Endorphins are among a group of electrochemical transmitters that when released translate experiences into pleasure. Brain-based translator Eric Jensen reports that studies show that when endorphin release is blocked, pleasure from music is substantially reduced (Jensen, 2000).

Changing the Learning Environment Through Music

Using music in teaching and training can increase your results in class by adding to the learning environment, and it can affect the state of the students. The feelings and physiology of your participants at any specific time determine how effective you can be as a teacher. In order for people to learn, they must be in a receptive state or a state of motivation that can lead to a learning state. If your audience is in a state of apathy, it's very difficult for them to absorb the material you want to teach. You can change the state of a learner with music. It can put people in a more receptive state for learning, and if one understands how to match the tempo and pacing of a musical piece with the activity, music can enhance the presentation and tie an emotion to what is to be learned.

Going Digital

To "prime" the brains of your students for learning you will need a compact disc player or a cassette player and a basic library of musical selections. CDs and CD players provide instant access to selections without the cueing necessary with cassette tapes. Tapes still have some advantages because you can record a single song and label it easily. If you plan to play a tape with a single recording, finding the starting point of a specific selection is not an issue. However, this analog technology is the last form of nondigital music to be phased out of production. You can now purchase almost any song you desire online for a fraction of the cost to convert your old music (see "iTunes and MP3 players").

Get comfortable by using just a few musical choices in the beginning. Generally speaking, plan to use instrumental rather than vocal music. Lyrics tend to intrude on the thinking process and will not provide the effect you want on your students. Be patient and try

Compact disc player

music with your students for one or two specific purposes. The most effective way to introduce your integration of music with students is to play music as a background when students are entering the classroom. Upbeat music like CDs from Bond or Strunz and Farah will provide you with songs that are great backgrounds and require no intervention while you are setting up for class or presentation (for more suggestions, see the end of this chapter). It's great to do this when you first get to class and start your day. Start the music and see what impact it has on you for anticipating a wonderful day of teaching.

As you get comfortable with your stereo or more advanced technology, gradually add music to start or intercede with lessons and events in the classroom or presentations. After your comfort level increases with selecting music for activities, your students start to enjoy it and anticipate your use of music with glee! The key is to know when and how much music to use. Sometimes no music is the best option. Many teachers just starting to use music tend to overuse the strategy at first.

iTunes and MP3 Players: A New World of Goodies!

With the popularity and lower prices of CD players, thievery is hardly a concern anymore. You can purchase a decent CD stereo player for less than seventy-five dollars. But why do that? New technology is being offered at lower prices every month. The storage format popular now is MP3. It produces great quality sound and takes up much less memory in your computer than previously required for music. Now with free downloadable computer programs for your PC or Mac like Apple's iTunes, you can start for free! Teachers can place all of their music selections on a laptop or a desktop computer. Add an inexpensive set of speakers; the fidelity is amazing for a classroom-sized space. Some of the better quality speakers sets have so much power (80–100 watts) that you can obtain excellent fidelity and sharpness at a volume high enough to power a lecture hall. Having a great selection of music with the ease and speed of these programs makes using music a snap!

One stop further along the technology train is the addition of an MP3 player like the iPod. In these wonderful, but still expensive, little devices, one can download all of their stored songs from a computer and have them immediately available to play. The iPod Nano is the newest model and unbelievably small and light. When purchasing a set of speakers for your iPod, make sure the manufacturer has included a stereo minijack input so you can also link your laptop or desktop computer to the set.

MP3 player

The world of buying and collecting music has changed. The days of pirated downloads have merged into legitimate Web sites that sell songs for a reasonable price. The iTunes music store has developed huge archives of songs available for download at ninety-nine cents each. Once you establish an account with a Web site like the iTunes music store, you can retrieve almost any song from almost any genre.

One of the most exciting options when purchasing music from the iTunes music store is that you can hear the first twenty seconds before you decide to purchase it! This gives you alternatives for hearing different artists playing the same song, and it allows you to be more secure in your choice before you purchase it. How many times have you gone to a music store and purchased a CD for $18, then taken it home to find that you don't like most of the cuts? Music store Web sites like iTunes are a song buyer's heaven.

Beginning Suggestions

Some students might be sensitive to sounds. Try turning the sound down slightly or seating them away from your speakers. With a good set of speakers you can keep the volume low. This means you should still have the ability to speak at a conversational level without raising your voice.

Students who are musically trained may also be bothered. They tend to hear musical sounds as a language, and it interferes with their normal language processing. Generally speaking, use music about 30 percent of the time or less. Any more may be too much of a good thing.

Explain to your students why you are using music. Depending on their age, a few of them may feel classical music is tragically unhip, but usually not only will they come to accept it, they will develop favorite composers. If you are using a CD player, leave the case cover beside it so students can reference what is playing. As students become familiar with the music you have available, give them the opportunity to choose what they listen to.

Beats per minute	Type of usage recommended
45–50	Imagery, physical/mental relaxation, concentration, and thinking. This is great for study, testing, work groups, and computer time.
55–70	Effective for learning new material. Also great for writing in journals and thinking creatively.
70–80	Group work, moderate activity, inspiration for creative groupwork.
80–130	Motivation and productivity. Great for task completion and kinesthetic activities. Seldom effective otherwise, except at break time or to call back a group from a break.

Knowing the Fundamentals About Music

You can get great results from knowing just the fundamentals about music. Here are the key things to know:

- The beat or tempo is most important. The beat of the music affects both the heart rate and breathing, the two most important determiners of mood, feeling, and state.

- In general, your selections will be instrumentals. Exceptions should be only for breaks or for special effects.

- Try to match each type of tempo to a particular activity.

- Using music too often reduces effectiveness. Limit its use to 30 percent of class time or less.

THE EDUCATIONAL CONNECTION

As teachers and presenters, you want the very best for your students and those whom you present to. If you are an energetic teacher like John Kiefer, you will try to involve your charges in as many enjoyable, constructive activities as the classroom/workshop space will allow. The high-stakes testing program sweeping this country may control your time as a teacher. However, using music can help to provide creative elements of learning and to compensate for the freedom that existed in classrooms of the past. While testing may or may not contribute to a child's physical, intellectual, and social development, scientists and educators are beginning to realize that early, positive musical experiences are uniquely important for students (Bjorkvold, 1989).

Students take to music naturally. Musical sounds are among the first stimuli an infant responds to, and if you observe very young children at play you will see them instinctively weave music into their activities. Solitary play is almost always accompanied by tunes, fragments of songs from Disney movies, and rhythmic sounds from TV ads they are subconsciously recalling. Children of all cultures bring music into their games, and their play with other children and use it to explore the new world around them (Bjorkvold, 1989).

continues

Musical activities create important experiences that can help students develop physical coordination, timing, memory, and visual and language skills. When you play music in the classroom your students will gain important subtle skills that trigger the desire to start playing an instrument, or at the very least, become interested in the variety of music you can introduce through playing music in the classroom. Your students will gain important experience with self-paced learning, mental concentration, and a heightened personal and social awareness.

Music has been largely pushed aside in many public schools and often completely cut from curriculum, only to be taught at the teacher's discretion. School districts began raising goals for basic curricula through creating new educational standards and testing, a trend that is with us in ever-increasing stringency. In cutting the "fat" to tighten up programs, some schools have often been forced to leave out the arts. Unfortunately, more drill and practice by themselves have not increased scores on high-stakes testing to sufficiently reach the goals for many states (Sanchez, 2005).

Educators are now wondering if the arts did, after all, add significantly to the educational experience. Research suggests that teachers who use music as a teaching strategy can increase student attentiveness, thus leading to better transitions, better student control, and eventually a better climate for taking standardized tests (Miller, 1999).

10 Effective Ways to Use Music in the Classroom

1. **While students are changing class** or, at elementary, coming from a break: to create an anticipatory mood. Use upbeat or soaring orchestral music or an epic movie theme. This identifies your room as a special place and tends to draw students in. Suggestions: Handel's *Water Music; Ancient Dances,* by Respighi; "Also Sprach Zarathustra" (the movie theme from *2001: A Space Odyssey*); themes from *Rocky, Raiders of the Lost Ark,* or *Star Wars.* Try the theme from *The Rocketeer,* "Takeoff." Another set of inspiring music can be found in CDs from Bond: try *Shine* or *Born.*

2. **To start or conclude an activity**, try to establish a "callback" song. This is something that students will recognize every time you play it. The conditioning that results after using the same piece of music will allow you to control transitions with ease. Instead of trying to yell for students to clean up after and activity or lab, try using a song they recognize to signal cleaning up. Try "Celestial Soda Pop" by Ray Lynch or "Elysian Fields" by Tingstad and Rumbel.

3. **During energizer breaks** or to change the state of a lethargic group: put energy into a room with up-tempo music and a strong beat. Use for only two or three minutes at most; sometimes only a minute is enough. A fun alternative to the standard energizer activities is to have the group "conduct" vigorously while a rousing piece is played. Try it with the "Lone Ranger" section from the *William Tell Overture* or the overture from *The Phantom of the Opera*.

4. **If a group tends to come into your room in a drowsy, sleepy mood** (right after lunch or perhaps late in the day), consider using this music providing an entry to the learning activity. Suggestions: Rock music with a fast, hard beat, such as the Pointer Sisters' "Jump (For My Love)" "New Attitude" by Patti LaBelle, or Roy Orbison's "Pretty Woman." You might also try the soundtrack from *Flash Dance*, Beethoven symphonies, Tchaikovsky's *1812 Overture*, "Classical Gas" by Mason Williams, *Hooked on Classics* (familiar classical music scored as pop music), or *Stadium Rock* (the rock music played at sporting events to energize the crowd, available in album form by that or similar names).

5. **Music to enter your classroom** needs to put you at ease, too. Try turning on your computer music system or iPod immediately after entering your classroom. Try something that is soothing and will relax you as you set up. Most important is to select a CD playlist that has very predictable recording throughout. This will allow you to do other things and to leave it on for a longer period. When students are walking in to your environment, this is the first impression they have of you. Try Andean music: The flutes, drums, and rhythms are a great mix and very easy to listen to yet upbeat. Experiment with classical guitars like CDs from The Heat of the Sun, or *Give and Take* from Tingstad and Rumbel.

6. **Transitioning music** ("switch seats, find a partner") that creates a sense of urgency in the group includes Khachaturian's *Sabre Dance*, the "Lone Ranger" section from Rossini's *William Tell Overture*, and "Flight of the Bumble Bee."

7. **Create a calm, relaxed atmosphere** to relieve a tense or stressed group. A hospital study showed that critical-care patients' need for sedatives was lessened when music by Bach, Debussy, Haydn, Mendelssohn, and Mozart was played. Suggestions: Pachelbel's Canon in D (one of the most soothing pieces of music ever written, available in hundreds of versions), Mozart violin concertos and string quartets, or Strauss waltzes. Other suggestions include *Serenade for Strings*, "Amazing Grace," soft piano or guitar music, or environmental music (music played over the sound of waterfalls, ocean surf, rain). Some new age music also works for this purpose. Consider Michael Jones's *After the Rain*, Bill Douglas's *Deep Peace*, or David Arkenstone's *Papillon*. Look for new age music especially designed for meditation or to create a relaxed alertness. Many of these selections also work as background noise for quiet class activities (silent reading, journal writing).

8. **To create a creative, brainstorming atmosphere** or to ready the brain for complex mental activity (like problem solving or test taking): Research indicates the brain can be primed for complex mental activity in a manner analogous to the way an athlete warms up before an athletic event.

Experiments have shown that complex pieces of music played for ten to fifteen minutes increased student performance temporarily on spatial-temporal tests; see the discussion of the "Mozart Effect" in Chapter 1. Its effects are often overstated; however, any complex piece should accomplish the same end. Almost anything by Mozart, but especially his piano concertos (specifically no.s 20, 21, 23, 26, and 27); Bach's *Brandenburg Concertos*, Beethoven's Piano Concerto No. 5, or "Clair de Lune" by Debussy will work. You might also experiment with gospel or country music played with a hammered dulcimer, such as *Country Mountain Classics*.

9. **To create a special effect or celebrate a special occasion:** Certain situations call for a special piece of music that allows the class to celebrate, share humor, or note a special occasion. Suggestions: "Celebrate" by Kool & the Gang, "You Say It's Your Birthday" by the Beatles, Tina Turner's "Simply the Best," Elgar's "Pomp and Circumstance," and "Stars and Stripes Forever" by Sousa. There are numerous special effects tapes available as well as TV and movie soundtrack CDs, for example: *The Twilight Zone, Rawhide, Jaws, Rocky, Star Wars, Chariots of Fire, Out of Africa*, or "Lara's Theme" from *Dr. Zhivago*.

10. **To end the class period or day** you may want to consider a musical selection that becomes the closing signature piece for your time with your students. This piece could be upbeat and bouncy or wistful, depending on the atmosphere you and your students want to evoke as your ending. You could use the same piece all year or change at some regular interval. Suggestions: "I Can See Clearly Now" by Johnny Nash; "Happy Trails to You," the *Roy Rogers* theme song; the *Happy Days* theme; "What a Wonderful World," by Louis Armstrong; "Here Comes the Sun," by the Beatles; or "The Goodbye Song," from Steam. This is a place where lyrics are not a problem.

A Word of Caution

Once you open the floodgates of using music in the classroom on a regular basis, students will ask you to bring in their favorite music. You will want to preview it first—not just for alternative lyrics, but also to evaluate whether you are going to reach your goals by playing it. It's hard to say "no thanks" when students offer to bring in music; sometimes it's best to take the CD home, listen to it, and thank the student the next day. Explain that you appreciate the offer but you won't be able to work it in because, while it might be great to listen to privately, it isn't part of what you are trying to accomplish.

Types of Music to Consider

Classical Music: What many people call classical music was actually composed in three distinct periods: Baroque, Classical, and Romantic. They can all be used to create an atmosphere while students are transitioning from one activity to another or as background for a variety of activities, including brainstorming or discussion in small groups; reading, writing, test taking; or as a soft accompaniment to a whole-class activity. Classical music selections can often be found in discount stores or the bargain bin at the record store for less than five dollars. Look for treatments by a full orchestra in a major key. Often you can find something titled "The Best of . . . (Bach, Mozart, etc.)" or "A Treasury of . . . (Baroque, Romantic, etc.)." These collections are a good place to start finding what you like without spending a lot of money.

The piano, like the flute, is an instrument that can be heard in nearly all genres of music.

Baroque music tends to be simple and harmonious and is best used as background or to create a restful but alert state. Familiar and popular possibilities include music by Handel, like *Water Music* or *Music for the Royal Fireworks; Concerto* by Grosso; Vivaldi's *The Four Seasons;* and Bach's *The Brandenburg Concertos.* Other names include Albinoni, Corelli, Purcell, and Telemann.

Classical music is more complex than Baroque and contrasts between rousing, energetic sections and beautifully subtle moments. It works well for priming, to enhance creativity, and as soft background to stories or lectures. Mozart is the master of it all. Consider overtures to *The Magic Flute* and *The Marriage of Figaro; Eine kleine Nachtmusik,* especially "The Romanza"; Symphony No. 39; and his piano concertos. Beethoven is wonderful for both powerful symphonies and elegant piano sonatas. Try *The Eroica Symphony,* Symphony No. 5, *The Egmont Overture, Für Elise,* or the *Moonlight Sonata.* Other names are Haydn and Schumann.

Romantic music is usually lush, often florid and emotional. Much of it will sound familiar, as it is often used in movie scores. Familiar names include Tchaikovsky, Wagner, Verdi, Brahms, Chopin, and Debussy.

New age music can be used to establish a restful, relaxed atmosphere. There is a multitude of choices. Depending on your taste and that of your learners you might consider the music of Enigma, Enya, Michael Jones, David Arkenstone, Tingstad and Rumbel, Kitaro, Tony O'Connor, Vangelis, George Winston, or Yanni.

Rock and roll, jazz, rap, hip-hop, techno, and other variations provide exceptions to the no-lyrics rule and can be popular music played for a specific purpose, usually to inject energy into the room, to accompany a short (two- to three-minute) energizer break, or to end the day on an up note. There are hundreds

of collections available. Try "Gonna Make You Sweat" by C + C Music Factory—it's used to get groups going.

Country-western provides some very recognizable songs that can be used for special effects. When getting kids back in their seats you might use some special effects like "Back in the Saddle Again" by Gene Autry or "Give Me One More Shot" by Alabama. When you think your learners are overloaded with material, try "Am I Losing You" by Jim Reeves. You will get a laugh every time and change the state of your students—just as you wanted to do!

THE EDUCATIONAL CONNECTION

In general, your students will love music. Experiment. Try purchasing some music online and you will never go back—it's so easy and convenient. Use music with a purpose, and avoid saturation. Selective use of music provides interest and catches the attention of the learner in a way that's hard to duplicate. The use of music in your classroom is a form of self-expression: it's a universal language, and you are capable of using it as a wonderful teaching tool. Take the opportunity to enjoy the use of it and see if it makes a difference.

Summary of Chapter 8

- Playing music in the classroom can assist in the development of physical coordination, timing, memory, and visual and language skills.

- Music affects many functions of the body with its rhythmic patterns and vibratory rates.

- Using music in the classroom can assist in managing the state of the learner.

- Computers and digital improvements in recording and copying music have provided ease in collecting, organizing play lists, and playing music in the classroom.

- Selecting music for specific uses involves knowing and applying an understanding of tempo.

ENGAGING THE BRAIN THROUGH ACTIVITIES

Activity #1

The Concert Review

Background: The term "concert review" refers to playing music while reviewing the lesson or content presented. By displaying transparencies or PowerPoint slides in sequence to selected music, the student can recall the content and flow of the lesson. It works best when the lesson to be reviewed is presented with transparencies or PowerPoint slides.

Concert reviews provide a wonderful way to assist students in recalling material presented during the class period. The brain needs repetition to help retain information. Using this strategy, you can help your students retain information for a longer period of time and provide them with a comprehensive review of the content enhanced by the emotional additive of music.

What music should I use? Music to accompany the activity might suggest relaxation and imagery. Instrumentals seem to work best. Vocals tend to distract from concentrating on what students have just learned and the sequence they have learned it. Try music selections from Windham Hill, George Winston, and new age artists like Ray Lynch. Use music that is not very complex and ranges in tempo from sixty to eighty beats per minute. Music featuring oboes, cellos, and classical string guitars work well, too.

Directions

1. Start with selecting slides or transparencies from your lesson presentation. Careful selection of slides containing key information is important. Fewer slides are better representatives for one class period. Keep the maximum number of slides at about fifteen, even if the concert review is for more than one class period of content.

2. Practice before class with several musical selections to establish which music you prefer to use with your slides.

3. Tell your students to get comfortable and relax. Say, "I am going to show you some of the visuals we used today in class. Please sit back and take a few moments to reflect on the lesson in the sequence that we presented it as I play some music for background."

4. Start the music and display the slides in the order that you presented them. If you are in front of an overhead projector, stay low so your image won't distract from the focus of the transparencies. Change the slides every five seconds; this seems to be an adequate amount of time for the students to reflect on the content without boring them.

5. The entire process should only take about two minutes. Plan on leaving the last slide on the screen as you slowly lower the sound level while the music is still playing. You might want to experiment with the last slide, including a culminating thought for the day.

Activity #2

Recognizing the Physical Impact of Music

To affirm the power of music in modifying the physiological state of the learner, try the following experiment with your students:

1. Ask each person to take an informal check of his or her pulse rate and to note it. Tell them to determine personally how awake they feel on a scale of one to five, five being "highly active."

2. Indicate that in about thirty seconds, they are going to hear a piece of music that may affect how they feel at this time. Inform students that it's okay if they wish to close their eyes to become more comfortable to listen to the selection.

3. After about thirty seconds, play Pachelbel's Canon in D. Watch what happens to their body language and facial expressions (you may observe an easing or relaxing reaction in the students).

4. After about two minutes, slowly reduce the volume to zero and ask students, "Did you observe any change in your body while listening to Pachelbel's Canon in D? Would you rate yourself lower or higher on your personal 'awake scale'? How do you feel now compared to when we first started the experiment?"

5. Tell students that in about thirty seconds you will play another selection. Ask them to informally check their pulse rate and to note how they feel now on their "awake scale." Again, request that they close their eyes if it is comfortable for them to do so.

6. Play "Gonna Make You Sweat" by C + C Music Factory. Make sure the volume is high to start so the music starts rather abruptly. Watch what happens to their body language and facial expressions. (Note: You may observe some of them keeping up with the beat as the music swells in amplitude and rhythm.)

7. After two minutes reduce the volume to zero and say, "Please turn to your neighbor and share whether you think your pulse rate may have changed and whether you think your awake scale may have changed." Allow partners to converse for about two minutes.

8. Ask students to share any changes they observed in themselves after hearing "Gonna Make You Sweat."

9. What you will find with any age group is rather interesting: Most students will become aware that unconsciously, music changes the way they feel.

Selected Books to Enhance This Chapter	
Jensen, Eric	*Music With the Brain in Mind.* Corwin Press: Thousand Oaks, CA 2000 A book with excellent support from the research on the value of music in the school. Includes translation of the latest brain and musical research plus provides lots of practical strategies for using music at all levels in the school. For teachers there are many tips on choosing music and the benefits of various types of music in the classroom. Applicable from K–12.
Jensen, Eric	*Top Tunes for Teaching: 977 Song Titles & Practical Tools for Choosing the Right Music Every* Time. Corwin Press: Thousand Oaks, CA 2005 A compilation of almost 1,000 music titles organized in over 30 play lists to get teachers started in making their own collection. A must-have book for the beginning collector and a good reference for anyone who wants to improve the way music is used in the classroom. Applicable from K–12.
Miles, Elizabeth	*Tune Your Brain: Using Music to Manage Your Mind, Body, and Mood.* Berkeley Books: NY 1997 A wonderful treatise of how music affects the brain and the body. Miles provides a useful and very readable guide to musical psychology. Teachers serious about learning this subject will find her suggestions helpful for the classroom.

9

This Is Your Brain on . . . :
Understanding and Curbing
Adolescent Substance Abuse

Chapter 9
This Is Your Brain on . . . : Understanding and Curbing Adolescent Substance Abuse

The fact is, drug addiction is a brain disease. While every type of drug has its own individual "trigger" for affecting or transforming the brain, many of the results of the transformation are strikingly similar regardless of the addictive drug that is used.

—Alan I. Leshner, scientist

There are a variety of reasons why one teenager becomes addicted to drugs and another does not. No single cause for addictions exists; rather, a combination of factors is usually involved. The combination and timing of these factors can also determine who becomes addicted and who does not. The availability of prescription drugs through the Internet and other sources has increased the risk of drug abuse markedly in the United States and beyond during the past decade. The concern today focuses on what we have learned about the teenage brain and the impact drugs can have on it. It is well documented that early use of drugs and alcohol can have a devastating effect on brain development. One of the dilemmas facing parents, teachers, and schools is how to convince teenagers that this is a real problem without resorting to scare tactics. We know from the past that this methodology for changing behavior and reducing risk behavior isn't effective and probably never has been.

Teenagers diagnosed with attention deficit/hyperactivity disorder (AD/HD) are especially vulnerable to abusing any mind-altering substance to diminish feelings. With effective intervention, young people who take prescribed drugs for AD/HD turn out to be no more susceptible than those not affected for drug abuse.

A Drug Dilemma

Josh appeared to his friends like any other fourteen-year-old. He was a nice-looking boy who had the beginning of chiseled features, thick dark brown hair, and a winning smile as the result of the freshly removed braces. His teachers would have commented that his presence in class was unremarkable. He was a solid C+ to B- student and never caused behavior problems.

That was what you got on the outside. Few of his teachers and friends knew what Josh had gone through during elementary school as a result of being diagnosed with AD/HD coupled with anxiety problems. His life in elementary school had been a living hell even with supportive, informed, and loving parents; Josh's problems had consumed the family for the past six years.

It started in the first and second grade. Reports of poor social behavior and the inability to stay on task plagued his daily life. Bad behavior and poorly developed reading and math skills were topics of conversation during numerous parent-teacher conferences.

Josh suffered from constant stomach pains, nervousness, worry, distractibility, and the overwhelming feeling that he was incapable. All these things grew to consume him. He seemed pretty much defeated by everything and everybody until the summer after he finished the fifth grade.

It's been a difficult issue for Josh's parents and his doctors. Every child has his share of worry, shyness around strangers, or fear of heights, but severe social anxieties are something else. These kids have anxieties that far exceed normal bounds. Fear overtakes them; they can't sleep alone, can't separate from their parents, can't bear to go to school, and can't make or keep friends. Add the diagnosis of AD/HD, and you have people clambering to prescribe any drug that might alleviate the symptoms.

He was clinically diagnosed when he was in the fourth grade. His preadolescent brain was the victim of the neurochemical storms typical of children suffering from AD/HD, excess worry, and depression. "If this was happening in elementary school, what was middle school going to be like?" worried his parents.

But that was the old Josh. Today, as a teenager, his life is back, thanks to the chemical stabilizing provided by two drugs: Luvox, an antidepressant, and Adderall, a relatively new anti-AD/HD drug. For the first time in as long as he could remember, Josh was able to rid himself of his demons and join in on the life that most middle-schoolers enjoyed. Good news for Josh!

Although psychotropic drugs are helping affected teens, the effects on their developing brains remains undocumented.

But was it really good news? Luvox seems to be a good answer for anxiety, even though it works by artificially manipulating the very chemicals responsible for feeling and thought. Adderall appears to be a good answer for AD/HD, except that it's a stimulant containing Dexedrine. There are side effects, such as weigh loss and sleeplessness, and both drugs are being poured into a young brain that has years to go before it's finally fully formed. The bottom line, however, is that Josh is now capable of acting like a normal teenage boy without the baggage so evident in elementary school.

A physician recently said, "Treating mental disease with drugs today is comparable to treating a tonsillectomy with an axe!" But restoring a neurochemical balance in the brain, however imprecise the method, has allowed Josh to function normally and master the social skills he lacked in elementary school. Only after receiving the medications was he able to benefit from psychological treatment and counseling offered. The Joshes of the world might say, "Those who call these medications a quick fix have never suffered from one of these debilitating diseases."

Within the medical community and the families of the troubled children there is concern growing about just what psychotropic drugs can do to still-developing brains. Few people deny that the drugs are helping, but all acknowledge that we haven't given enough thought to long-term consequences. "The problem," warns Dr. Glen Elliott, director of the Langley Porter Psychiatric Institute's children's center at the University of California, San Francisco, "is that our usage has outstripped our knowledge base. Let's face it, we're experimenting on these kids without tracking the results" (Kluger, 2003).

The other side of this issue has reached the courts. Parents who were coerced by schools to medicate their children for attentional dysfunctions (O'Leary, 1993) have brought their cases before the judge. Indirect coercion is already likely to be at work in schools where 30 percent or more of the boys take Ritalin (Diller, 1996).

The Impact of AD/HD on Substance Abuse

Some researchers indicate youngsters with untreated AD/HD are more likely than other populations to abuse addictive substances such as alcohol, marijuana, heroin, prescription tranquilizers, pain medication, nicotine, caffeine, sugar, cocaine, and street amphetamines (Richardson, 2005). Using these substances makes these untreated teenagers feel better and numbs their feelings by self-medication. Regardless of treatment, individuals with AD/HD have several characteristics that make them more vulnerable to substance abuse: First, they tend to suffer from impulsivity, have social skills problems, and have a tendency to associate with others who are not doing well in school. Second, if they have been treated with prescription drugs for the disorder, they are probably more knowledgeable about taking drugs than their counterparts.

An encouraging finding showed recently that when AD/HD children used prescribed medication and were monitored properly by adults, there was no increase in the chance of later substance abuse when compared to the normal population. Carol Watkins suggested that adolescents with AD/HD who were treated with stimulant medication were less likely to develop drug problems than those who were not treated (Watkins, 2000). Adding evidence to this concept is Daniel Amen, director of the Amen Clinic and well-known author on SPECT brain imaging. He says, "A common myth is that the use of medications to treat AD/HD children somehow predisposes them to drug abuse in later life." According to Amen, there is no proof that giving teens medicine to help them with the challenges of AD/HD will somehow teach them to abuse substances later.

It's suggested that parents of an adolescent with AD/HD should start talking about drug abuse and risky behavior early and maintain an open dialogue. Children and adolescents who are aggressive or who habitually break rules are at increased risk. Therefore, substance abuse–prevention classes in school need to help all students distinguish the difference between legitimately prescribed drugs and illegal drugs.

THE EDUCATIONAL CONNECTION

Teachers and administrators of middle and high schools should be aware of the increasing problem of prescription drug abuse and the impact this problem is having on more and more adolescents. Schools and communities should incorporate prescription drug abuse, including steroid abuse, into evidence-based substance use–prevention programs, beginning with elementary school and continuing through high school. Educators should be aware that adolescents are using the Internet to acquire controlled prescription drugs. The appeal of ordering off harder-to-track school computers makes this a challenge for teachers who have students use Internet-linked computers for student research.

Additionally, parents of teenagers should safeguard their prescription medications from their children, refrain from conveying through words or actions messages that condone casual use of prescription drugs, and be vigilant about their children's use of controlled medications prescribed to them to ensure that their children are taking the drugs appropriately and not selling or sharing them. Parents also should take steps to make sure their teenagers are not using the Internet to acquire controlled prescription drugs.

That Was the Good News!

The National Center on Addiction and Substance Abuse (CASA) at Columbia University recently released a comprehensive report on the abuse of prescription drugs in America. Astoundingly, more than two million abusers are under the age of seventeen. The licit drugs most likely to be abused were opioids or pain relievers (OxyContin, Vicodin), central nervous system depressants (Valium, Xanax), stimulants (Ritalin, Adderall), and anabolic-androgenic steroids (Anadrol, Equipoise).

"Our nation is in the throes of an epidemic of controlled prescription-drug abuse and addiction. While America has been congratulating itself in recent years on curbing increases in alcohol and illicit-drug abuse, and an the decline in teen smoking, the abuse of prescription drugs has been stealthily, but sharply, rising," says Joseph A. Califano Jr., CASA chairman and former U.S. Secretary of Health, Education and Welfare.

The most disturbing finding in the report shows that in the past ten years, the number of twelve- to seventeen-year-olds who abused controlled prescription drugs rose 212 percent, while the number of adults jumped 81 percent.

The explosion in the prescription of addictive opioids, depressants, and stimulants has, for many children, made their parents' medicine cabinet a greater temptation and threat than the illegal street drug dealer. "Parents who do not want to become inadvertent drug pushers should consider locking their medicine cabinets," says Califano.

Perhaps one of the deleterious side effects of the Internet has been the availability of controlled prescription drugs from hundreds of Web sites offering drugs for sale without requiring a prescription or proof of age. The report indicates that only 6 percent of online pharmacies required a prescription, while 41 percent indicated that no prescription was needed and 4 percent didn't mention prescriptions at all. Virtually no Web site restricted the sale of controlled prescription drugs to children. "Anyone with a credit card and Internet access can get their hands on these dangerous drugs," said Beau Dietl, CEO and chairman of Beau, Dietl & Associates, CASA's investigatory partner, who compared Internet pharmacies to "predators in the forest" and "vultures" feeding on America's youth.

Teen Brains and Psychoactive Drugs

A psychoactive drug crosses the blood/brain barrier and enters into direct contact with the brain. All psychoactive drugs affect the person's perceptions, cognitions, emotions, and behaviors by distorting, amplifying, dulling, and exaggerating these functions of the brain.

The specific impact and effect of psychoactive drug use on adolescent development depends on several factors: First, the amount or dose of the drug and which category the drugs fits into, whether depressants, hallucinogens, or stimulants. Second, the method of getting the effects of the drug to the brain can determine how fast and intense the reaction is. Typical methods of delivery include ingesting, smoking, injecting, and sniffing. In addition, the teenager's expectations of the drug effect will influence the effect. This is also known as the placebo effect, and can have a powerful impact on the person's experience (Childress, 2000).

Finally—and unfortunately, left to chance—is how the chemistry of the drug interacts with the neurochemistry of the adolescent taking it. This is the great unknown factor because there is no simple mechanism for determining a person's neurochemistry. How each individual reacts to a drug is a matter of Russian roulette.

It is generally accepted that the use of psychoactive drugs, especially by adolescents undergoing intense personal changes, can distort perceptions, thoughts, emotions, and behaviors. This disruption in turn has an adverse effect on the adolescent's achieving the developmental tasks of maturing physically, cognitively, emotionally, and socially.

Shifting Paradigms on Addiction and the Brain

Neuroscientists are beginning to understand more about how drugs can hijack the brain of teenagers and how addiction works to change the brain. Researchers using functional magnetic resonance imaging (fMRI) are revealing new ideas and gaining confidence in their understanding of the brain and drug interventions.

A better understanding of dopamine, the brain chemical involved in motivation, pleasure, and learning, supports key evidence for recent findings. Because addictive drugs like cocaine and nicotine cause a flood of dopamine in the brain, researchers once thought that the neurochemical was a simple pleasure switch, the body's own "reward" button. This theory has been dominating the literature for the past twenty years. However, if dopamine delivers the pleasure message, addicts should be in a continual state of bliss. In reality, most of them get very little pleasure from the drug, despite the surge of neurochemicals. "I've seen hundreds of addicted people, and never have I come across one who wanted to be addicted," says Nora Volker, head of the National Institute on Drug Abuse (NIDA). As she began examining drug addicts' MRIs she realized that something was different.

In response, Dr. Volkow and other researchers are developing a new understanding of addiction: Rather than just telling us to feel good, dopamine tells us what is relevant—the bits of new information we pay attention to in order to survive, like alerts about sex, food, and pleasure, as well as danger and pain. For instance, if you are hungry after getting off of an airplane in the morning and you get a whiff of a cinnamon roll as you head for the airport exit, your dopamine levels increase in the brain. According to Volkow, the chemical will also surge if a dog were to pop out at you while walking. Dopamine's role is to shout, "Hey! Pay attention to this!" Only as an afterthought might it whisper, "Wow, this feels great." Volkow says that maybe drug-addicted people aren't just chasing a good time. Perhaps their brains have somehow mistakenly learned that drugs are the most important thing to pay attention to, as crucial to survival as food or sex (Childress, 2002).

Maybe drug-addicted people aren't just chasing a good time. Perhaps their brains have somehow mistakenly learned that drugs are the most important thing to pay attention to.

Using this theory on the importance of dopamine and the brain might help explain other self-destructive human tendencies, from sexual addictions to obesity. The experiments that Volkow and her team are conducting may also reveal some of the most powerful behavioral machinery in our brains, the equipment that motivates and inspires us. If they are right, dopamine research may become more important in future years for trying to solve the problems of addiction.

According to the Salient Theory of Dopamine as proposed by Volkow and others, drugs appear to hijack the sectors of the brain where dopamine is involved. This includes the nucleus accumbens (NA), an area known as part of the pleasure center. When drugs are introduced into the brain, as much as five to ten times more dopamine surges through the NA and forces the brain's motivational and attentional mechanisms to focus purely on the drug. It becomes the most interesting and important thing in the world. "In any addicted person, what's salient is the drug," says Volkow. "There's no competition."

Over time, the addict's brain adapts to the increase of dopamine by dampening the system down. Volkow's research has also shown that addicts have fewer dopamine D2 receptors, which are found in parts of the brain involved in motivation and reward behavior. With fewer receptors, the dopamine system is desensitized, and the now understimulated addict needs more and more of the drug to feel anything at all. Meanwhile, pathways associated with other interesting stimuli are left idle and lose strength. The prefrontal cortex—the part of the brain associated with judgment and inhibitory control—also stops functioning normally. What appears to be enhanced motivation for the drug can lead to an impaired prefrontal cortex. This hijacking then leads to an enhanced motivation for the drug. If the person wants the drug and has a reduced control of behavior through a damaged prefrontal cortex, he or she has the perfect recipe for substance abuse and addiction (Robinson, 2003).

Adolescents Are More Vulnerable

Again, no single cause for addiction exists. There are a variety of reasons why one teenager becomes addicted to drugs and another does not. Genetic predisposition, neurochemistry, family history, trauma, life stress, and other physical and emotional problems contribute (Robinson, 2003). Part of what determines who becomes addicted and who does not is the combination and timing of these factors. Adolescents may be more vulnerable to drug, alcohol, and tobacco addiction due to the way their growing brains are wired.

Certainly social pressures are part of adolescent vulnerability, but perhaps more important is that the teenage brain lends itself to highly motivated exploration of the world in order to learn how to be an adult. This is the time to take risks! (See Chapter 5). Apparently the stage of brain construction during adolescence makes the brain more vulnerable to addiction that at any other time in life (Childress, 2002).

As stated in Chapter 5, the adolescent brain is still developing and undergoing dramatic transformations. In some brain regions, more than 50 percent of neuronal connections are lost (Guidd, 2002). Some new connections are formed, and the net effect is pruning. These brain changes are relevant to adolescent behavior. According to Ken Winter, professor in the department of psychiatry at the University of Minnesota, the prefrontal cortex is pruned and not fully developed until a person's mid-twenties. During the teenage years, the amygdala and nucleus accumbens show less pruning and tend to dominate the prefrontal cortex. This imbalance leads to less planned thinking and more impulsiveness, less self-control, and more risk taking. "There is more hot talking than cool thinking going on in the teenage brain," says Dr. Winters.

Hijacking the Amygdala

The amygdala appears to play a very large part in the decision-making process during adolescence (Winters, 2003). In light of this imbalance between the prefrontal cortex and the amygdala, one has to consider the levels of stress that teenagers are going through during this phase of their lives (see Chapter 6). In the presence of the high levels of stress hormones coursing through teenager's blood, the amygdala takes an even greater hit as a decision maker! "I hate school; I am going to skip classes and get smashed!" says the amygdala with little or no tempering by the soon-to-be-developed prefrontal cortex. Again, decision-making is handicapped by the factors of brain growth and maturation in the teenage brain.

Oops? Brian!

He wasn't at the top of his class, but Brian loved the social part of being a high-school senior enough to keep him in school and to take the college prep classes his friends were enrolled in. A popular lineman on the varsity football team, Brain had lots of casual dates and had been experimenting with tobacco, alcohol, and marijuana at the weekend parties so popular with his friends. It just seemed to be the thing to do on Friday nights after the game, and it gave everyone plenty to talk about on Monday morning at school. He figured it was OK because he would probably get into college next year, so for now, he wanted to enjoy all the perks of being a senior classman.

Julie had only attended Livingston High for her senior year and was considered a cool girl from the big city. After a few months on the scene, she started bringing more than marijuana to the parties. At first Brian kept clear of the white lines available late on Friday night, but he noted that almost everybody else was taking a hit of cocaine...why not try it?

He intended to try it just once, for "the experience" of it. It turned out, though, that he enjoyed the drug's euphoric effect so much that in ensuing weeks and months on Friday nights he used it again and again. Some of his buddies stopped and expressed concerns over getting caught, the influence it had on them, and the high costs. Julie's supply began to dwindle, so she was asking friends to help share the costs; $200 was the going rate for enough lines to get that good feeling for the partygoers on Friday nights. Brian decided he really should quit, too. He knew that despite the incomparable short-term high he received from using cocaine, the long-term consequences of its use are perilous. So he vowed to stop using it. "Whew, what a good decision. I was draining my money supply, and anyway, I know my folks would ground me for sure if they found out," thought Brian.

Unfortunately Brian's brain had a different agenda. It now demanded cocaine. While his rational mind knew very well that he shouldn't use it again, his brain overrode such warnings. Unbeknownst to him, repeated use of cocaine had brought about dramatic changes in both the structure and function of his brain. In fact, if he'd known the danger signs for which to be on the lookout, he would have realized that as time passed and the drug was used with increasing regularity, these changes would becomes more pronounced, and indelible, until finally his brain had become addicted to the drug. And so, despite his heartfelt vow never again to use cocaine, he continued using it. His drug use was now compulsive, beyond his control. He was addicted. While this turn of events is a shock to the drug user, it is no surprise at all to researchers who study the effects of addictive drugs. To them, it is a predictable outcome.

To be sure, no one ever starts out using drugs intending to become a drug addict. Every drug user starts out as an occasional user, and that initial use is a voluntary and controllable decision. But as time passes and drug use continues, a person goes from being a voluntary to a compulsive drug user. This change occurs because over time, use of addictive drugs changes the brain—at times in big, dramatic ways, at others in more subtle ways, but always in destructive ways that can result in compulsive and even uncontrollable drug use.

The brain changes range from fundamental and long-lasting changes in the biochemical makeup of the brain to mood changes to changes in memory processes and motor skills. These changes have a tremendous impact on all aspects of a person's behavior. In fact, in addiction the drug becomes the single most powerful motivator in the life of the drug user. He will do virtually anything for the drug.

This unexpected consequence of drug use is what Alan I. Leshner, former director of the National Institute of Drug Abuse, National Institutes of Health, calls the "oops phenomenon." Why oops? Dr. Leshner says, "Because the harmful outcome is in no way intentional. Just as no one starts out to have lung cancer when they smoke, or no one starts out to have clogged arteries when they eat fried foods, which in turn usually cause heart attacks, no one starts out to become a drug addict when they use drugs. But in each case, though no one meant to behave in a way that would lead to tragic health consequences, that is what happened just the same, because of the inexorable, and undetected, destructive biochemical processes at work."

While we haven't yet pinpointed precisely all the triggers for the changes in the brain's structure and function that culminate in the "oops" phenomenon, a vast body of hard evidence shows that it is virtually inevitable that prolonged drug use will lead to addiction. From this we can soundly conclude that drug addiction is indeed a brain disease.

Story modified with permission from an article by Alan Leshner, Ph.D., National Institute on Drug Abuse.

A Popular Drug of Choice

Because of its recent popularity with teenagers and relative ease in obtaining, methamphetamine is increasingly a problem at schools. Commonly known as "speed," "meth," "ice," or "crystal," it is a powerfully addictive stimulant that acts on the central nervous system to produce increased wakefulness and physical

Meth can be ingested, smoked, shot intravenously, or inhaled through a straw.

activity as well as irritability, insomnia, confusion, tremors, convulsions, anxiety, paranoia, and aggressiveness. The drug increases heart rate and blood pressure and can irreversibly damage blood vessels in the brain (Ernst, 2000).

Dr. Thomas Ernst and Dr. Linda Chang at the Harbor-UCLA Medical Center in Torrance, California, used a noninvasive brain imaging technique called magnetic resonance spectroscopy (MRS) to study whether meth users' brain cells were healthy, diseased, or damaged. "We found abnormal brain chemistry in methamphetamine users in all the brain regions we studied. In one of the regions, the amount of damage was also related to the history of drug use—those abusers who had the greatest cumulative lifetime methamphetamine use had the strongest indications of cell damage," Dr. Chang says.

"Methamphetamine may be substantially toxic to the cells we use in thinking," Dr. Ernst says. "This long-term, and perhaps permanent, alteration in basic brain chemistry is additional evidence that methamphetamine abuse, like abuse of other drugs, should be considered a brain disease and treated accordingly."

Alcohol and the Teenage Brain

The drinking-and-driving prevention message of the past twenty years is more important today than ever before. However, there haven't been many other new compelling reasons to stop young people from drinking other than a moral or authoritarian message. While there have been many attempts to thwart teenage experimentation with alcohol, the campaign hasn't been entirely successful. The results of the Youth Risk Behavioral Survey for 2003 show that 44.9 percent of high-school students had had one or more drinks of alcohol on more than one of the thirty days preceding the survey, and approximately three-fourths (74.9 percent) of students nationwide had had one or more drinks of alcohol on more than one occasion in their lifetime. These numbers are fairly high for consumption; researchers are now saying there is strong scientific evidence that even occasional and moderate drinking can impact a teenager's memory system.

As we know, the adolescent brain changes a lot during the teen years (see Chapter 5). Neuroscientists say those changes are what make them especially vulnerable to the effects of alcohol. "The parts of the brain that are very important in things like judgment, decision making, impulse control, and memory formation are hit pretty hard by alcohol," said researcher Aaron White, assistant research professor in the department of psychiatry and behavioral sciences at Duke University Medical Center.

When teenagers drink too much and too fast, cells in the hippocampus, which is involved with learning and memory, quit functioning and stop the brain from forming new memories. The changes that are taking place in the hippocampus during the teenage years make it more sensitive to alcohol (White, 2003). Research indicates that the damage could be a long-term problem: Since the hippocampus appears to be more sensitive to alcohol at a young age it appears that damage is done even if a heavy-drinking teenager quits. "If we look at the cognitive abilities of teenagers who are in drug and alcohol treatment, for at least three weeks after an adolescent's last drink, they show memory impairments and other cognitive deficits," says Dr. White.

Did They Believe the Research?

Thirty years ago, preliminary evidence was that the impact of smoking marijuana on the body was deleterious. Studies at the University of California at Los Angeles and other locations were shared with teenagers in high schools as a preventive measure. The assumption was that teenagers are at risk if they don't have the facts and the knowledge about what marijuana will do to them. These studies and many others were summarized and shared with students in high schools all over the nation. At the time, we didn't have any long-term evidence that marijuana was harmful to the body or could cause brain damage.

Researchers are now saying there is strong scientific evidence that even occasional and moderate drinking can impact a teenager's memory system.

Two problems arose. First, the percentage of the psychoactive ingredient called tetrahydrocannabinol (THC) in the plants being ingested orally or by smoking at that time was very low. Compared to what teenagers are using today, marijuana contained only about 25 percent as much of the active ingredient in the 1970s. The studies so popularized then suggested that even experimenting with marijuana could lead to dire health consequences. When teenagers tried it they disbelieved what the authorities were saying because nothing was happening to them except what they deemed as positive. They were convinced that the data were incorrect and became quite cynical about long-range studies that later indicated a more serious problem with higher levels of THC.

Second, teenagers see state governments trying to determine the legality of using medical marijuana. "It must also be safe for recreational use if they will allow it to be used for medicine," cry the youthful experimenters. This pervasive argument has reached our courts in many states. The legal right to smoke marijuana for any medical purposes lends credence to the belief that marijuana is not only safe to treat serious illness but somehow safe for general use and for all society.

The challenge is making the material meaningful to the students. How do you link the impact of drugs on the teenage brain and make it relevant to their world? The topic is of interest to students, but can we rely on their ability to transfer the knowledge gained into a behavioral awareness about a positive changes in behavior?

THE EDUCATIONAL CONNECTION

Teenagers believe that there has always been an association between fried eggs and your brain! However, the evidence is very clear that "scare tactics" do not work with most teenagers. The days of the "black lung" demonstrations for tobacco abuse are fading. As much as we would hope that students understand the basic elements of how their brains function, knowledge alone has not reduced risk-taking behavior in many students (YRBS, 2003).

Whatever your role in the school, a teacher, principal, coach, nurse, or guidance counselor, you can play an important role in preventing underage drinking and illicit drug abuse. In the school settings, teenagers draw conclusions about alcohol and drug abuse from what they see and hear from their friends, classmates, and teachers. When schools establish drug and alcohol policies that clearly state expectations and penalties regarding use by students, they help reinforce the fact that underage drug use is not an acceptable form of behavior.

In the school consider these steps: First, assess student drinking to determine the extent of the problem by looking for local and state data collected on high risk behavior (See the YRBS Studies and state and local Department of Health Surveys) Find out what factors may be contributing to student drug and alcohol use in your school or community (e.g., easy access to alcohol, peer pressure, adults' failure to address the issue). Then determine what steps, if any, are being taken within your school system to help young people resist the pressure to drink. Work with the health teachers to determine if a research-based prevention program is available to all students. Educate parents about alcohol and drug abuse. Develop an active partnership with the families of your students, and implement school policies prohibiting alcohol use on school grounds.

What We Know About Drug-Prevention Programs

In 1997, the U.S. Department of Education released a study that required researchers to collect data over four years from about ten thousand students. The results were consistent with national trends and include some key findings.

1. Some drug prevention programs improved student outcomes by delaying or reducing drug use, but the effects were small.

2. The most commonly used approaches did not show evidence of effectiveness or were not evaluated properly.

3. Student outcomes were greater in districts where prevention programs had been in place for some time and had targeted general and high-risk students.

4. The most effective approaches teach students how to resist and deal with powerful social influences. These approaches rely on interactive teaching methods and require a commitment to teacher training.

Learning how to deal with powerful social influences such
as peer pressure can reduce the risk of teenage drug and alcohol abuse.

Summary of Chapter 9

- The abuse of prescription drugs by adolescents is at an all-time high.

- Schools should incorporate prescription drug abuse into evidence-based substance abuse–prevention programs.

- The interaction between drugs and the neurochemistry of the adolescent may be more significant in terms of long-team damage than earlier research suggested.

- A better understanding of the dopamine receptors is leading to new theories on addiction.

- The relationship between the amygdala and the prefrontal cortex makes adolescents more vulnerable to the effects of alcohol and drugs than adults.

- The most effective approaches to drug-abuse prevention teach students how to resist and deal with powerful social influences.

ENGAGING THE BRAIN THROUGH ACTIVITIES

There are some wonderful programs available to middle- and high-school teachers for linking neurobiology with drug abuse. The National Institutes of Health (NIH) has released free standards-based supplemental units in recent years that teachers and students can use effectively. All of them are free and can be downloaded easily.

Activity #1

Programs for High School
The Brain: Understanding Neurobiology Through the Study of Addiction
A standards-based curriculum supplement brings research discoveries from the labs of NIH to the classroom. Five lessons are accompanied with excellent graphics and easy-to-follow instructions. Students draw upon real science to discover the impact of addiction on the brain. Publication No. 00-4871
http://science.education.nih.gov/supplements/nih2/addiction/default.htm

Activity #2

Programs Available for Middle School
Understanding Alcohol: Investigations Into Biology and Behavior
This is a standards-based curriculum that focuses on the science underlying the effects of alcohol on human biology and behavior. Office of Science Education, National Institute on Alcohol Abuse and Alcoholism and Office of Science Education.
http://science.education.nih.gov/Customers.nsf/MSAlcohol?OpenForm

The Brain: Our Sense of Self
This program expands on the basic understanding of brain function and the
nervous system. (National Institute of Neurological Disorders and Stroke and
Office of Science Education)
http://science.education.nih.gov/customers.nsf/MSSelf?OpenForm

How Your Brain Understands What Your Ear Hears
This is a standards-based curriculum that investigates the multisensory process
of human communication. It assists students in understanding the fundamentals
of sound and how to prevent hearing loss. Publication No. 04-4990, National
Institute on Deafness and Other Communication Disorders and Office of Science
Education.
http://science.education.nih.gov/Customers.nsf/MSHearing?OpenForm

Activity #3

National Science Teacher (NSTA) Conferences
At each of the NSTA regional and national conferences, materials from the NIH
Office of Education are distributed free at the NIH display booths. They also
offer free teacher-training workshops at many conferences.
http://science-education.nih.gov/exhibits

Many other commercial sources represented at the NSTA conferences offer both
free and purchasable materials for teachers on the brain and addiction. For a
conference in your area go to the NSTA Web site:
http://www.nsta.org/conventions

Selected Books for Enhancing This Chapter	
Amen, Daniel, G.	*Healing ADD: The Breakthrough Program That Allows You to See and Heal the 6 Types of ADD.* Berkeley Books: New York, 2002 A very comprehensive and interesting background on ADD or AD/HD. Amen's work in SPECT brain imaging influences this work and helps laypersons understand Amen's six types of attention deficit disorder.
California Department of Education	*Getting Results: Part I and Part II.* California Action Guide to Creating Safe and Drug Free Schools (1998) This well-edited guide is somewhat dated; however, it provides a comprehensive, unbiased resource to schools on drug prevention, from research summaries to recommendations for research-based curricula.

10

Drugs That Enhance
Student Achievement:
Good Kids Making Bad Decisions

Chapter 10
Drugs That Enhance Student Achievement:
Good Kids Making Bad Decisions

To have the wisdom of age and the memory of a young person…That'd be a very good combination.

—Martha Farah, psychologist

New drugs to improve memory and cognitive performance are under intense study and testing on people impaired by brain deficiencies. The possibility of their use on healthy adults, let alone adolescents, triggers debate from the laboratory to the legislature. Within a short time, the smart drugs will become an issue of some concern in education. Although many of these new-generation drugs may be years away from government approval, their social impact has already been profound. With best-selling drugs like Modafil successfully being used as "off-label," it's only a matter of time before schools and governments will be faced with contemplating the social ramifications of chemical memory enhancement.

Todd Was a Good Kid

Todd was a good kid, admired by most of the students he knew at school and their parents. He was the kind of boy that his friends' parents would say to themselves, "I wish our boy had Todd's looks" or "I wish our daughter would fall in love with a wonderful guy like Todd."

It would be hard to imagine improving on the Todd that everybody knew and respected. His teachers placed him in that category usually reserved for the top athletes and valedictorian candidates in class. He was blessed with good penmanship and knew how to make his assignments look good from acquiring excellent computer skills. Often unknowingly, teachers prejudge students by their appearance and their first week's assignments. Todd knew that his first assignments turned in at the beginning of a term had to be outstanding. That benchmark left an impression on his teachers, and it carried over for him in every class.

During the spring of his junior year, Todd would take the PSAT like all the other college-bound hopefuls. He knew it would have predictive value and how important it was to his goal—getting into a top university! Maybe Harvard or Princeton in the east, maybe Stanford in the west. Why not? His parents had encouraged him and set up a college fund that would pay for an Ivy League school even at today's prices. His only worry was getting a good PSAT score so he would be eligible to become a merit scholar.

For all of his looks, personality, and maturity, Todd lacked confidence in himself. He knew how highly adults and teenagers thought of him, yet when he was honest with himself, he suffered like most other teenagers with nagging doubts about his abilities. He knew how to play the "good grades game," but frequently he felt a lack of confidence with his long-term memory because he had trouble doing well on tests that required lots of memory skills.

He would find himself studying world history, for example: Queen Isabella of Spain financed Columbus for his later voyages. He could remember that fact for just about a minute after reading it but then on sample tests would not be able to recall that fact. He couldn't get it into his long-term memory. He had always compensated for this by writing well and spending considerable effort on assignments to offset his test scores. What would he do with the PSAT coming up? Wouldn't it be great if he could swallow a pill rather than study for the test? Perhaps he could take a pill and get a "mental tune-up" for the PSAT.

That is exactly what Todd was to do! On Saturday morning, the day he was scheduled to take the PSAT, Todd downed a green gelatin cap containing a drug called Modafinil. Within an hour, his attention sharpened. So did his memory.

He aced the PSAT. If his brainpower would normally rate a 10, the drug raised it to 15. "I was quite focused," said Todd. "It was also kind of fun, and I felt very confident. Why go through the pangs of self-doubt even when I study hard, if I can get something like this to power me up! I'll do it every time because it helps so much and doesn't seem to be illegal."

Modafinil, the drug that improved Todd's powers of concentration, is used to treat narcolepsy and other sleep disorders. It is one of three prescription medications on the market that have been shown to enhance certain mental powers. He was able to get it from a buddy whose father had a prescription for Modafinil because of a sleep disorder.

Studies on this medicine have been done only in adult patients, and there is no specific information comparing use of Modafinil in children with use in other age groups. The Food and Drug Administration originally approved Modafinil, sold under the name Provigil, in 1998. Since its introduction, the number of off-label prescriptions for Provigil has skyrocketed, with an estimated 80 percent of prescriptions for the drug going to night-shift workers, truck drivers, pilots, and soldiers—jobs in which it's crucial to remain awake and alert. Now the FDA may approve it for wider use—a move that has met with some controversy.

The pill has been found to increase both wakefulness and what researchers call "vigilance," the ability to stay on task, thinking clearly and functioning normally. The drug that Todd took may change the way we think about regulating standardized tests and whether the use of them should be allowed when taking any competitive examination. These are decisions that could change what criteria we have for gaining entrance to the universities in this nation.

In a series of experiments researchers found that in games that test mental skill, subjects who took a 200-milligram dose of Modafinil paid closer attention and used information more effectively than subjects given a sugar pill.

Confronted with conflicting demands, the people on Modafinil moved more smoothly from one task to the next and adjusted their strategies of play with greater agility. In short, they worked smarter and were better at multitasking (Turner, et al., 2003). Modafinil is especially intriguing to researchers and the labs that will profit greatly from its use by the public. Its developers aren't sure exactly how it keeps drowsiness at bay, but in even in healthy people, the medication appears to deliver measurable improvements with few side effects.

Studies have shown that that Modafinil can produce significant mental gains in normal, healthy subjects. It has not has been approved for that purpose, nor have any of the other "smart drugs" now in development for treating Alzheimer's. Nevertheless, a growing number of healthy Americans are taking them to get a mental edge. Some obtain the medications from doctors who write prescriptions for "off-label" uses not approved by the Food and Drug Administration—a practice both legal and common. Others buy the drugs through unregulated Internet pharmacies. The Internet pharmacy problem has tremendous implications for student purchases.

There Is No Free Lunch!

The big question, of course, is whether these drugs will in fact do what is expected of them. Some scientists are skeptical about what will happen to the healthy people taking smart drugs to enhance cognitive ability. "There's no free lunch," said Tom Tully, a researcher at Cold Springs Harbor Laboratory, who has a long history of being keenly attentive to the social implications of scientific research. Consumers will have to consider what level of discomfort or risk they're willing to accept in exchange for sharper recall or enhanced powers of concentration (Healy, 2004).

The side effect that most neuroscientists fear is not physical discomfort but subtle mental change. Over time, a memory-enhancing drug might cause people to remember too much detail, cluttering the brain. Similarly, a drug that sharpens attention might cause users to focus too intently on a particular task, failing to shift their attention in response to new developments. In short, someone who notices or remembers everything may end up understanding nothing. If you are an Alzheimer's victim, the balance point might be quite different from that of a healthy teenager. In comparison with other comparably elective treatments such as cosmetic surgery, "smart drugs" involve intervening in a complex and not fully understood nervous system. The likelihood of unanticipated problems is consequently higher.

Off-Label Drugs

Researchers are resigned to the continuing bioethical debate on the drugs. "We've got our hands full just showing that these drugs will work," admitted Tullly. "Having said that, do I think there will be off-label use if it works clinically? Yes, I do. In principle, these compounds could improve the motor skills required to play the piano or second-language acquisition."

Examine for a moment the recent history with off-label prescriptions for Viagra. Although some problems with vision now are surfacing in a few cases, it can be argued that Viagra is probably the most successful off-label prescription of all time. Ritalin and amphetamines are not far behind, and both have been popularly prescribed for uses other than their original release purpose.

Is It Cheating?

We have seen a market in the past ten years for over-the-counter smart drinks, smart power bars, and diet supplements containing certain "smart" chemicals, but there is little evidence to suggest that these products really work. Results from different laboratories show mixed results. There are very few well-designed studies using normal healthy people (Chudler, 2005).

Now, things are different. Not to be confused with what you can buy at your favorite health food store, we are faced with an entire new world of drugs. We are seeing the results in laboratories with animal models, and human testing is well under way.

While President George W. Bush's bioethics panel has characterized the use of drugs by healthy people to enhance cognitive performance as a form of cheating, another branch of the government, the military, has aggressively explored the capacity of new pharmaceutical agents to increase cognitive alertness and performance in fatigued but essentially normal individuals (Hall, 2003).

The growing demand for Ritalin, which can be addictive, has prompted the U.S. Drug Enforcement Administration to classify it as a "drug of concern."

This quickly leads to the discussion of cognitive enhancement for students who are competing for limited space in colleges and universities. Eventually, ambitious parents will start giving mind-enhancing pills to their children, said James McGaugh, the University of California at Irvine neurobiologist. "If there is a drug which is safe and effective and not too expensive for enhancing memory in normal adults, why not normal children?" he said. "After all, they're going to school, and what's more important than education of the young? Some parents will consider it more important to give their children a little chemical edge than think of the long-term consequences."

Ritalin is prescribed to alleviate the symptoms of attention deficit disorder. College students preparing for exams frequently discuss the benefits of taking Ritalin or similar drugs on exam day. The growing demand for Ritalin, which can be addictive, has prompted the U.S. Drug Enforcement Administration to classify it as a "drug of concern." Students justify the illegal use by rationalizing that "if some test takers are using it, why shouldn't I?" (Hall, 2003) Many college and graduate students want an edge badly enough to take Ritalin, even if they do not suffer from attention deficit disorder. At campuses, test sites and, increasingly, workplaces across the country, people are popping "vitamin R." Some users persuade a doctor to prescribe it; others get it from friends who have been diagnosed with attention deficit disorder.

Remembering More, Thinking Faster, Staying Awake Longer

Air Force pilots and truck drivers have long popped amphetamines to ward off drowsiness. Generations of college students have swallowed over-the-counter caffeine tablets to get through all-nighters. But such stimulants provide only a temporary edge, and their effect is broad and blunt—they boost the brain by focusing the entire nervous system.

The new mind-enhancing drugs, in contrast, hold the potential for more powerful, more targeted, and more lasting improvements in mental acuity. Some of the most promising have reached the stage of testing in human subjects and could become available in the next decade, brain scientists say.

"There are things cooking here that couldn't have been done one to two decades ago," said James L. McGaugh, director of UC Irvine's Center for the Neurobiology of Learning and Memory. Many leading scientists working on human memory are now saying that it's not a question of if this will happen, but when these drugs will be ready for release for consumption (Tully, 2003).

Defense Department scientists are pursuing mind-enhancing drugs for U.S. combat forces. The Pentagon spends $20 million per year exploring ways to "expand available memory" and build "sleep-resistant circuitry" in the brain. Among its aims: to develop stimulants capable of keeping soldiers awake, alert, and effective for as long as seven days straight. The armed forces have taken leading roles in testing performance enhancers for pilots and soldiers (Healy, 2004).

The Impetus for Memory Research

A scientific understanding of the human immune system has been advanced greatly in the last twenty years. Just as the crusade for solving the riddles of AIDS brought millions of dollars to research laboratories, so too has Alzheimer's disease brought large sums of money to the neuroscientists working on memory and the loss of it. In the neurodegenerative disorder Alzheimer's, the patient's brain undergoes a rapid and devastating decline. Chemicals known to be toxic to neurons accumulate into tangled plaques that prevent communication between synapses. As these plaques build up, neurons throughout the brain are gradually strangled to death. When these neurons are destroyed, levels of crucial neurotransmitters, especially acetylcholine and glutamate, drop off. The result: severe and, until recently, irreversible memory loss. Scientists are now better able to target potential sites for drug intervention. To date, some two hundred different compounds are in various stages of clinical trials for Alzheimer's (Healy, 2004).

In recent years some of the mechanics of memory have been identified (Kandel, 2000). The new brain boosters stem in part from research to develop treatments for Alzheimer's disease, spinal cord injuries, schizophrenia, and other conditions.

However, the promise of improved learning and memory of healthy people makes these classes of drugs a very controversial problem.

Neuron with neurofibrillary tangles

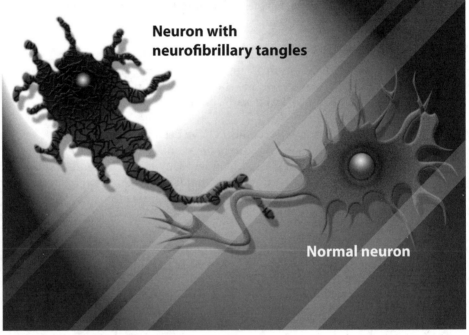

Illustration of tangles in an Alzheimer's patient's neuron compared to a normal person's neuron.

While cognitive enhancers were originally developed for the treatment of Alzheimer's patients, they can also be used as biochemical memory aids for the general population. In today's increasingly competitive marketplace, what struggling junior or senior in high school wouldn't welcome the edge a memory pill could offer? What about university students, overworked air traffic controllers, medical students, and aspiring actors whose livelihoods depend on being able to flawlessly recall large quantities of information?

In the last two decades, scientists have made important discoveries about which regions of the brain perform specific functions and how those regions work together to absorb, store, and retrieve information. Researchers also have begun to grasp how and where neurotransmitters are manufactured and which ones help perform which mental tasks. Research has gotten further stimulus from a deep-pocketed investor: the U.S. military, which is looking for ways to help pilots and soldiers stay sharp under the stress and exhaustion of combat.

"On the horizon are other potential smart drugs, each operating on different systems in the brain. If they progress through tests of safety and effectiveness, the first of them could be available as early as 2008," says Tom Tully.

The potential market for cognitive enhancers has never been bigger, or more receptive. An estimated 77 million members of the baby boom generation will turn 50 in the next 10 years, joining 11 million who have already passed the half-century mark—a stage at which memory and speed of response show noticeable decline (Langreth, 2002).

What's Out There?

Smart drugs are emerging from medications developed for the search for improving the lives of people suffering from brain impairments such as Alzheimer's, depression, schizophrenia, multiple sclerosis, and stroke. Here are a few under development:

Company	Drug	How It Works	When
Cephlon Corp. Frazer, PA	Modafinil Sold as Provigil	Acts on the central nervous system as a mild stimulant	Has been approved for treating narcolepsy since 1998. Under FDA consideration.
Cortex Pharmaceuticals Irvine, CA	Drug: CX516 Ampakines	Acts as hearing aid for aging neurons, magnifying signals from other brain cells.	Human trials under way.
GlaxoSmithKline Middlesex, UK	SB271046	Blocks a serotonin receptor that is prevalent in the hippocampus.	Human trials in Alzheimer's patients starting.
Johnson & Johnson New Brunswick, NJ	H3-blocker	Blocks histamine-3 receptor, which may be involved in alertness, attention, and memory.	Entering human trials for jet lag or memory loss.
Helicon Therapeutics Farmingdale, NY	PDE-4 inhibitors and others	Indirectly boosts CREB memory protein.	Human trials within two years.
Merck & Co. Whitehouse Station, NJ	GABA inverse agonists	Modulates GABA receptors to increase alertness in brain regions central to learning and memory.	In lab testing; plans for human tests undisclosed.

Company	Drug	How it Works	When
Axonyx New York, NY	Gilatide	Activates various memory genes.	Human tests under way.
Pfizer/National Institute on Aging New York, NY	Aricept (Donepezil)	Assists in protecting people with mild memory loss from Alzheimer's; has been found to boost the brain function in healthy people.	NIA now testing.
Ceregene Inc. San Diego, CA	"Gene Therapy" (Genetically engineered cells are deeply implanted inside the cortex, acting as miniature pumps secreting nerve growth factor.)	Nerve growth factor revitalizes brain cells that atrophy and shrink as their host's age advances. Helps prevent against the early stages of Alzheimer's disease, in hopes of slowing its progress.	Human trials underway.

Sources: *Los Angeles Times*, 12/20/04; *Scientific American*, 11/2003; *Trends in Neuroscience*, 1/2005

What's the Future?

Some scientists predict that the development of even more effective brain-enhancing drugs will usher in an age of "cosmetic neurology." "If people can gain a millimeter, they're going to want to take it," said Jerome Yesavage, director of Stanford University's Aging Clinical Research Center. Judy Illes, a psychologist at Stanford's Center for Biomedical Ethics, said mind-enhancing medicine could become "as ordinary as a cup of coffee." This could be good for society, helping people learn faster and retain more, she said. The trend also raises questions: Will the rich get smarter while the poor fall further behind? (Drugs such as Modafinil can cost as much as $6 per dose.) Will people feel compelled to use the medications to keep up in school or in the workplace? In a world where mental function can be tweaked with a pill, will our notion of "normal intelligence" be changed forever?

In Internet chat rooms every day, high-school and college students are discussing the benefits of taking Ritalin or similar drugs on exam day. "The brain was designed by evolution over the millennia to be well-adapted because of the lives we lead," said Martha Farah, a psychologist at the University of Pennsylvania. "Our lives are better served by being able to focus on the essential information than being able to remember every little detail. . . . We meddle with these designs at our peril." Despite such qualms, Farah is drawn to the idea that a mind, enriched by a life of experience, might not have to lose the speed of recall it enjoyed in its youth.

THE EDUCATIONAL CONNECTION

We suspect there are possible health issues involved with mind-enhancing drugs. Safety in use by teenagers, side effects, and unintended consequences become questions for parents and teachers when students are using them to enhance performance. There are concerns for all medications and procedures, but the educational community's tolerance for risk is probably lower for enhancement than for therapy.

The ethical issues surrounding brain enhancement concern the social effects of brain enhancement: How will it affect the lives of all of our students, including those who may prefer not to enhance their brains? For example, the freedom to remain without the use of these drugs may be difficult to maintain in a society where one's competition is using enhancement. Conversely, barriers such as cost will prevent some who would like to enhance from doing so. This would exacerbate the disadvantages already faced by people of low socioeconomic status in education and employment.

These issues can provide social studies and science teachers with excellent opportunities to engage students in discussions about their future choices. (See "Facilitating Discussion" in Chapter 3.)

Summary of Chapter 10

- New drugs are rapidly being developed to improve memory and cognitive performance in people with brain deficiencies.

- The possibility of new mind-enhancing drugs being used "off-label" for healthy people is a concern.

- The long-term impact on the brain after using memory or mind-enhancing drugs is unknown.

- The social implications of using chemical memory-enhancement drugs in youth and adults are far reaching.

ENGAGING THE BRAIN THROUGH ACTIVITIES

Activity:

My Values Discussion Strategies

Neuroscientists have demonstrated through brain imaging studies that when students are talking about an issue, their brains are much more active as opposed to just seeing or thinking about an issue (Carter, 1999). During My Values (MV) discussions, students are encouraged to talk about the issue posed, thereby increasing the chances that the discussion about those issues will be transferred to long-term memory. More important, when students exchange ideas and hear other students express their ideas without the teacher intervening, students are more likely to form opinions and values that represent who they are that time in their lives. Ideas for MV discussions incorporate material drawn from *Values Awareness Teaching Strategies* by Gus T. Dalis and Ben B. Strasser.

The MV Discussion Strategy requires that teachers understand how to respond specifically to student comments. It's what the teacher does or doesn't do that determines what students learn about what values or opinions are important to them.

The key to a successful MV lesson is for the teacher to withhold his or her personal values during the discussion and remain impartial. Teacher-directed discussions allow teachers to express their personal values on an issue and try to persuade or convince students of their viewpoint. **A well-conducted MV lesson doesn't provide that opportunity**. When teachers refrain from providing their personal values about an issue, students begin to think about their own values and listen carefully to values that other students pose. Often those students who normally would not actively share in class will express some profound ideas and values of their own.

Criteria for Good Questions for MV Discussions

A good question to begin a MV discussion is critical. The teacher must be able to identify a specific topic, phrase the discussion question, and create a setting to make the question real. There are three criteria that each question should pass. Is the topic:

1. Within the knowledge of the students?

2. Relevant to the students?

3. A question that invites students to discuss their values?

Definition of Values

A value is a preferred or important quality, characteristic, attribute, or property. Examples would include honesty, reliability, being devoted, being colorful.

Values include those that serve as a moral creed to live by: "One of my values about life is that a person doesn't take drugs to gain an advantage on tests, just as one shouldn't take steroids to gain an advantage in competitive sport." Values can influence individual decisions about more day-to-day matters such as, "What shirt will I wear today?" (Dalis & Strasser, 1977, p. 7)

Using the MV Discussion With the "Smart Drugs" Controversy

Using drugs originally designed for people with brain deficiencies on healthy people to increase learning and cognitive abilities will be quite controversial. We have already seen this happen with Modafinil. More drugs are in development that attack shyness, forgetfulness, and the mental decline of aging. Others add muscle mass and boost the ability to learn. Students in middle and high school will be facing the problem of how the use of these drugs should be regulated by society.

There are many moral and ethical questions about the use of "smart drugs." Here are some questions that could be used for MV discussions after students know something about the concept:

• What would happen if people got smarter? Is this a good thing or a bad thing?

• How do you feel about the use of a legal drug for some other purpose than it was licensed for?

• How do you feel about using mind-enhancing drugs to improve test scores?

• What are the possible advantages and disadvantages of short-term and long-term smartness? How do you feel about those?

- If such drugs become available for the general public, should they be regulated, and by whom?

- Who should get these smart drugs, and how should they be used?

- Should the smart drugs be banned like stimulants and steroids in athletics?

- Is going to special schools or classes and getting a tutor different from taking a smart drug?

- Should it be legal to take a smart pill before a PSAT or the SAT? Would this be cheating?

- What are the benefits of the smart drugs? Could these substances make people better at what they do?

The MV Behaviors

The teacher behaviors are actions taken to establish and maintain open lines of student-student and student-teacher communication. They also help students realize their own values. Deciding which of these behaviors to use at a given moment is based on what the student does and where the student is in his or her development as a discussion participant. The teaching behaviors and student behaviors listed below can be explored in depth in *Teaching Strategies for Values Awareness and Decision Making in Health Education* by Gus T. Dalis and Ben B. Strasser (1977, pp. 78–88 for teaching behaviors, pp. 131–138 for student behaviors).

Constructing

Students need to know what is expected of them and how they are to work. The teacher must communicate the roles of the student-teacher and student-student relationship. It's designed to protect the openness or freedom of the class members. Here is a typical constructing behavior used by a teacher to get the process started:

"The purpose of today's lesson is to make it possible for you to get some insight into what your values are about. Here is how we are going to work:

1. You don't have to agree with other students.

2. If you have a value about X, we would like you to share it, but it will be up to you to decide to do that.

3. It is okay to disagree with someone, but no put-downs are acceptable.

4. If you want some information, ask for it, and I will try to get it for you.

5. This is your discussion. While I may have some personal thoughts and opinions on this subject, I will maintain a neutral position during this discussion.

6. Remember that only one person speaks at a time.

7. If you want a conference, you can ask me, and we will take time for small-group discussions."

This all takes place in a social context. Students state their values in the presence of other students, and the teacher must take deliberate action to maintain open lines of communication between students and between him or her and the students. This requires a nonjudgmental environment.

Topic Setting

This occurs when a teacher states a topic to be explored by the students. The topic must offer students several courses of action and should be somewhat controversial to be an effective MV question. Issues chosen to discuss should provide students with a diverse range of opinions on how to resolve them. If the focus shifts because of student or teacher interaction, it is the job of the teacher to inform students that they are now working on another topic.

Acknowledging

Too often students look for those students that are called on frequently by the teacher because they usually have valid ideas. In MV discussions, the teacher acknowledges and sometimes identifies the behavior by the student **without** making a judgment about the appropriateness or validity of those ideas. This is critical to the development of a good MV discussion. By using the same response to student comments, students are affirmed for their opinions but not affirmed for the value of their opinions. Here are some effective responses:

"I see what you are saying, Jan." "I understand, Dayna." "That's certainly possible, Zoe." "I understand, thanks for sharing your ideas with us, Kenny."

Clarifying

This may be done by asking the student to explain more or by restating or rephrasing a student's comments. The clarifying behavior is used because the teacher didn't understand and not because he or she thinks the other students didn't understand. Typical clarifying behaviors might sound like this:

"Juan, would you repeat your thought? I need to hear it again from you." "Heather, are you saying that . . .?" "Thomas, I am having difficulty in understanding your idea. What do you mean by . . .?" "Could you explain more about what it means when you say 'get rid of them,' Ward?"

Responding

A teacher uses this behavior to make it possible for a student to get the information requested. This may allow the student to substantiate, modify, or reject a value or opinion he or she has stated. The teacher only responds when the student asks for some information. To assist students with the MV discussion, a teacher might identify the response needed to fulfill the request. Examples could include:

"Yes Martha, the drug you are talking about is a stimulant." "No Leroy, there isn't a legal question here." "If it would help you with your opinion Samuel, I can share some background on why the drug was developed."

Teacher Silence

This is one of the best ways to affirm that it's the students' responsibility to develop opinions and values regarding the problem. It is a great nonverbal message that teachers fail to use as often as they should. An effective time to wait is at least five seconds. Students will begin to feel the pressure because most teachers are talking all the time, and students are accustomed to that pattern.

Labeling

It can be a powerful tool to help students realize the products of thinking through an MV discussion. Examples include:

"You have reported a value, Ruth." "Willow, is it fair to say that one of your values about taking tests is that you shouldn't rely on smart drugs to improve your score?"

Conference

One of the most valuable tools to use during MV discussion is calling for a conference on the part of the student. They need to know that it's okay to call for a conference.

Student Behaviors

Teacher responses are determined by the student behaviors.

Topic Setting

Students may inadvertently engage in topic setting by changing the question. It is imperative that the teacher recognize that the topic has been changed. In most cases the teacher's job will be to return to the original question. Examples include:

- *Student Response:* I think it's wrong to import the drug Modafinil to this country.
- *Teacher Response:* Graham, when you ask whether the drug was imported from another country, you changed the original question: How do you feel about using mind-enhancing drugs to improve testing? We can discuss importing issues later as another issue if you would like to.

Reporting Data

Some data from student observations may be accurate; some may be inaccurate. Other sources of data will include what they have previously learned and are able to recall. Your task is not to sort out the accurate from the inaccurate but to identify the reporting of data. Judging the value of the reported data will be the responsibility of the students.

Reporting Action

This is used when students state what might be done relative to a given topic. The emphasis is on proposing some action to be taken. The reporting carries an implicit value judgment about it.

- *Student Response:* One thing we might do is to ask whether a student has taken one of the smart pills before taking a test.
- *Teacher Behavior:* Francisca, you have just reported an action that can be taken.

Reporting Prediction

When students make observations and report them to the class, they often do this in a prediction. As a way of helping students explore the strength or limitations of their own values, the teacher needs to use this behavior to help students identify what they are doing.

- *Student Response:* I know what's going to happen if we allow students to take smart pills before tests: The entire testing program will not be accurate.
- *Teacher Behavior:* Lydia, you have just reported a prediction. That could happen.

Reporting My Values

Reporting a value is the presentation of a statement intended to communicate whether something is good or bad. Students make value statements about their own behavior, the behavior of others, an object, an event, an idea, a particular person, or people.

This is what teachers would like students to get comfortable sharing during MV discussions. At this point, he or she becomes aware of what is important to that individual. Teachers skilled in the MV discussion techniques will be able to label the student behavior:

- *Student Response:* I think the smart drugs should be available to any student who wants them.
- *Teacher Behavior:* Thanks, Sean, you have shared your value about smart drugs being available to anyone who wants them.

Student Silence

Students need time to reflect and think without the teacher talking. Sometimes students want to contribute but are afraid to do so. An effective MV discussion often involves time for student reflection without pressure from a teacher urging them to contribute.

Summary of Student and Teacher Behaviors

* Students may request a conference at any time

Student Behaviors*	Teacher Behaviors
⟶	Constructing/Topic Setting/ Teacher Silence
Generating Information ⟶	Acknowledging/Clarifying/ Labeling/Responding/Conference
Reporting Action ⟶	Acknowledging/Clarifying/ Labeling/Responding/Conference
Reporting Data ⟶	Acknowledging/Clarifying/ Labeling/Responding/Conference
Reporting Prediction ⟶	Acknowledging/Clarifying/ Labeling/Responding/Conference
Topic Setting ⟶	Acknowledging/ Topic Setting
Reporting My Values ⟶	Labeling
Student Silence ⟶	Teacher Silence

Selected Books for Enhancing This Chapter	
Restak, Richard	*The New Brain: How the New Age Is Rewiring Your Brain.* Rodale: New York, 2003 Dr. Restak tells an interesting story of how technology and biology are converging to influence brain development. His chapter on cosmetic psychopharmacology is fascinating and will be the subject of entire books in the future.
McGaugh, James	*Memory and Emotion: The Making of Lasting Memories.* Columbia University Press: New York, 2003 James McGaugh is most respected for his work on emotion and memory. This very readable book is a mix of autobiographical detail and the latest research on questions about memory. It's written for the general reader in practical and sometimes humorous accounts from McGaugh's past and present. One chapter is partially devoted to the speculations of how the development of mind-enhancing drugs for Alzheimer's patients may impact healthy brains.

Conclusion

There are a few key points that I have tried to convey throughout this book:

1. With the advent of neuro-imaging technology and supercomputers, scientists have been able to delve into the brain and its workings in new ways only dreamed about by researchers three decades ago. Perhaps no more important information has emerged out of this era than the findings about the adolescent brain.

2. We now know that the brain goes through profound growth and changes from childhood to adulthood. The neural networks established during this period will serve to shape the individual and guide him or her throughout life, making this an even more critical time for an enriched environment. By being aware of this, the influential adults in a teenager's life become even more important. Learning auto mechanics from an uncle, helping manage a family business, and studying history from a brilliant teacher all have a weighty impact on the brain's developing neural networks.

3. The brain becomes leaner and more efficient though an extensive pruning during adolescence. Impulse control, planning, and decision making are largely functions of the frontal cortex, one of the last regions of the brain to fully mature. The process is often associated with behavior that may be erratic and unpredictable . . . Anybody you know?

It seems prudent for parents, teachers, and health-care providers to know that, neurologically, teens are not the same as adults. While they are full of promise, energetic, and caring, they do not have a prefrontal cortex that controls many higher-order skills. When confronted with the need to make sound judgments in complex situations or control impulses, many adolescents will and do fall short.

It's our job to act as safety nets, repairing damaged egos, setting up reasonable barriers, conveying the risks of drug abuse, and being empathetic teachers. What's promising is evidence from neuroscience that helps explains adolescent behavior. The data suggest that teens need to be surrounded by compassionate adults, families, good schools, and communities that will help them learn how to make better risk-reducing decisions.

While reading this book I hope you have enriched your scientific knowledge of the brain, improved your teaching tool kit, and now understand where adolescents are coming from—even if they don't! The more you know about this age, the more exciting it is to work with them.

References

Amen, D. (2001). *Healing ADD: The breakthrough program that allows you to see and heal the 6 types of ADD.* New York: Berkeley Publishing Group.

Arnsten, A. F. T. (1998). The biology of being frazzled. *Science. 280*(5370), 1711–2.

Bechara, A., Damasio, H., & Damasio, A. R. (2003). Role of the amygdala in decision-making. *Annals of the New York Academy of Sciences, 985,* 356–69.

Bjorkvold, J. (1989). *Roar: The music within.* New York: HarperCollins.

Bogin, B. A. (1994). Adolescence in evolutionary perspective. *Acta Paediatrica* (Suppl.), *406,* 29–35.

Bookheimer, S. (2004). *Overview on learning and memory: Insights from functional brain imaging.* Keynote presentation at the Learning Brain Expo, San Diego, CA.

Brazelton, T. B. (1992). Optimistic infants, head start: The emotional foundations of school readiness. Arlington, VA: National Center for Clinical Infant Programs.

Bruer, J. (1999). In search of brain-based education. *Phi Delta Kappan, 80,* 9.

Cahill, L. (2004). *An overview of emotions and memory.* Presentation at the Learning Brain Expo, January 19, San Diego, CA.

Caine, R., & Caine, G. (1998). Building a bridge between neurosciences and education: Cautions and possibilities. *NASSP Bulletin, 82* (598), 1–6.

Campbell, D. (1997). *The Mozart effect.* New York: Avon Books.

Carey, B. (2005). Genders really do think differently: Men use more gray matter, women use more white. Retrieved Jan. 20, 2005, MSNBC. http://www.msnbc. msn.com/id/6849058.

Carskadon, M. (2002). In Inside the teenage brain. [Television series episode]. Spinks, S. (Producer-Writer), *Frontline,* January 2002. Retrieved November 2005 from http://www.pbs.org/wgbh/pages/frontline/shows/teenbrain

Carter, R. (1999). *Mapping the mind.* Berkeley: University of Califorina Press.

Califano, J. A. (2005). *Under the counter: The diversion and abuse of controlled prescription drugs in the U.S.* New York: The National Center on Addiction and Substance Abuse at Columbia University.

Childress, A. R. (2000). Imaging the brain vulnerability to disorders of desire: Opiates, brownies, sex and cocaine. *Psychiatry Today.* University of Florida. Retrieved February 2006 from http://www.psychiatry.ufl.edu/Newsletters/ Content/childress.pdf.

Chudler, E. (2005). Neuroscience for kids. Retrieved from http://faculty. washington.edu/chudler/neurok.html

Chugani, H. T., Behen, M. E., Muzik, O., Juhasz, C., Nagy, F., & Chugani, D. C. (2001). *Local brain functional activity following early deprivation: A study of postinstitutionalized Romanian orphans.* Detroit: Department of Pediatrics, Children's Hospital of Michigan, Detroit Medical Center, Wayne State University School of Medicine.

Csikszentmihalyi, M. (1990). *Flow: The psychology of optimal experience.* New York: Harper Row Publishers, Inc.

Dalis, G. T., & Strasser, B. B. (1977). *Teaching strategies for values awareness and decision making in health education.* Thorofare, NJ: Charles B. Slack, Inc.

Damasio, A. (1994). *Descartes' error: Emotion, reason, and the human brain.* New York: Grosset/Putnam.

Damasio, A. (1999). *The feeling of what happens: Body and emotion in the making of consciousness.* Orlando, FL: Harcourt Brace.

Diamond, M., & Hobson, J. (1998). *Magic trees of the mind: How to nurture your child's intelligence, creativity, and healthy emotions from birth through adolescence.* New York: Dutton.

Diller, L. H. (1996).The run on Ritalin: Attention deficit disorder and stimulant treatment. *Hastings Center Report, 26,* 12–14.

Ernst, T., Chang, L., Leonido-Lee, M., & Speck, O. (2000). Evidence for longterm neurotoxicity associated with methamphetamine abuse: a 1H MRS study. *Neurology, 54*(6), 1344–49.

Farah, M. J. (2005). Neuroethics: The practical and the philosophical. *Trends in Cognitive Sciences, 9*(1), 34–40.

Farah, M. J., Illes, J., Cook-Deegan, R., Gardner, H., King, P., Parens, E., Sahakian, B., & Root, P. (2004). Neurocognitive enhancement: What can we do and what should we do? *Neuroscience, 5,* 421–425.

Forger, N. G. (2001). The development of sex differences in the nervous system. In Blass E. (Ed.), *The Handbook of Behavioral Neurobiology,* Vol. 13: Developmental Psychobiology. (pp. 153–208), New York: Kluwer/Plenum.

Franklin Institute. The human brain: Stress and the brain. Retrieved February 2006 from http://www.fi.edu/brain/stress.htm.

Gazzaniga, M. S. (1992). *Nature's mind: The biological roots of thinking, emotions, sexuality, language, and intelligence.* New York: Basic Books.

Gerald, G. (2000). What is emotional intelligence? Retrieved February 2006 from http://www.brainconnection.com.

Geyer, G. (2003). *Creating optimum learning.* Paper presented at the learning and the Brain Conference, Boston, MA, April 26, 2003.

Gibbs, N. (1995, October 2). The EQ factor: New brain research suggests that emotions, not IQ, may be the true measure of human intelligence. *TIME Magazine.*

Giedd, J., Blumenthal, J., Jeffries, N.O., Castellanos, F., Liu, H., Zijdenbos, A., Paus, T., Evans, A., & Rapoport, J. (1999). Brain development during childhood and adolescence: A longitudinal MRI study. *Nature Neuroscience, 2*(10), 861–3.

Giedd, J. (2002). In Inside the teenage brain. [Television series episode]. Spinks, S. (Producer-Writer), *Frontline,* January 2002. Retrieved November 2005 from http://www.pbs.org/wgbh/pages/frontline/shows/teenbrain

Gogtay, N., Giedd, J. N., Lusk, L., Hayashi, K. M., Greenstein, D., Vaituzis, A. C., Nugent, T. F. III, Herman, D. H., Clasen, L. S., Toga, A. W., Rapoport, J. L., & Thompson, P. M. (2004). *Dynamic mapping of human cortical development during childhood through early adolescence.* Bethesda, MD: National Institutes of Mental Health. Retrieved February 2006 from http://www.loni.ucla.edu/~thompson/DEVEL/PR.html

Goleman, D. (1995). *Emotional intelligence: Why it can matter more than IQ.* New York: Bantam Books.

Goleman, D. (2005). *Working with emotional intelligence.* New York: Bantam Books.

Greenfield, D. N. (2000). Internet addiction. In P. Fanning, and M. McKay (Eds.), *Family guide to emotional wellness* (pp. 301–8). Oakland, CA: New Harbinger Publications.

Greenfield, P. M., Gross, E. F., Subrahmanyam, K., Suzuki, L. K., & Tynes, B. (2005). Teens on the Internet: Interpersonal connection, identity, and information. In R. Kraut (Ed.), *Information technology at home.* Oxford, UK: Oxford University Press.

Grieco, A. (1986). Sitting posture: An old problem and a new one. *Ergonomics, 29,* 345–62.

Gunnar, M. R., Brodersen, L., Krueger, K., & Rigatuso, R. (1996). Dampening of behavioral and adrenocortical reactivity during early infancy: Normative changes and individual differences. *Child Development, 67,* 877–889.

Gurian, M. (2003). *The boys and girls learn differently: Action guide for teachers.* San Francisco, CA: Jossey-Bass.

Hagemeier, C. (2004). *Laughter and learning: How to enhance learning by filling your trainings with fun.* Paper presented at the Learning Brain Expo, San Diego, CA.

Hall, S. S. (2003). The quest for a smart pill. *Scientific American, 289,* 54–57; 60–65.

Hawkins, J. D., & Catalano, R. R. (1992). *Communities that care: Action for drug abuse prevention.* San Francisco, CA: Jossey-Bass.

Healy, D. (2004). *Let them eat Prozac: The unhealthy relationship between the pharmaceutical industry and depression.* New York: New York University Press.

Healy, M. (2004, December 20). Sharper minds. TIME.

Hickok, G., Bellugi, U., & Klima, E. S. (2001). Sign language in the brain. *Scientific American, 284*(6).

Hickok, G. (2005). *How Is Language Processed in the Brain?* Paper presented at the Learning Brain Expo, San Diego, CA.

Hobson, A. (2003). *Sleep, memory, and learning.* A paper presented on April 26, 2003, at the Learning and Brain Conference: To Leave No Child Behind at MIT, Boston, MA.

Hollon, T. (2003). Dead man's curve. Field Journal, February, Earthwatch, Boston, MA.

Hyman, S. (2000). An interview with Steven Hyman, M. D. *Moyers on addiction. Close To Home* [TV series episode]. http://www.pbs.org/wnet/closetohome/science/html/hyman.html

Jensen, E. (1996). *Completing the puzzle: A brain-based approach to learning.* Thousand Oaks, CA: Corwin Press.

Jensen, E. (1998). *Teaching with the brain in mind.* Alexandria, VA: Association for Supervision and Curriculum Development.

Jensen, E. (2000). *Music with the brain in mind.* Thousand Oaks, CA: Corwin Press.

Jensen, E. (2003). *Tools for engagement: Managing emotional states for learner success.* Thousand Oaks, CA: Corwin Press.

Jensen, E. (2005). *Top tunes for teaching: 977 song titles and practical tools for choosing the right music every time.* Thousand Oaks, CA: Corwin Press.

Kagan, J. (2002). *Temperamental contributions to the affect family of anxiety.* A paper presented on May 11, 2002, at the Learning and Brain Conference: To Leave No Child Behind at MIT, Boston, MA.

Kaiser Family Foundation. (2005). *Generation M: Media in the lives of 8–18 year-olds.* Retrieved February 2006 from http://www.kff.org/entmedia/entmedia030905pkg.cfm.

Kandel, E. R. (1976). *Cellular basis of behavior: An introduction to behavioral neurobiology.* San Francisco, CA: W. H. Freeman & Co.

Kandel, E. (2000). Memory and learning. "Science Friday" with host Ira Flatow. International Public Radio, rebroadcast of an interview on October 13, 2000.

Kastleman, M. (2001). The difference between the male and female brain. *Article Archives—Content Watch.* Retrieved May 2005 from URL- http://www.contentwatch.com/learn_center/article.php?id=165

Kimura, D. (1992, September). Sex differences in the brain. *Scientific American,* pp. 119–124.

Kluger, J. (2003, November 3). Medicating young minds. TIME, *162,* 14.

Klutky, N. (1990). Sex differences in memory performance for odors, tone sequences and colors. *Zeitschrift für experimentelle und angewandte Psychologie,* 37(3), 437–46. Retrieved March 2005 from http://www.ncbi.nlm.nih.gov/entrez/query.fcgi?cmd=Retrieve&db=Pub Med&list_uids=2238732&dopt=Abstract

Kohn, A. (1993). *Punished by rewards: The trouble with gold stars, incentive plans, A's, praise, and other bribes.* New York: Houghton Mifflin.

Kotulak, R. (1997). *Inside the brain: Revolutionary discoveries of how the mind works.* Kansas City, MO: Andrews McMeel Publishing.

Lally, R. (1997). *Brain development in infancy: A critical period.* Bridges, CA: California Department of Education.

Langreth, R. (2002). Viagra for the brain. *Forbes Magazine on-line.* Retrieved in February 2006 from http://nootropics.com/smartdrugs/brainviagra.html

Laursen, N. (2003). A presentation on storytelling delivered on May 8, 2003, at Rowland Unified School District, Rowland Heights, CA.

Lavoie, R. D. (2002). The teacher's role in developing social skills. Retrieved February 2006 http://www.ricklavoie.com/teacherart.html

LeDoux, J. (1996). *The emotional brain: The mysterious underpinnings of emotional life.* New York: Touchstone.

Levine, M. (2002). *A mind at a time.* New York: Simon & Schuster.

Levine, S. (2005). Grey matters: The teenage brain. Podcast, The Dana Alliance for Brain Initiatives.

Lockyer, B. (2001). *Safe from the start: Reducing children's exposure to violence.* Sacramento, CA: California Attorney General's Office.

Lynch, R. (1999). Response to a question from a composer. Retrieved February 2006 from http://www.raylynch.com/intro.html

MacLean, P. (1970). The triune brain, emotion, and scientific bias. In F. O. Schmitt (Ed.), *The Neurosciences: Second Study Programs.* New York: Rockefeller University Press.

McEwen, B. (2002). *The end of stress as we know it.* Washington, DC: Joseph Henry Press.

McGaugh, J. L. (2003). *Memory and emotion: The making of lasting memories.* New York: Columbia University Press.

Miles, E. (1997). *Tune your brain.* New York: Berkeley Books.

Miller, L. (1999). *A monograph on the use of music in schools.* Caesar Rodney School District: DE.

Moore, P. (2005). The inferential focus: A human resources newsletter. Retrieved May 2005 from http://www.inferentialfocus.com/research/restopics.html

National Sleep Foundation. (n.d.). Teens and sleep. Retrieved February 2006 from http://www.sleepfoundation.org/hottopics/index. php?secid=18&id=185

O'Leary, J. C. (1993). An analysis of the legal issue surrounding the forced use of Ritalin. *New England Law Review, 27,* 1173–1209.

Ornstein, R., & Thompson, R. F. (1986). *The amazing brain.* New York: Houghton Mifflin.

Perry, B. (2002). *The power of early intervention: The impact of abuse and neglect on the developing child.* An address to the Orange County Department of Education, November 14, 2002, in Anaheim, CA.

Perry, B. (2005). *Bonding and attachment in maltreated children.* Presented on April 27, 2005, in San Luis Obispo, CA.

Pert, C. B. (1997). *Molecules of emotion: The science behind mind-body medicine.* New York: Scribner.

Post, J. M. (2003, December 21). Rathole under the palace. *Los Angeles Times.*

Prensky, M. (2001). Digital natives, digital immigrants, part 2: Do they really think differently? *On the Horizon, 9,* 6.

Ramey, C., & Ramey, S. (1999). *Right from birth: Building your child's foundation for life.* Lanham, MD: Goddard Press.

Ratey, J. J. (2001). *A user's guide to the brain: Perception, attention, and the four theaters of the brain.* New York: Pantheon Books.

Rauscher, F., Shaw, G., & Key, K. (1993). Music and spatial task performance. *Nature, 365,* 611.

Richardson, W. (2005). *ADD and stimulant medication: The destructive cycle of AD/HD and addictive behavior.* Colorado Springs, CO: Piñon Press.

Ripley, A. (2005, February 27). Who says a woman can't be Einstein? TIME Magazine.

Robichaud, M., Dugas, M. J., & Conway, M. (2003). Gender differences in worry and associated cognitive-behavioral variables. *Journal of Anxiety Disorders, 17*(5), 501–16.

Robinson, T. E., & Berridge, K. C. (2003). Addiction. *Annual Review of Psychology, 54*(1), 25, 29.

Rogers, C. R. (1974). Remarks on the future of client-centered therapy. In D. A. Wexler & L. N. Rice (Eds.), *Innovations in client-centered therapy.* New York: John Wiley & Sons.

Ruhl, K. L., Hughes, C. A., & Schloss, P. J. (1987). Using the pause procedure to enhance lecture recall. *Teacher Education and Special Education, 10,* 14–18.

Rutter, M., & O'Connor, T. G. (1999). *Are there biological programming effects for psychological development? Findings from a study of Romanian adoptees.* London: Social, Genetic & Developmental Psychiatry Research Centre, Institute of Psychiatry.

Salovey, P., & Mayer, J. (2002). Emotional intelligence. Retrieved February 2006 from http://www.eqtoday.com/02/emotional.php.

Sanchez, C. (2005). Poverty holds back No Child Left Behind law. *All Things Considered,* National Public Radio, July 20, 2005.

Sapolsky, R. (1999). *Why zebras don't get ulcers: An updated guide to stress, stress-related diseases, and coping.* New York: W. H. Freeman and Company.

Scales, P. (2004). *A gateway asset for school success and healthy development.* Minneapolis, MN: The Search Institute.

Scheibel, A. B. (1998). Embryological development of the human brain. Seattle, WA: New Horizons for Learning. Retrieved in February, 2006. http://www.newhorizons.org/neuro/scheibel.htm

Shedler, J., & Block, J. (1990). Adolescent drug use and psychological health: A longitudinal inquiry. *American Psychology, 45*(5), 612–30.

Shiu, E., & Lenhart, A. (2000). *How Americans use instant messaging.* Washington, DC: Pew Internet and American Life Project. Retrieved February 2006 from http://www.pewinternet.org/PPF/r/133/report_display.asp

Siegel, D. J. (1999). *The developing mind: Towards a neurobiology of interpersonal experience.* New York: Guilford Press.

Society of Neuroscience (2004). *Brain facts: A primer on the brain and nervous system.* Washington, DC.

Sossin, W. (1997). Selected papers from the Sossin Lab Website. Retrieved February 2006 from http://www.mni.mcgill.ca/cbet/waynes/references.html

Spinks, S., (Producer). (2002). Inside the teenage brain: An interview. *FrontLine.* Retrieved June 2005 from: http://www.pbs.org/wgbh/pages/frontline/shows/teenbrain/work/adolescent.html

Subrahmanyam, K., Kraut, R. E., Greenfield, P. M., & Gross, E. F. (1995). *The impact of home computer use on children's activities and development.* Retrieved February 2006 from http://www.futureofchildren.org/information2826/information_show.htm?doc_id=69826

Sweatt, D. J. (2002). *Mechanisms of memory.* San Diego, CA: Elsevier/Academic Press.

Sylwester, R. (2001). *The Developing Adolescent Brain.* Paper presented at the Learning Brain Expo, San Diego, CA.

Sylwester, R. (2003). *A biological brain in a cultural classroom: Enhancing cognitive and social development through collaborative classroom management* (2nd ed.). Thousand Oaks, CA: Corwin Press.

Talukder, G. (2000). Decision-making is still a work in progress for teenagers. Retrieved February 2006 from http://www.brainconnection.com.

The Nemours Foundation. (2000). *TeensHealth.* Updated 2005 and reviewed by D. Lyness, Originally reviewed by S. Dowshen, & E. Woomer. Retrieved February 2006 from http://kidshealth.org/PageManager.jsp?dn=KidsHealth&lic=1&ps=207&cat_id=20124&article_set=20400

Thompson, P. M., Giedd, J. N., Woods, R. P., MacDonald, D., Evans, A. C., & Toga, A. W. (2000). Growth patterns in the developing human brain detected by using continuum-mechanical human brain tensor maps. *Nature, 404*(6774), 190–193.

Tully, T., Bourtchouladze, R., Scott, R., & Tallman, J. (2003). Targeting the CREB pathway for memory enhancers. *Nature Reviews, Drug Discovery, 2*(4), 267–177.

Turner, D. C., Robbins, T. W., Clark, L., Aron, A. R., Dowson, J., Sahakian, B. J. (2003). Cognitive Enhancing Effects of Modafinil in Healthy Volunteers. *Psychopharmacology, 165*, 260–269.

U.S. Department of Education. (2004). 1.1 million home-schooled students in the US in 2003. *NCES Bulletin*, p. 115.

Watkins, C. (2004). *Attention Deficit Disorder and addiction.* Baltimore, MD: Northern Counties Psychiatric Association. Retrieved February 2006 from http://www.baltimorepsych.com/add_and_addiction.htm

Webb, T., & Webb, D. (1990). *Accelerated learning with music.* Norcross, GA: Accelerated Learning Systems.

Weisfeld, G. E., & Billings, R. L. (1988). *Observations on adolescence: Sociobiological perspectives on human development.* New York: Springer-Verlag.

White, A. (2003). Alcohol hits teen brain hard. *Duke Health Brief.* Retrieved February 2006 from http://www.dukemednews.org/av/medminute. php?id=7041

Wild, B., Rodden, F., Grodd, W., & Ruch, W. (2003). Neural correlates of laughter and humour. *Brain, 126,* 2121–2138.

Winters, K. (2004). The effects of alcohol on the adolescent brain. An audio teleconference, March 18, 2004. Center for Substance Abuse Prevention, U.S. Department of Health and Human Services.

Wolfe, P. (2001). *Brain matters: Translating research into classroom practice.* Alexandria, VA: Association for Supervision and Curriculum Development.

Wulfert, E., Block, J. A., Santa Ana, E., Rodriguez, M. L., & Colsman, M. (2002). Delay of gratification: Impulsive choices and problem behaviors in early and late adolescence. *Journal of Personality, 70*(4), 533–552.

Yesavage J. A., Mumenthaler, M. S., Taylor J. L., Friedman, L., O'Hara, R., Sheikh, J., Tinklenberg, J., & Whitehouse, P. J. (2002). Donepezil and flight simulator performance: Effects on retention of complex skills. *Neurology, 59,* 123–5.

Youth risk behavior surveillance (2003). Center for Disease Control, U. S. Department of Health and Human Services.

Yurgelun-Todd, D. (2002). In Inside the teenage brain. [Television series episode]. Spinks, S. (Producer-Writer), *Frontline,* January 2002. Retrieved November 2005 from http://www.pbs.org/wgbh/pages/frontline/shows/teenbrain

Zeidner, M., Roberts, R. D., & Matthews, G. (2002). Can emotional intelligence be schooled? A critical review. *Educational Psychologist, 37*(4), 215–231.

Zull, J. (2002). *The art of changing the brain: Enriching the practice of teaching by exploring the biology of learning.* Sterling, VA: Stylus Publishing.

Index

ABCs (alphabetical brain connections), 12–14
Abraham, C., 17
Acknowledging behavior, 189
ACTH (adrenocorticotropic hormone), 12, 113
Action, 191
Activities:
  brain, guided tour of, 15
  cerebrospinal fluid, 36–37
  discussions, 38–39
  field trips, 106
  games, 105
  impact on adolescent brain, 72
  Labels game, 87–88
  for learning state, 137–139
  mind mapping, 16–17
  music, 153–155
  Musical Shares, 16
  Penfield's experiments, simulating, 37
  project-based learning, 105
  rituals, 104–105
  Scissors game, 85–87
  simulations, role-playing, 106
  smart drugs, 186–192
  storytelling, 59–60
  stress, helping students deal with, 121–122
  stroke, viewing effects of, 36
  substance abuse and brain, 172–173
ADD (Attention Deficit Disorder), 27, 180
Adderall, 160
Addiction:
  brain and, 164–165
  factors of, 159
AD/HD. See Attention Deficit Hyperactivity Disorder
Adolescence, brain during:

activities, 85–88
alcohol and, 168–169
books on, 89
cultural gap, 76–77
digital learning, 78
in general, 65
interpretation by adolescents, 79–81
key points about, 195
listening to adolescents, 83
mammoth analogy, 65–67
media, technology and, 74–76
music and visualization, 77
pre-puberty brain development, 71
risk taking, 67
sculpted brain, 72–73
sleep, 81–82, 84
social functioning, 84
success expectations, 67–68
success in education, 69
tests, success and, 70
Adolescents:
  addiction vulnerability of, 165
  biological brain of, 99–100
  emotions, communication, 93–94
  emotions, learning, 94–95
  neural networks and, 8
  search for meaning, 100–101
  See also Students
Adolescents, substance abuse and:
  activities, 172–173
  addiction and brain, 164–165
  AD/HD impact on, 161
  alcohol, 168–169
  amygdala and, 166

books on, 173
cocaine addiction, 166–167
drug dilemma story, 159–161
drug-prevention programs, 171
marijuana, 169
methamphetamine, 167–168
prescription drug abuse, 162–163
prevention of, 170
psychoactive drugs, 163
by teenagers, 159
vulnerability to, 165
Adrenal glands, 113–115
Adrenaline:
  definition of, 12
  rush, 113–114
Adrenocorticotropic hormone (ACTH), 12, 113
Agenbroad, L., 66–67
Alcohol, 168–169
Allostatic load:
  description of, 115–116
  effects of, 118–119
  of teachers, students, 120
Alphabetical brain connections (ABCs), 12–14
Alzheimer's disease:
  memory research for, 181–183
  smart drugs for, 179
Amen, D.:
  ADD book by, 173
  on AD/HD, substance abuse, 161
  on size of brain tissue, 9
  SPECT work of, 27
Amphetamines, 180, 181
Amygdala:
  in adolescence, 65
  emotional memories with, 9
  men/women and, 32

processing of emotions, 96, 97
response to emotions and, 80
substance abuse and, 166
of teenage brain, 165, 166
Amygdala response (AR), 97
Anxiety, 48
Aplysia californica (California sea slug), 131–132
Apoptosis, 7
Apple iPod, 144
Apple iTunes, 144–145
AR (amygdala response), 97
Aricept (Donepezil), 184
Arnsten, A. F. T., 119
Arts with the Brain in Mind (Jensen), 89
Attachment:
  educational connection, 54
  forming/maintaining relationships, 51–53
Attention Deficit Disorder (ADD), 27, 180
Attention Deficit Hyperactivity Disorder (AD/HD):
  book on, 173
  drug dilemma story, 159–161
  impact on substance abuse, 161
Autonomic nervous system, 114–115
Axons, 13, 29

Baroque music, 151
Barry, D., 31
Beat, of music, 146, 147
Bechara, A., 97
Behaviors, for My Values discussion, 188–192
Berridge, K. C., 165
Billings, R. L., 67
Biological brain, 99–100
Biological clock, 81

Bjorkvold, J., 147
Block, J., 67
Block, J.A., 56
Blood, 114
Blood pressure, 119
Body:
  allostatic load, 115–116, 118–119
  functions, music and, 144
  music's impact on, activity for, 154–155
Bogin, B., 67
Books:
  on adolescent brain, 89
  on brain and learning, 17
  on brain development, 61
  on brain research, 39
  on emotions, 107
  on learning state, 140
  on music, 155
  on smart drugs, 193
  on stress, 123
  on substance abuse and brain, 173
Boys, brains of, 33–34
Brain:
  activities, 15–17
  addiction and, 164–165
  alcohol and, 168–169
  alphabetical brain connections, 12–14
  Alzheimer's disease, 181–183
  biological brain, 99–100
  description of, 10
  development in early childhood, 8
  development in womb, 7–8
  educational connection, 14
  emotions and learning, 94–96
  key points about, 195
  links with psychology, neuroscience, 5–7
  mechanic/neurosurgeon story, 3–4
  memory functions, 96–97

methamphetamine and, 168
multifunctions of, 9
neuroscience caution, 4–5
parts of, 10–12
peptide molecules, 97–98
physiological states, 128–129
psychoactive drugs and, 163
search for meaning, 100–101
smart drug side effects, 179
stress and, 112
substance abuse, impact on, 159
technological changes and, 4
See also Adolescence, brain during; Substance abuse
Brain, stress and:
  activity to deal with, 121–122
  adrenaline rush, 113–114
  allostatic load, 115–116, 118
  autonomic nervous system/adrenals, 114–115
  books on, 123
  chronic stress, effects of, 118–119
  educational connection, 117, 120
  endorphins, 113
  science fair example, 111–112
  too much stress, 115
"The Brain: A Road Map to the Mind" (MSNBC Interactive) activity, 15
Brain breaks, 127–128
Brain damage, 22
Brain development, environmental/genetic effects on:
  activities, 59–60

attachment, emotional
relationships, 51–53
books, 61
early brain, 46–47
emotional intelligence,
53–58
experience-dependent
mechanisms, 50–51
maps of growth patterns,
48–50
sequential brain
development, 47
traumatic experiences,
malleability, 45–46
use of brain, 46
violence exposure, 43–44
Brain hemispheres, 34, 35
Brain injuries:
research on, 24–25
sources of, 22–23
Brain mapping:
development mapping,
48–49
research/development,
25–27
Brain research:
activities, 36–39
brain injuries, 22–23
California sea slug and,
131–132
educational connection,
27, 33–34
gender differences in
brain, 30–33
mapping brain, 25–27
Mel High School and,
21–22
neural networks, 27–30
new/old findings, 23–25
right brain/left brain,
34–35
The Brain series
(Public Broadcasting
System), 34
Brain stem, 11
Brain-enhancing drugs.
See Smart drugs
Brain-imaging technology:
education and, 28
types of, 25–27

Broca, P., 25
Broca's area, 12
Brookheimer, S. Y., 3, 27
Brooks, Robert, 69
Bruer, John, 6
Bush, George W., 180

Cahill, L., 95, 100
Caine, G., 100, 102
Caine, R., 100, 102
Califano, J. A., Jr., 162–163
California, 50
California Department of
Education, 173
California sea slug (Aplysia
californica), 131–132
Caregiver, 51–53
Carpenter, Tom, 68
Carskadon, M., 81, 82
Carter, R.:
brain differences by
sex, 31
Mapping the Mind,
39, 103
talking benefits, 186
CASA (National Center
on Addiction and
Substance Abuse), 162
CAT (Computerized Axil
Tomography) scan,
26, 27
Catalano, R. R., 73
A Celebration of Neurons:
An Educator's
Guide to the Brain
(Sylwester), 39
"Celestial Soda Pop"
(Lynch), 143
Cell phone, 75
Cerebellum, 11
Cerebral cortex, 12
Cerebrospinal fluid,
36–37
Cerebrum, 11
Chang, L., 168
Childress, A. R.:
on addiction, 165
on drug addiction, 164
on placebo effect, 163
Chudler, E.:

Neuroscience for Kids
website, 37
on smart drugs, 180
on stress, 113
Chugani, H., 48–49, 53
Cingulate gyrus, 13
Clarifying behavior, 189
Classical music, 150–151
Classroom Activators:
64 Novel Ways to
Energize Learners
(Evanski), 140
Cobain, K., 76
Cocaine addiction,
166–167
Colsman, M., 56
Columbian mammoth,
65–67
Communication, neuron,
29–30
Community service, 57
Compact disc (CD)
player, 144
Compact discs (CDs), 144
Completing the Puzzle
(Jensen), 10
Computer, 75
Computerized Axil
Tomography (CAT)
scan, 26, 27
Computers, 27
Concert review activity,
153–154
Conference, 190
Consciousness, 9
Constructing behavior,
188–189
Corpus callosum, 13, 31
Cortex, 11
Country Western
music, 152
Cultural gap, 76–77
Curry, Mr., 101–103

Dalis, G. T., 186, 187
Damasio, A. R.:
amygdala, 97
book by, 17
on consciousness, 9
Descartes' Error, 25

Damasio, H., 97
Daunas, Mr., 21–22
Dendrites, 13
Deoxyribonucleic acid
    (DNA), 28
Descartes' Error
    (Damasio), 25
Diamond, M., 45, 61
Dietl, B., 163
Digital age:
    cell phones, instant
        messaging, 74–75
    education and, 78
    educational
        connection, 76
    impact on adolescent
        brain, 74
Diller, L. H., 161
Discussions:
    activity to facilitate,
        38–39
    My Values discussion
        strategies, 186–192
DNA (deoxyribonucleic
    acid), 28
Dopamine, 13, 164–165
Drug abuse. See Substance
    abuse
Drug: CX516
    Ampakines, 183
Drug-prevention
    programs, 171
Drugs, smart. See Smart
    drugs
Dugas, M. J., 32

Education:
    biological brain and,
        99–100
    brain development
        and, 3
    emotions and, 101–103
    emotions and learning,
        94–96
    link with neuroscience,
        psychology, 5–7
    search for meaning,
        100–101
    sleep deprivation and,
        81–82, 84

specialization and, 67–69
talking about
    learning, 103
technology and, 4, 5
Educational connection:
    activities, 72
    adolescent
        interpretation, 79
    anxiety of student, 48
    attachment, 54
    brain development, 51
    brain differences by sex
        and, 33–34
    brain hemispheres, 35
    brain plasticity, 71
    brain research and, 28
    brain sculpting, 73
    brain structures,
        functions and, 14
    delayed gratification, 57
    digital age, 78
    emotions and learning,
        99, 102
    environment shapes
        brain, 23
    learning state, 133
    listening to
        adolescents, 83
    music for learning,
        147–148, 152
    prescription drug
        abuse, 162
    sleep, 82
    smart drugs, 185
    specialization, 69
    stress, 117, 120
    substance abuse
        prevention, 170
    technology and
        adolescent
        brain, 76
    violence, trauma
        effects, 50
Educational
    Psychologist (journal),
    56–57
Egyptians, 24
Einstein, A., 24
Eliot, L., 43, 61
Elliott, G., 161

The Emotional Brain:
    The Mysterious
    Underpinnings of
    Emotional Life
    (LeDoux), 96–97, 107
Emotional intelligence:
    critics of, 56–58
    signs of success,
        struggle, 53–56
    strength of, 43
Emotional Intelligence:
    Why It Can Matter
    More Than IQ
    (Goleman), 53–54, 61
Emotions:
    activities for, 104–106
    biological brain, 99–100
    books on, 107
    communication and,
        93–94
    consciousness and, 9
    emotional intelligence,
        53–56
    emotional relationships,
        51–53
    learning and, 94–96, 99
    limbic system and, 11
    memory of, 96–97
    of men/women, 32
    molecules and, 97–98
    music and, 144
    physiological state
        and, 129
    search for meaning and,
        100–101
    teaching and, 101–103
    teenage interpretation
        of, 79–80
The End of Stress
    As We Know It
    (McEwen), 123
Endorphins:
    definition of, 13
    effect on emotions, 98
    response to music, 144
    stress and, 113
Enriching the Brain
    (Jensen), 61
Environment, effects on
    brain development:

activities, 59–60
attachment, emotional
    relationships,
    51–53
books, 61
early brain, 46–47
emotional intelligence,
    53–56
emotional intelligence
    critics, 56–58
experience-dependent
    mechanisms,
    50–51
maps of growth patterns,
    48–50
sequential brain
    development, 47
shapes brain, 23
traumatic experiences,
    malleability, 45–46
use of brain, 46
violence exposure, 43–44
Epinephrine. *See*
    Adrenaline
Episodic memory, 94
Ernst, T., 168
Ethics:
    of brain enhancement,
        185
    My Values discussion
        strategies, 186–192
    of smart drugs, 180
Evanski, J., 140
Everett, E., 136
Excitatory
    neurotransmitter,
    29–30
Experience:
    neural template and, 8
    traumatic, 45–46
    violence exposure, brain
        development and,
        43–44
Experience-dependent
    mechanisms, 50–51

Failure, 69, 70
"Falsefiability," 23–24
Farah, M., 177, 184–185
Fat, 119

The Feeling of What
    Happens: Body
    and Emotion in
    the Making of
    Consciousness
    (Damasio), 9, 17
Feinstein, S., 89
Ferris Bueller's Day Off
    (movie), 130
Field trips, 106
50 Cent, 76–77
Food, stress and, 112
Food and Drug
    Administration
    (FDA), 178
Forger, N., 31
Forgetfulness, 119
Frontal cortex, 79, 80
Frontal lobe, 12, 73
Functional MRI (fMRI),
    27, 164

GABA inverse
    agonists, 183
Gage, P., 25
Games, 105
Gazzaniga, M., 10, 115
Gender, brain differences,
    30–34
Gene therapy, 184
Generalism, 67–68
Genetics, effects on brain
    development:
activities, 59–60
attachment, emotional
    relationships, 51–53
books, 61
early brain, 46–47
emotional intelligence,
    53–56
emotional intelligence
    critics, 56–58
experience-dependent
    mechanisms, 50–51
maps of growth patterns,
    48–50
sequential brain
    development, 47
traumatic experiences,
    malleability, 45–46

use of brain, 46
violence exposure,
    43–44
*Getting Results: Part I and
    Part II* (California
    Department of
    Education), 173
Geyer, G., 31
Gibbs, N., 55–56
Giedd, J.:
    adolescent brain
        findings, 71, 72
    on brain development, 7
Gilatide, 184
Girls, brains of, 33–34
Glial cells:
    definition of, 13
    function of, 7
    support of neurons, 28
Glucocorticoids:
    allostatic load and,
        116, 118
    chronic stress and, 119
    effect of, 98
    response to stress,
        114–115
    stress of students, 117
Glutamate, 29–30
Gogtay, N., 48
Goleman, D.:
    books by, 61
    on emotional intelligence,
        53–54, 55
    impact of work of, 56
Gratification:
    delay of, 55–56
    education and, 57
Gray matter, 71
Greenfield, D., 75
Greenfield, P. M., 74
Grieco, A., 132
Gross, E. F., 74
"A Guided Tour of the
    Human Brain"
    (HOPES) activity, 15
Gunnar, M., 45
Gurian, M., 33

H3-blocker, 183
Haier, R., 32

Happiness, 94, 95
Hawkin, J. D., 73
Healing ADD: The
    Breakthrough
    Program that Allows
    You To See and Heal
    the 6 Types of ADD
    (Amen), 173
Health:
    problems from
        stress, 111
    smart drugs and, 185
Healy, D., 179, 181
Hearing, 32, 49
    See also Music
Heart, 24
Heder, J., 84
Hickock, G., 34
Hip-Hop, 151
Hippocampus:
    alcohol and, 168–169
    damage from stress,
        115, 119
    long-term memory
        with, 9
    neurons/memory and, 29
    in temporal lobe, 12
Hitler, A., 44
Hobson, A., 81
Hollon, T., 65–67
Homeostasis, 115
Home-schooling, 84
Hormones:
    ACTH, adrenaline
        definitions, 12
    adrenaline rush,
        113–114
    brain differences by sex
        and, 30
    chronic stress and, 119
    emotions and, 95
    glucocorticoids, 114–115,
        116, 118
    over-secretion of stress
        hormones, 115
    stress and, 112
Hounsfield, G., 26
How the Brain Learns
    (Sousa), 103
Hubel, D., 50

"Human Brain, Human
    Jungle" (Jensen), 10
Hussein, S., 43–44
Huttenlocker, J., 30
Hyman, S., 27
Hypothalamus, 13, 113

Illes, J., 184
Immune system, 119
Instant messaging, 75
Intelligence Quotient (IQ),
    53–54
Internet:
    changes with, 4
    impact on adolescent
        brain, 74, 75
    prescription drugs from,
        162, 163
Interneurons. See Glial
    cells
Interpretation, by
    adolescents, 79–81
iPod, Apple, 144
iTunes, Apple, 144–145

Jazz, 151
Jensen, E.:
    books by, 17, 61, 89, 140
    books on music, 155
    on brain hemispheres, 34
    on emotions, 129
    on endorphins,
        music, 144
    "Human Brain, Human
        Jungle," 10
    on meaning, 100, 101
    neuroscience work
        of, 5
Joke, posting, 138–139

Kagan, J., 56
Kaiser Family Foundation,
    75, 77
Kandel, E., 131–132, 181
Key, K., 5
Kiefer, J., 143–144
Kimura, D., 33
Klutky, N., 32
Kohn, A., 69
Kotulak, R., 30, 49

Labeling, 190
Labels game, 87–88
Language:
    learning, brain
        development and,
        48–49
    social language
        dysfunction, 84
Lanqreth, R., 183
Lateralization, 13
Laughter activity, 137–138
Learning:
    brain breaks for, 127–128
    brain development and,
        3, 48–49
    brain differences by sex
        and, 33–34
    brain structures,
        functions and, 14
    emotional intelligence,
        53–56
    emotions and, 94–96,
        99, 102
    experience-dependent
        mechanisms, 50–51
    fatigue, 132–133
    generalism,
        specialization, 67–68
    music to enhance,
        143–152
    neuron communication
        and, 29–30
    neuroscience caution,
        4–5
    physiological states and,
        129–130
    punctuated lesson, 136
    search for meaning,
        100–101
    social world and, 84
    state, activities for,
        137–139
    state, books on, 140
    state changers, 133–135
    talking about, 103
    technological changes
        and, 4
    use of brain, 46
Learning Brain Expo (San
    Diego, CA), 34

Learning environment, 144
LeDoux, J.:
  book by, 107
  on emotion, learning, 100
  on emotional brain, 96–97
  on emotions and
    brain, 11
Left brain, 34, 35
Lenhart, A., 75
Leshner, A. I., 159, 167
Levine, M.:
  on brain specialization,
    68
  on child development, 30
  A Mind At A Time, 39
  social language
    dysfunction, 84
Levine, S., 79
Limbic system, 11
Lincoln, A., 136
Lobes, 11, 12
Locker, B., 50
Long-term memory, 95
Long-term potentiation, 30
Lowry, L., 74
Luvox, 160
Lynch, R., 77, 143

MacLean, P., 10–11, 24
Madonna, 76
Magic Trees of the Mind
  (Diamond), 61
Magnetic Resonance
  Imaging (MRI), 27, 48
Mahan, S., 127–128
Malleability, 45–46
Mammoth, Columbian,
  65–67
Mapping:
  brain mapping research/
    development, 25–27
  development mapping,
    48–49
  mind mapping activity,
    16–17
Mapping the Mind (Carter),
  39, 103
Marijuana, 169
Marshmallow experiment,
  55–56

Matthews, G., 56–57
Mayer, J., 53, 55
McEwen, B.:
  on adrenaline rush, 114
  on allostasis, 116
  The End of Stress As We
    Know It, 123
  on fat, 119
  on stress, 111, 112
McGaugh, J.:
  on amygdala, 97
  book by, 193
  on emotions, 95
  on smart drugs, 180, 181
  on stress response, 115
Meaning:
  search for, 100–101
  true life story about,
    101–103
Media, impact on
    adolescent brain,
    74–76
Medulla, 13
Mel High School, 21–22
Melatonin, 81
Memory:
  alcohol use and,
    168–169
  brain structure for,
    96–97
  emotions/long-term
    memory, 95
  episodic, 94
  neurons in hippocampus
    for, 29
  smart drugs for, 181–183
  stress and, 115
Memory and Emotion:
    The Making of Lasting
    Memories (McGaugh),
    193
Men, brains of, 30–33
Methamphetamine,
    167–168
Miles, E., 143, 144
Miller, Z., 5
A Mind At A Time
    (Levine), 39
Mind mapping activity,
    16–17

Mischel, W., 55–56
Modafinil (Provigil):
  controversy over, 187
  development of, 183
  as off-label drug, 177
  use of, 178–179
Molecules, 97–98
Molecules of Emotion:
    The Science Behind
    Mind-Body Medicine
    (Pert), 97–98, 107
Moore, P., 74
Mother, 47
"Mozart effect," 5
MP3 player, 144
MRI (Magnetic Resonance
    Imaging), 27, 48
MTV, 77
Mulligan, R., 102
Music:
  activities, 153–155
  body functions and, 144
  books on, 155
  brain processing of, 34
  caution about, 150
  educational connection,
    147–148, 152
  impact on adolescent
    brain, 78
  iTunes, MP3 players,
    145–146
  learning state
    management
    with, 143
  Mozart effect, 5
  selection, use in
    classroom, 144–145
  for storytelling, 60
  types to consider, 150–152
  usage suggestions,
    146–147
  visualization and, 77
  ways to use, 148–150
Music with the Brain in
    Mind (Jensen), 155
Musical Shares activity, 16
My Values (MV) discussion
    strategies, 186–192
Myelin, 13
Mylenation, 8

Napoleon Dynamite
  (movie), 84
National Center on
  Addiction and
  Substance Abuse
  (CASA), 162
National Institutes of
  Health, 172–173
National Institutes of
  Mental Health, 48
National Science
  Teacher (NSTA)
  conference, 173
National Sleep
  Foundation, 82
Nature *vs.* nurture debate:
  early brain development
    and, 47
  experience-dependent
    mechanisms and,
    50–51
  revision to, 43
  See also Brain
    development,
    environmental/
    genetic effects on
Neocortex, 11, 97
Nervous system:
  autonomic, response to
    stress, 114–115
  of California sea slug,
    131–132
  methamphetamine and,
    167–168
  music and, 144
Neural network:
  activities for, 72
  description of, 28–30
  use of, 71
Neural plasticity, 45–46
Neural templates, 8
Neurogenesis, 7
Neurons:
  Alzheimer's disease and,
    181, 182
  brain damage/repair
    and, 22
  in brain development,
    7–8
  of cerebral cortex, 12

definition of, 13
environment and
  brain, 23
networks of, 9, 28–30
use of brain, 46
Neuroscience:
  brain as jungle, 10
  brain development,
    3, 7–8
  brain parts, 10–12
  caution about, 4–5
  definition of terms, 12–14
  functions of brain, 9
  link with psychology,
    education, 5–7
  new/old findings, 23–25
Neurotransmitter:
  definition of, 13
  excitatory, 29–30
  noradrenaline, 115
New Age music, 151
The New Brain: How the
  New Age is Rewiring
  Your Brain
  (Restak), 193
Nirvana, 76
Nolte, N., 102
Noradrenaline, 115
Norepinephrine, 13
NSTA (National Science
  Teacher)
  conference, 173
Nucleus accumbens:
  dopamine and, 164–165
  pleasure and, 11
  of teenage brain, 165

Obesity, 119
Occipital lobe, 12
Off-label drugs, 178,
  179–180
O'Leary, J. C., 161
"Oops phenomenon," 167

Pain, 113
Parents:
  adolescent brain
    development and, 73
  attachment formation in
    child, 51–53

Parietal lobe, 12
Patterns:
  search for meaning and,
    100, 101
  teaching story about,
    101–103
PBS (Public Broadcasting
  System), 34
PDE-4 inhibitors, 183
Penfield, W., 25–26, 37
Peptide molecules, 97–98
Perry, B.:
  on effects of violence,
    trauma, 50
  on relationships, 52
  on sequential brain
    development, 47
  on trauma, 48
Pert, C. B., 97–98, 107
PET (Positron Emission
  Tomography) scan, 26
Photosynthesis, 101–102
Physiological states of
  students:
  activities for, 137–139
  books on, 140
  brain breaks, 127–128
  California sea slug
    research, 131–132
  description of, 128–129
  learning, "Twenty
    Minute Rule,"
    132–133
  learning and, 129–130
  punctuated lesson, 136
  state changers, 133–135
Placebo effect, 163
Plasticity:
  ability for change, 71
  of brain, 45–46
Pons, 14
Positron Emission
  Tomography (PET)
  scan, 26
Possessing Genius: The
  Bizarre Odyssey
  of Einstein's Brain
  (Abraham), 17
The Practical Cogitator
  (Einstein), 24

Prediction, reporting, 191
Prefrontal cortex:
  in adolescence, 65, 195
  development of, 165
  drug addiction and, 165
  stress and, 119
Pregnancy, brain
    development during,
    7–8
Prensky, M., 74, 78
Pre-puberty, brain
    development in, 71
Prescription drugs:
  abuse of, 162–163
  for AD/HD, 159–161
  See also Smart drugs
Prevention:
  of prescription drug
      abuse, 162
  of substance abuse in
      school, 170–171
Project-based learning, 106
Protein kinease C, 119
Provigil, 178
  See also Modafinil
Psychoactive drugs, 163
Psychology:
  brain development
      and, 3
  link with neuroscience,
      education, 5–7
Psychotropic drugs,
    159–161
Public Broadcasting
    System (PBS), 34
Punctuated lesson, 136

Questions, for My Values
    discussion, 187

Radiation, 26
Ramey, S., 47
Ratey, J. J.:
  on attachment, 53
  on brain damage/repair,
      22
  on endorphins, 98
  on use of brain, 46
Rauscher, F., 5
Relationships:

attachment, 54
emotional intelligence,
    53–56
forming/maintaining,
    51–53
Reporting, 191–192
Research. See Brain
    research
Responding behavior, 190
Restak, R., 193
Reticular formation, 14
Richardson, W., 161
Right brain, 34, 35
Ripley, A., 32
Risk-taking, 66–67
Ritalin:
  number of boys
      taking, 161
  as off-label drug, 180
  use of, 180
Rituals activity, 104–105
Roberts, R. D., 56–57
Roberts Military Academy,
    82, 84
Robinson, T. E., 165
Rock and Roll music, 151
Rodriguez, M.L., 56
Rogers, C. R., 112
Romantic music, 151
Ruhl, K., 136

Sadness, 94, 95
Sahakian, B., 179
Salient Theory of
    Dopamine, 164–165
Salovey, P., 53, 55
Sanchez, C., 148
Santa Ana, E., 56
Sapolsky, R.:
  book by, 123
  on excitatory
      neurotransmitter,
      29, 30
  on hippocampus, 119
  on nervous system, 114
  on noradrenaline, 115
SB271046 drug, 183
Scales, P., 57
Scans:
  of brain, 26–27

of brain development,
    48–49
Scheibel, A. B., 7
Scissors game, 85–87
Search, for meaning,
    100–101
Search Institute-
    Developmental
    Assets, 56
Secrets of the Teenage
    Brain: Research-
    Based Strategies for
    Reaching and Teaching
    Today's Adolescents
    (Feinstein), 89
Senses:
  brain functioning and, 9
  of men/women, 32
  in sequential brain
      development, 49–50
  See also Music
Sequential brain
    development:
  brain development
      scans/research,
      48–50
  experience, genetic
      signals and, 47
Serotonin, 14
Sex, brain differences by,
    30–34
Shaw, G., 5
Shedler, J., 67
Side effects, of smart
    drugs, 179, 185
Siegal, D. J., 45, 52
Silence, 190, 192
Single Photon Emission
    Computed
    Tomography (SPECT)
    scans, 26–27
Sleep:
  deprivation, school and,
      81–82, 84
  Modafinil and, 178
Smart drugs:
  books on, 193
  educational
      connection, 185
  ethics of, 180

future of, 184–185
impact of, 177
for memory, sleep-
    resistance, 181
memory research
    impetus, 181–183
My Values discussion
    strategies, 186–192
off-label drugs, 179–180
side effects of, 179
story about use of,
    177–179
types of, 183–184
Smell, 32
"Smells Like Teen Spirit"
    (Nirvana), 76
Society:
    ethics of smart drugs, 185
    social life of
        teenagers, 84
Society for
    Neuroscience, 21
Sossin, W., 131
Sousa, D., 5, 103
Specialization, 67–69
SPECT (Single Photon
    Emission Computed
    Tomography) scans,
    26–27
Speech, 25
Sperry, R., 24, 34
Spinks, S., 50
Stalin, J., 44
State changers, 133–135
States. See Physiological
    states of students
Stein, B., 130
Steinbeck, J., 127
Stimuli, 131–132
Storytelling activity, 59–60
Strasser, B. B., 186, 187
Stress:
    activity to deal with,
        121–122
    adrenaline rush, 113–114
    allostatic load, 115–116,
        118
    books on, 123
    brain development
        and, 47

chronic stress, effects of,
    118–119
definition of, 112
educational connection,
    117, 120
endorphins and, 113
glucocorticoids and, 98
nervous system/adrenals
    and, 114–115
science fair example,
    111–112
too much, 115
Stroke:
    activity to view effects
        of, 36
    brain and, 21–22
Students:
    emotions, learning and,
        94–96, 99–100
    emotions, molecules
        and, 98
    learning time for,
        132–133
    music for learning,
        143–150, 152
    My Values discussion,
        186–192
    search for meaning,
        100–102
    stress, activity to deal
        with, 121–122
    stress, effects of, 118–120
    stress, learning and, 117
    talking about
        learning, 103
    See also Adolescents;
        Smart drugs
Students, physiological
    states of:
activities for, 137–139
books on, 140
brain breaks, 127–128
California sea slug
    research, 131–132
description of, 128–129
learning and, 129–130
learning time, 132–133
punctuated lesson, 136
state changers, 133–135
Substance abuse:

activities, 172–173
addiction and brain,
    164–165
AD/HD impact on, 161
adolescent vulnerability
    to, 165
alcohol, 168–169
amygdala and, 166
books on, 173
cocaine addiction,
    166–167
drug dilemma story,
    159–161
drug-prevention
    programs, 171
marijuana, 169
methamphetamine,
    167–168
prescription drug abuse,
    162–163
prevention of, 170
psychoactive drugs, 163
by teenagers, 159
Success:
    specialization,
        expectations, 67–69
    test failure, life
        success, 70
Supercomputer, 27
Sweatt, D. J., 132
Sylwester, R.:
    book by, 39
    on brain sculpting, 73
    on emotions, 94–95
    on fMRI, 27
    on gender differences,
        32–33
    on molecules,
        emotions, 98
    neuroscience work
        of, 5
Synapse, 14

Talk:
    about learning, 103
    My Values discussion
        strategies,
        186–192
    punctuated lesson, 136
Tape, 144

Teachers:
  adolescent brain
    development and, 73
  job of, 195
  learning time and,
    132–133
  My Values discussion
    strategies, 186–192
  stress and, 120
  See also Educational
    connection
Teachers (movie), 102
Teaching:
  brain structures,
    functions and, 14
  learning state and,
    132–133
  physiological states and,
    129–130
  punctuated lesson, 136
  state changers, 133–135
Teaching with the Brain in
  Mind (Jensen), 17
Techno music, 151
Technology:
  cell phones, instant
    messaging, 74–75
  educational
    connection, 76
  impact on adolescent
    brain, 74
  impact on education, 5
  learning and, 4
Teenagers. *See*
  Adolescence, brain
    during; Adolescents;
    Students
Telephone, 75
Television, 74
Temporal lobe, 12
Testing:
  music and, 147, 148
  smart drugs and, 178–179
Testosterone, 32
Tetrahydrocannabinol
  (THC), 169
Thalamus, 14, 97
Thomson, P.:
  adolescent brain
    findings, 71

MRI scanning of brain,
    48, 49
Time, for sleep, 81–82
TIME magazine, 56
Tools of Engagement:
    Managing Emotional
    States for Learner
    Success (Jensen), 140
Top Tunes for Teaching: 977
    Song Titles & Practical
    Tools for Choosing
    the Right Music Every
    Time (Jensen), 155
Topic setting, 189, 190–191
Touch, 32
Transitions, music for,
    148–149
Traumatic experience:
  brain development and,
    45–46
  effects of, 50
  learning and, 95
Triune Brain model:
  description of, 10–11
  replacement of, 24
Tully, T.:
  on side effects of smart
    drugs, 179
  on smart drugs, 181, 182
"Twenty Minute Rule,"
    132–133

University of California at
    Irvine, 5
University of California at
    Los Angeles (UCLA):
  marijuana study at, 169
  MRI scanning of brain,
    48, 49
U.S. Department of
    Education, 84, 171
U.S. Drug Enforcement
    Administration, 180
U.S. military, use of smart
    drugs, 180, 181

Values, 186–192
Values Awareness Teaching
    Strategies (Dalis and
    Strasser), 186

Vasopressin, 14
Vesalius, A., 24
Viagra, 180
Video games, 74
Violence, 43–44
Vision, 32, 49–50
Visualization, 77
Volkow, N., 164–165

Watkins, C., 161
Weight gain, 119
Weisfeld, G. E., 67
Wernicke, C., 25
Wernicke's area, 12
What's Going on in There?
    How the Brain and the
    Mind Develop in the
    First Five Years of Life
    (Eliot), 61
White, A., 168–169
Why Zebras Don't Get
    Ulcers: An Updated
    Guide to Stress,
    Stress-Related
    Diseases and Coping
    (Sapolsky), 29, 123
Wiesel, T., 50
Winters, K.:
  on amygdala, 166
  on nucleus
    accumbens, 11
  on teenage brain, 165
Witelson, S., 21
Wolfe, P., 5, 80
Women, brains of, 30–33
Working with Emotional
    Intelligence
    (Goleman), 56, 61
Wulfert, E., 56

X-rays, 26

Yesavage, J., 184
Youth Risk Behavioral
    Survey, 168, 170
Yurgelan-Todd, D., 80

Zeidner, M., 56–57
Zola, S., 65
Zull, J., 11

CORWIN PRESS

The Corwin Press logo—a raven striding across an open book—represents the union of courage and learning. Corwin Press is committed to improving education for all learners by publishing books and other professional development resources for those serving the field of PreK–12 education. By providing practical, hands-on materials, Corwin Press continues to carry out the promise of its motto: **"Helping Educators Do Their Work Better."**